Handing One
Another Along

Handing One Another Along

Literature and Social Reflection

ROBERT COLES

Edited by Trevor Hall and Vicki Kennedy

RANDOM HOUSE

NEW YORK

Published in the United States by Random House,
an imprint of The Random House Publishing Group,
a division of Random House, Inc., New York.

RANDOM HOUSE and colophon are registered
trademarks of Random House, Inc.

Permissions acknowledgments for previously published material
can be found beginning on page 255.

LIBRARY OF CONGRESS CATALOGING-IN-PUBLICATION DATA

Coles, Robert.
Handing one another along: literature and social reflection /
edited by Trevor Hall and Vicki Kennedy.
American ed.
p. cm.
ISBN 978-1-4000-6203-4
eBook ISBN 978-0-679-60403-7
1. American literature—History and criticism—Theory, etc. 2. English literature—
History and criticism—Theory, etc. 3. Literature and morals. 4. Literature and society.
I. Hall, Trevor H. II. Kennedy, Vicki. III. Title.
PS169.E83C65 2010   820.9'355—dc22   2009047337

Printed in the United States of America on acid-free paper

www.atrandom.com

2 4 6 8 9 7 5 3 1

First Edition

Book design by Jo Anne Metsch

To our many Literature of Social Reflection
("Gen. Ed. 105") students, teachers—
with much gratitude, appreciation, thankfulness
for all the stories shared

CONTENTS

PART I. HEADING OUT

*The literary and journalistic documentary tradition of
social observation—the call to venture outside of what
we know and attend the stories of others.*

Featured: James Agee, George Orwell, and William Carlos Williams

PART II. WHEN STRANGERS MEET

*Meeting so-called ordinary American working-class men and women:
courage, challenge, kindness, and complexity in everyday living.*

*Featured: The Old Ones of New Mexico, Raymond Carver, Edward
Hopper, Tillie Olsen, and Ruby Bridges*

PART III. A STORYTELLING HUMANITY

Ways of seeing race and identity—encounters through the eyes of another.

Featured: Ralph Ellison, Flannery O'Connor

PART IV. BRINGING IT HOME

Intellectuals and the religious search—finding meaning in the life given to us.

Featured: Dorothy Day, Ignazio Silone, Elie Wiesel, John Cheever, Walker Percy, Zora Neale Hurston, and a Potato Chip Truck

PART V. BOUNDARIES, BORDERS, AND BREAKTHROUGHS

Finding simple clarity amidst moral, psychological, and social complexity.

Featured: Paul Gauguin, Charles Dickens, Thomas Hardy, and George Eliot

INTRODUCTION

Handing One Another Along

I f I could have a sound track running for you as you read this book, you would be listening to Billie Holiday. In fact, when I taught the Harvard University course upon which this book is based, a course aimed at reflecting on life and moral courage, and how we might develop character and moral courage in our own lives, I began each class with one of her songs. Right now you might be hearing "Black and Blue" or "Body and Soul" or "Them There Eyes." She was another narrator of sorts, for us, as we talk about life, literature, and art, about how we reflect upon and understand the stories around us. Billie would be singing her bloody heart out, her voice soothing, searching, telling, confessing, bringing to life all the pain and love and loss that a gifted singer can render, causing us to become more aware of our own yearnings, and the yearnings of others. Billie would join the other people, the writers, poets, photographers, and artists whose works help inspire us and are examined in the pages ahead, individuals who help us think about personal character, people who have struggled hard to reconcile scholarly, literary, artistic interests and pursuits with moral concerns, with the enduring questions of where do we come from, what are we, and where are we going. These and other questions are directly and artistically rendered—for example, by Paul Gauguin in his painting *D'où venons-nous? Que sommes-nous? Où Allons-nous?*, a work we will visit toward the end of this book. With written and visual stories as our guides, we embark on a journey, exploring the world through social reflection and observation of a particular kind. The idea is to venture outside of our own immediate experiences, to wonder about and wander with others in search of an understanding that will enable us to hand one another along.

With Billie Holiday providing the ambient accompaniment, we join James Agee in Alabama and George Orwell in the Midlands of England. We meet Dr. William Carlos Williams, a physician from Rutherford, New Jersey, who every day made house calls to his patients, carrying his black bag up tenement stairs. In the evening, stethoscope put aside and typewriter picked up, Williams composed poems and stories and worked on novels, trying to give us a sense of what it meant to be with particular Americans, as he knew them in the 1920s, '30s, and '40s.

While Billie sings of longing, we meet the writer Raymond Carver, whose family moved from Arkansas to the West Coast, working in factories and in the fields. We meet the people who populate his poems and short stories: blue-collar workers, waitresses, motel workers, people who are washed out, or who are drying out. Yet for all their pain, their marginality and vulnerability, the redemptive epiphanies in Carver's stories are not unlike the epiphanies all of us have, or hope to have, as we come to terms with the deep beauty and deep disruptions of life.

We meet Tillie Olsen, born in Nebraska, a writer who spent most of her life in California. She will give us stories that ask us to think about what it means to be a mother and at the same time a full-time worker. It isn't long before she moves us toward the current discussion about welfare. Olsen was a tough and active labor organizer, but she also fought hard for the recognition of her fellow women writers. She asks us, through her fiction, to consider what many women have tried to do, to be.

We will move on to the huge subject of race in America. It's been with us from the very beginning, since the first pioneers stepped foot on American soil and found others here waiting for them. Those others wondered who these people coming ashore with their boats were, wondered why they were there, and for what purpose. We will begin our own travels on the subject of race with the guiding help of Ralph Ellison, a college dropout, a jazz musician, a photographer who stumbled his way north to Manhattan, trying to figure out what he was going to do with his life. He had been denigrated and denied by certain teachers ("What's the matter with him?" many of them thought), and out of that life, from those rejections and uncertainties, came the novel *Invisible Man*.

We meet Flannery O'Connor, a white woman from rural Georgia who, ailing from lupus, died at thirty-nine. Some will wonder who she is to tell us about race, she who was privileged, and cultured, and very much a private person. We will see how a writer who had such limited physical capacity could nevertheless feel and see and write in a way that transcended her limitations and experiences to shed light on all of our lives.

Soon enough we meet Walker Percy, who gives us characters "who made straight A's and flunked ordinary living." Well, how can you and I do better than that, how can we think about our lives in such a way that we don't fail at ordinary living? That is the question we will consider in the context of Walker Percy and "Intellectuals and the Religious Search." Walker Percy, having begun as a scientifically oriented young man, majored in chemistry at college, went on to medical school, worked as a physician, became interested in psychiatry, gave us philosophical essays, gave us, as well, six novels before his death in 1990. He was a man from the South, from privilege, from a family of authority and renown. But he also knew suffering and the pain of family suicide. Out of all that, he created novels such as *The Moviegoer*, which, in a way, tells us what this book is, finally, about. At the end of *The Moviegoer*, we are given the metaphor of "handing one another along" and of being helped along—a sturdy reminder that amidst life's potential for loneliness or despair, we are ultimately, and ideally, deeply connected to one another, always handing one another along in our journeys.

All of this is then brought to us again, certainly, by Zora Neale Hurston in her novel *Their Eyes Were Watching God*. Hurston was a folklorist writer, a black woman with a stubborn, idiosyncratic nature that found its most valuable expression through writing. We readers will be lucky to wonder who she is and what she is telling us, which has a way of reaching over barriers of race and time. Finally, we take into account the personal lives and challenges put forth by spiritual wanderers such as Dorothy Day and Georges Bernanos, by Elie Wiesel and Ignazio Silone. At the very end of our exploration, we take to heart three deeply searching Victorian novelists and moralists, Charles Dickens, Thomas Hardy, and George Eliot, who wondered about nothing more or less, really, than you and me, and about how we find our way through life's confrontations.

This book's reflections will also be guided by particular moments in history—by the constraints that history imposes on us and the inspiration and opportunity it allows us. Without exception, our thinking, our values, even our reading of books that have been handed down over generations, are influenced by the historical moment in which we live. What was it like for people who wrote or read these same books fifty years ago, a hundred years ago? When we read books or look at pictures, we do so at a time, in a place, at our own behest or that of another called a friend or a teacher. We might ask ourselves what inspires us to put forth one line of inquiry and what discourages or prevents us from pursuing another. Each historical moment is yours and mine, and our personal experiences connect with this moment—they go back and forth, influencing one another: who we are, our race, our class, the homes we come from, what we are learning in those homes, the times in which we are living and learning. Furthermore, we are influenced by where we've lived, the town, the neighborhood, the nation, as well as our cultural background. National and personal heritage influence the way we think, what we do. In essence, then, what you get out of any book and what you bring to experiencing a book, or the viewing of a painting or a photograph, is an aspect of your experience, a personal, reflective response, what you bring to the table. This book is an attempt to help you make your perspective broader—so that you can reflect on life in a wider sense, and on moral matters through the more universal lens that writers and artists can provide.

Through stories, we are given the opportunity to search deeper into an understanding of what we make of our own stories, and of this world in which we live every day. What do we notice and why? What does that say about us, or others? How do we think about the stories of others, and about our own stories?

I can remember driving to work one day from my Massachusetts hometown, and when I reached Cambridge I saw people standing near Harvard Square holding placards with two names on them, each a candidate for state representative. The names were different, and I began to notice that the advocates holding the signs looked different, too. Were they really different, or was there something in me that noticed differences—was my mind subject to some external, objective "validation"? What was I picking up about the distinction that my head registered between the proponents of candidate X and those of candidate Y—in their dress, in their manner, in the way they were walking, soliciting attention? Our human subjectivity connects with the so-called objective world (people, places, and things, there, waiting to be apprehended). Then there is the observer in me: how my memories, experiences, and values shape who, how, and what I see—how what has been taught to me, told to me, emphasized to me can color things; what I stumbled into through fate, and luck, and chance, through the choices of my parents, the neighborhoods, the friends I have called mine. All of these things that we carry within us all the time, and that help us make sense of the world, can also limit what we take in. History is also working on us, on our personal experiences—and, too, in our schools, where we get offered so-called bodies of knowledge, which help shape what we notice, what we attend to seriously, and why.

If we want to reflect on the world around us, in terms of values, to whom might we appeal outside of friends or people in our immediate families? And what prompts us in our everyday lives to take a stand and say, "I'm for this and I believe that, and this is what I look for, and this is what matters"? Well, we know there's politics, and that politicians exhort us to see obligations in a certain way. So do ministers, priests, and rabbis, who also call upon us to look at things in a particular way. At times, moral education is delivered through attendance at a church, or a mosque, or a synagogue. Through listening to politicians and preachers and others who have our attention, we get prompted to reflect on the world.

We are stirred to reflect in other ways, too. We pick up the newspaper; we turn on the television; we listen to the radio. We are told: This is what matters, and this is how you might think about it. The *Boston Globe, Boston Herald, New York Times, Wall Street Journal, Los Angeles Times, Washington Post,* and on and on it goes, in every locale with each outlet choosing to emphasize this or that. You put on the TV and the broadcaster is saying, by implication, "There it is, the most important thing that happened today, and I'm going to start off with it."

Sometimes the news becomes a little more discursive and we get journalistic essays—reflective pieces. Those pieces are both shaped and constrained by the events that have taken place—a murder or an accident, for example. Then comes the social reflection of the commentators, the reporters. When those reporters go out, they, like you and me, notice particular things about whichever phenomena are available. Out of the entire scope of events taking place in your life and mine, there is a selection process for how the news gets reflected through the prisms of history, of time and place, which together tell us, "These are the things that ought to be on our minds, these are the values that matter." We can trace our paths through history, which culminate in where we are now. We reflect through journalism and news stories, and through our lives—as citizens of a country, as people who live here or there in that country, and at a given time in a country's ongoing history.

The word "literature" can also become its own abstraction. Literature is to storytelling as theology is to the practice of religion: the former, which is a broad concept, does not necessarily drive the latter, which is felt in daily application. A writer like Charles Dickens basically did not attend school, never got a degree, never taught literature or took a course in literature; indeed, he studied life, as he lived part of his childhood in a prison with his family, because they were so poor as to become criminal debtors. Dickens didn't write *Great Expectations* or *David Copperfield* because he had taken some courses in "literature" and wanted to be a writer. He wrote, as his journals tell us, out of personal aspiration and desperation. He was a poor unknown, we would have said of him if we were studying or teaching at Oxford or Cambridge. Despite his lack of educational background and credentials he became, well, Charles Dickens, one of our greatest novelists. He wrote stories, or "sketches," as he called them initially. Those sketches, in turn, were read by publishers and other people who thought (to paraphrase): "I want people to read this; I think I'll publish this; but who is this guy? Where did he come from? What kind of a person is he? I'd like to meet him! But whether I meet him or not, I'm excited by this story, so I'll publish it." It may have been just that simple.

Imagine that pretty soon people started thinking of him as "Charles Dickens the storyteller." They didn't know anything about him but that he was a storyteller and he had been published in some English newspaper or magazine. You and I know him as part of the Victorian period, as someone we study in literature courses. How we do that studying also has to do with history and the academy's notions of what history ought to be. We analyze, we theorize, we "deconstruct," we fit Dickens into a period, an era; above all, we classify. In my mind, I have these stories jumbled together in ways that I'm not even sure of myself; as William James put it, the mind is "one great blooming, buzzing confusion." But I'm not going to get away with that way of explaining things.

In this very book, the so-called literary and journalistic tradition is also an abstraction—an abstract classification and response to writers such as James Agee and George Orwell. If they were to come back here and join us, I imagine that they would likely laugh wryly and say, "Go ahead if that is what you have to do." Nevertheless, we do it and there are good reasons why we do it, and good reasons to go beyond longer works of literature to include short stories and poems. This book is about stories as a means of broad social and personal reflection. It's not a book on literature in the traditional sense of the way literature is taught or thought about, examined. It's not a book about social theory, although it deals with social questions, namely those rooted in events that have taken place in the world. This book is not only about the stories themselves; it is also about doing the work of social observation, of listening and reflecting upon the stories of others and of the world around us, and coming to terms with what one has done, how sometimes people have had experiences that won't let go of them and get into a confrontation with their own analytic sensibility and, yes, with the powers that be.

One of the major tensions in this book—I ought to level with you up front—is the tension between the analytic sensibility upon which each of us relies, and which thrives in academic institutions (for the students and the teachers alike), and the felt experience of people, of the writers as they bare themselves to us as readers, who, in turn, experience and feel with these writers and artists. I am also referring to the felt experience that you and I have all the time, and that we bring to these books, and that we work mightily to get out of our minds as we read them—encouraged, of course, by teachers who tell us, "No, no, no. Let's *figure* this book out, rather than emphasize feeling it." Now, there are hazards in both directions. The analytic sensibility runs amok, gives us brilliant theory, unconnected to the ordinary hurdles that face all of us every day. On the other hand, an emphasis on experience that does not allow us to occasionally get some distance from those often deeply emotional experiences, and try to develop a fair sense of the stories around us, can leave us wallowing in debilitating sentiment.

Thinking historically, we are going back to stories such as those of the Hebrew prophets of Israel, to Isaiah and Jeremiah, to their regular critique of power, the power of others to dismiss them and frighten them and send them outside the gates of acceptance. We are going back, also, to stories such as that of Jesus of Nazareth, and his relationship to power, and on and on that classic conflict goes, right down into our time and onward. Our country was settled by people who also rebuffed considerable social powers, who left lives that were acceptable and prominent, who crossed the ocean when death was not only around the corner but already present (during weeks of hard travel), who came to a world where there was no one to accept or welcome them. This story has gone on for several hundred years: people departing from what is, seeking some other life, some other interpretation of life, some other notion of what is valuable and desirable.

I remember when I was a resident at Children's Hospital in Boston, working with children who were dying of leukemia, I asked and heard about what was on their minds: life's purposes, its mysteries—what is on all of our minds as we fight against life's inevitable end. What was on their minds was what was on Tolstoy's mind when he wrote *Confession*. All struggled hard to reconcile the events of their lives, to take measure of the person they had been in this world. What was on their minds was what was on the minds of the other writers here: Dorothy Day and Georges Bernanos, and Elie Wiesel and Ignazio Silone. What does one live by and for? Knowledge, perhaps, but for what, and which knowledge? Power, perhaps, but power for what? Accomplishment, perhaps, but for what? Always the refrain: "For what?"

So there are works to inspire us toward moral reflections, and toward taking to heart the struggle within ourselves through each of these stories and through our own stories. The struggle to figure out a little bit more, with the help of others, about who and what we are. Human beings are creatures of awareness, of language. That is who we are. We know about time—its beginning for us and, certainly, its end. We are the creatures of stories; we tell stories to one another, and we know that we have our own stories to tell, sometimes over and over again. So in a world that has become, for me, all too categorical or deterministic in thought, we have the existential and the mysterious, which I hope this book exemplifies—a coming to terms with the rock-bottom nature of our storytelling humanity, which enables us to meet with and be helped and guided by others, including the writers featured in the pages ahead. Above all, no matter the outcome for each particular reader, I hope you will take to heart each of the authors and artists who join us on this reflective journey, perhaps even to the point that they, and the characters they introduce to us, become companions in your life. I hope that the stories, in sum, told through words and pictures, studied through a lens of our own personal and social reflections, can prompt you to stop and consider the way in which you perceive and interact with the world around you, and how you choose to participate in this one life given to you, to us.

Dr. Robert Coles

EDITORS' NOTE

This book is an invitation to think, listen, and participate in a discussion of moral inquiry and stories, through reading and through the reflections of Dr. Robert Coles, derived from the long-running Harvard University course A Literature of Social Reflection. This book, like the course itself, is about how literature can help us reflect on a broad range of social issues, and on what it means to find our way as human beings in this world.

At times the reader will be asked to follow a series of free associations and seemingly tangential lines of thought. The reader will, at times, want more illumination of a particular story, poem, or photograph. Although this book contains the context for many of these parenthetical references, we hope that the reader will also seek out those original stories, poems, or photographs and spend time with them—for it is these stories, coupled with Dr. Coles's thoughts, that form the core of this book, which requires the active engagement, participation, and imagination of its reader.

It is important to mention that along with reading the stories and listening to the lectures, the students in A Literature of Social Reflection were asked to participate in weekly section meetings. During these small, intimate gatherings, the students and their teaching fellows were able to make personal connections between their own lives and those of the authors, artists, and stories to which they had been introduced. We encourage you, the reader, to read the chapters presented in this book and then to enhance that experience with independent exploration of the stories and the artwork to which Dr. Coles refers throughout. When at all possible, we also encourage you to find the time to sit with friends, family members, or fellow readers to explore further the thoughts and narratives offered herein. It is, after all, through conversations with others that the greater implications of these stories will take on a broader meaning for each individual.

Much of what we read in newspapers and magazines and take in through television and the Internet seems to highlight our differences and instill mistrust in one another. It is our hope that this book, and the stories discussed, will do for you what they have done for us. We hope that the pages ahead will awaken in you a curiosity about the lives and stories of those around you, of people both familiar and unfamiliar—and so ultimately serve to narrow the distances between all of us through a contemplation and celebration of the stories, the narratives that we now hold in common.

Trevor Hall and Vicki Kennedy

PART I

Heading Out

The literary and journalistic documentary tradition of social observation—the call to venture outside of what we know and attend the stories of others.

Featured: James Agee, George Orwell, and William Carlos Williams

ONE

James Agee:
A Biting Irony

Let us start with an introduction to James Agee, born in Knoxville, Tennessee, in 1909. His parents were of different backgrounds. His father, Hugh James Agee, was of Appalachian yeoman stock, basically a workingman, one generation removed from the hollows of the Great Smoky Mountains. His mother was from what would be called today, by some, an upper-middle-class commercial family, and she was well educated. She received various periodicals, including the *Atlantic Monthly*—she had refinement and aspirations toward culture. When their first child, James (or Rufus, as he was called as a boy), was six years old, his father was killed in an automobile accident—an important moment in James's life. The last thing Agee wrote, the quasi-autobiographical novel *A Death in the Family*, would go on to win a Pulitzer Prize in 1957, although this was two years after his own untimely death, in 1955, from a heart attack suffered in the back of a taxicab; he was on his way to New York Hospital because he had been experiencing chest pains.

Agee's forty-five years proved to be tumultuous: the death of a parent at only six, and by ten or eleven he was sent off to the St. Andrew's School, an Episcopal boarding school in Sewanee, Tennessee, right near the University of the South, run at that time by a monastic Episcopalian order. He lived there for three or four years while his mother was getting her feet on the ground after the death of her husband and was tending to the boy's younger sister.★

When Agee was sixteen he left St. Andrew's for Phillips Exeter Academy, in New Hampshire—a fancy private school with a long intellectual tradition. He was a southern boy of a complex background, already in his own way a populist, an earthy, crunchy, idiosyncratic, rebellious—very rebellious—young man. He arrived at the staid New England private school at a time when it was much stiffer and more exclusionary, almost exclusively populated by wealthy East Coast scions of privilege. Within months, this sixteen-year-old youth began an affair with the forty-year-old school librarian, an affair that would last for the two years he attended classes. He was no stranger to that dark brown drink known as bourbon, and he smoked heavily. He also began writing and was soon enough contributing to the Exeter magazine, the *Monthly*. In no time, he was admitted to the fancy Lantern Club. Upon graduation in 1928, he went to Harvard.

While in Cambridge, at Harvard, he would give some courses his all; others he would ignore, to the point of flunking them. At times, he would just disappear—for days or even longer. He would frequent the Theater District in downtown Boston, where there were burlesque shows, lots of bars, and people who walked the streets, and women ready to take up the acquaintance of those who were interested in doing so. He would spend a lot of time there observing, but also striking up conversations. Back in Cambridge, he wrote feverishly—poetry and short stories, some of which began to be published in the *Harvard Advocate*. Eventually, he would become president of this undergraduate literary quarterly.

By the time he was ready to graduate, Agee had written a collec-

---

★While there, he got to know one of the priests very well, Father Flye. For those who want to pursue Agee—and many have, over the years—the correspondence between James Agee and Father Flye has been collected in a book that is still in print.

tion of poems, which he sent off for consideration to the Yale Younger Poets award. He won, which led to publication of his book *Permit Me Voyage* in 1934. During that time he was introduced to I. A. Richards, a distinguished professor of English on the New Haven campus. Richards, in turn, handed Agee on to a former student of his, Archibald MacLeish, who had gone to New York to work for Henry Robinson Luce, the publisher of *Time, Life,* and *Fortune.*

MacLeish, a poet who went on to become assistant secretary of state for cultural and public affairs, managed to secure Agee a job at *Fortune* magazine writing essays on finance and business, but all the while Agee was writing more and more poetry in his spare time. As Luce and his magazine were moving into the Chrysler Building in midtown Manhattan, the legend of James Agee was becoming known to the literary community of Manhattan: the enormously talented writer who drank a lot, slept around, and who would write while listening to Beethoven's Ninth Symphony so loudly and so often that people worried whether the Chrysler Building would withstand the orchestral blasts. He wrote pieces for *Fortune* on Mohawk rugs, orchids, the Tennessee Valley Authority (a group of dams that, under the aegis of the New Deal, were being built in Agee's home state to harness a river's threatening power of flooding); he wrote on Cuba, as it was ruled by none other than American gangsters in Havana; he wrote an essay on strawberries, which in the 1930s were an aristocratic indulgence for the upper class, and not widely familiar, as they now are to Americans. He also loved the movies, which had not yet become something called "film." Agee desperately wanted to write about the movies, but the top editors were not quite sure they were ready for that in any of the Luce publications. Those pieces would have to wait.

One day in early 1936, Mr. Luce called Agee in and said he had an assignment for him. He wanted Agee to go down to Alabama, find some sharecropping families, spend a few weeks there, then come back and write about them. Agee had become *Fortune's* ace reporter, the writer who knew how to take complicated social and economic matters and translate them for the businesspeople who needed to understand what was going on in America. At that time, *Fortune* was, without exception, an extraordinarily well-written magazine.

Agee agreed to go south, and as an afterthought Mr. Luce said, "Maybe get a photographer to go with you, and we'll get some good pictures." This was the 1930s, during the Great Depression, and when Luce said "sharecroppers" he did not have to spell out the qualifying word. What he meant was *white* sharecroppers; there were plenty of them. *Fortune* magazine (and, by extension, its readers) were not interested in black sharecroppers. They were interested in *white* yeomen, in finding out about them and how their experiences might reflect on larger social and economic issues.

What did Agee do before going on this assignment? Well, he didn't start looking at books, at statistics or studies about what he might see in Alabama. Rather, he started remembering courses he had taken at Harvard College, and it occurred to him that one Harvard lecturer had talked about the novelist Daniel Defoe, who in the eighteenth century wrote a book called *A Journal of the Plague Year,* an epic attempt to tell what happened when the plague hit London in the middle of the previous century. The book was a mix of factuality and evocations of individuals, put together by a novelist who'd created characters so that the reader would understand how it had felt back then: the sights and sounds of an epidemic, of the sick and dying. The dramatic power of storytelling, the intensity of characters stricken by a fatal illness, the concomitant atmosphere— all got worked into a narrative presentation. Agee remembered that book well, and he read it again in preparation for his trip.

Agee was then told by Dwight Macdonald (an important American writer of the earlier part of the twentieth century who started out with *Fortune* and would go on to found a journal called *Politics,* an idiosyncratic leftist magazine in the 1940s and '50s) to research the writing of Henry Mayhew. Agee went to the New York Public

Library and found out that Henry Mayhew was a London writer, an essayist and journalist of the mid-nineteenth century (a contemporary and friend of Dickens's) who, in essay after essay for a newspaper called the *Morning Chronicle,* described what he called "the London laboring class" or, at other times, "the London poor." Toymakers, tanners, tailors, milliners, shopkeepers they were called, or men and women who picked up garbage and cleaned floors. These were the people who made a great city work, and what he did was describe their work, their lives, and who they were, with respect and concern, with affection.

Mayhew came from a privileged background; had gone to a private school called Westminster, in London; and was a rebel within his family, among his friends. He was supported (with some mixed feelings) by his father. When he wrote, his objective was to make his reader "feel for these people," as he put it in one of his diary entries. Sometimes when his work was published in the *Morning Chronicle* and in the books in which these articles were collected, it was joined by illustrations done by George Cruikshank, the great nineteenth-century satirist and illustrator whose work adorned Dickens's writing when it first appeared in newspapers and books. Agee had encountered a connection of the visual to the textual that went back a couple hundred years—back, actually, to the late eighteenth century in France, and had flourished in the nineteenth century in England. Dickens used to say that he waited each week for Mayhew's stories and that they provoked and inspired some of his own writing. Of course, Dickens went one step further, beyond the tanners and jail keepers and factory workers of various kinds, described factually by Mayhew, in his own fictional depictions of these lives. Later on, in this country, the tradition was carried on by writers such as Jacob Riis and his famous *How the Other Half Lives* and Charles Loring Brace's book *The Dangerous Classes of New York*. These writers tried to tell us about a similar kind of disparity between themselves, as observers and writers, and those they were observing: the observer and the observed. Lewis Hine began taking photographs, which were often used to illustrate some of these essays. His photographs were of children and factories in Appalachia, and the border states of the South: Virginia, Tennessee, and Kentucky.

By the 1930s, we had the Farm Security Administration (FSA), and we had the whole tradition of documentary photography. One of those documentary photographers would ultimately be Walker Evans, another nonconformist who did not graduate from college. He went to Williams College, among others, for a while, then dropped out, took a fancy to the camera, and became a drinking buddy of Agee's in New York. The two of them finally set out for Alabama in July 1936—a reelection year for Roosevelt, and the first year that the New Deal would be tested by the American voting public.

Agee and Evans went down to Alabama. They ended up in a county located between Montgomery and Birmingham and undertook the chronicle that would eventually become *Let Us Now Praise Famous Men*. When you pick up this book and open its cover, the first thing you see is not words but pictures of people.

You see first a man with a well-worn suit jacket and a necktie. This is a book whose title, *Let Us Now Praise Famous Men,* comes from the Apocrypha, which is a book that didn't quite make the Bible. It has an annexed status to the Holy Book (kind of like Radcliffe once was to Harvard). It is no accident that "Let us now praise famous men" is a verse Agee includes in his book. In the photographs you see a man with a necktie and his jacket and then you turn the page and there is a man with overalls. When you meet the people, the homes, the furniture, the outhouses, the shoes, someone harvesting cotton, all through these photographs, you meet fellow American citizens in various stages of their existence and living various shades of that life.

As you begin to find your way into the book, you're given the title, told that the photographs were reproduced through the Farm Security Administration (then part of the Department of Agriculture), told the publisher, offered the dedication, and then, if you skip

From *Let Us Now Praise Famous Men* by James Agee. Photograph by Walker Evans.

From *Let Us Now Praise Famous Men* by James Agee. Photograph by Walker Evans.

the foreword written by Walker Evans, you learn that Agee never wrote the article for *Fortune.* He became so discombobulated, so upset, so engaged, so enraged that he quit the magazine, and he and his wife went to Frenchtown, in the western part of New Jersey, and for months, which turned into several years, he fretted over what we now have as a book.

The first words of the text proper come on page 33 in the Ballantine edition: "Poor naked wretches, wheresoe'er you are / That bide the pelting of this pitiless storm, / How shall your houseless heads and unfed sides, / Your loop'd and window'd raggedness, defend you / From seasons such as these?" That quote is taken from Shakespeare's *King Lear.* What does King Lear have to do with central Alabama, with its Depression-era brute poverty, with its extreme vulnerability and social marginality? Why *King Lear*? What is *King Lear* about? *King Lear* is about power and deception and betrayal; *King Lear* is about a family, a father and his daughters; *King Lear* is about trust and mistrust; *King Lear* is about patrimony gone awry.

Agee is telling us a lot without a single word of his own, drawing on his education and his sensibility, saying, "Folks, I'm gonna try and do justice to this world, boy am I going to try and do justice! I'm going to summon the best I can—yes, even Shakespeare: I'll bring him to nineteenth-century Alabama! I will sweat my words and thoughts and opinions so that you in turn will sweat, so that all of us will sweat about our American patrimony, about what it can mean to people to be an American in this fourth decade of the twentieth century, to be near starvation, to have little if anything."

Before you even pay attention to these people, stop and remember this: there is a context to all discussions, even political ones. *Let Us Now Praise Famous Men,* which takes up in its own way politics and race and privilege and poverty and power and vulnerability, nevertheless deserves a context. Agee asks us to remember that even the rich and the powerful, kings and their families, go through hurt and pain, and deception, and betrayal. Consider what happens when someone talks to you, coming out of this or that persuasion, about "these people and their special situation" or addresses you, me, or, most directly, the author, James Agee, the one who has the right to answer (and us with him) this implied skepticism, if not accusation: "Can you even understand them as an outsider, you well-to-do James Agee, coming down from the Chrysler Building with your relatively speaking huge salary? (He was extremely well paid.) Your huge salary, your Exeter and Harvard education, *you* are going to understand these people? Are you going to understand their hurt, and the way they feel and the struggles they have?" Agee seems to say to himself, "I do want to understand them, but I don't want to lose my moorings in our shared humanity. If I categorize them, describe them in such a way that sets them apart from the rest of us, especially those of us who are privileged, by way of upbringing or education or homes or jobs, then this is no favor done to them."

So he gives us King Lear, and then he gives us these well-known words: "Workers of the world, unite and fight. You have nothing to lose but your chains, and a world to win." Now, that is the kind of thing that might have gotten Mr. J. Edgar Hoover after him. That is Communist political rhetoric; but you and I, he would suggest, might look at those two sentences and say, "What is wrong with that? There is nothing wrong with advocating that workers unite and struggle for a better life. If they do so, they sure have a lot to win, so why not?!" On the other hand, there is a footnote—in which Agee observes how language can soon enough become the property of categorical politics, of betrayals, of Leninism and Stalinism, with their mass murder: the phrases go on, and the murder goes on too, in the name of those phrases. Agee is saying to us: I would like to call upon art and politics in a certain way—art through Shakespeare, and politics with a kind of language that frees us from clichés. There are many kinds of clichés, including the clichés we learn, unfortunately, in classrooms, from professors in our various kinds of postgraduate professional training instruction, where we are often trained—consciously or not—to throw around language and feel so good about ourselves being so well educated, so knowing at the expense of others.

One page is reproduced from a school textbook, one children of that era read in the elementary schools; they read about the great ball on which we live, and that "the world is our home." You may remember the books that were read to you when you were younger. I remember reading to my children books such as *Make Way for Ducklings*—nice, pretty, lovely books. The policemen are ever so friendly to the people crossing the street and to the ducks. Some of you will have different experiences with the police, but *which* police, and in *which* neighborhood, and doing *what*. So, there are the lovely books, telling us about "the great ball on which we live" and that "the world is our home," but Agee wants us to think of the homes of many other children, some of whom live in faraway lands, who are also our brothers and sisters. He wants us to wonder what every person needs in order to live securely, safely.

"Let us imagine that we are far out in the fields. The air is bitter cold and the wind is blowing. Snow is falling, and by and by it will turn into sleet and rain. We are almost naked. We have had nothing to eat and are suffering from hunger as well as cold. Suddenly the Queen of the Fairies floats down and offers us three wishes. What shall we choose? 'I shall wish for food because I'm hungry,' says Peter. 'I shall choose clothes to keep out the cold,' says John. 'And I shall ask for a house to shelter me from the wind, the snow, and the rain,' says little Nell with a shiver. Now everyone needs food, clothing and shelter"—and on and on this goes, in Agee's selection from *Around the World with the Children.* What does it mean when a child reads something like that? What kind of sensibility will stop that page and say, "Aha! This is the beginning of my story; I don't even have to mobilize my own language. I have found, noticed, read this."

What does Agee attempt here? He has here found irony, a biting irony—a beginning of his effort with us: the kind of irony he learned from novelists and playwrights and the kind of irony that he is going to make sure we read hard, and feel even harder, in this book.

Let Us Now Praise Famous Men challenges the very notion of what a book is (which is to say, it is sprawling, erudite, engaged, furious), offering pictures on their own, without words (not something that is typically done, not even within the literature of documentary writing). By placing Evans's photos first, Agee chooses to give the photographer initial authority—wordless authority—as if to suggest that if we just look we will see and understand. Then comes the Western tradition (Shakespeare) and the political tradition of valuable social rebelliousness that has been ultimately destroyed by institutional murder—those Utopian dreams that ended up in the Gulag of Stalin, a reminder of how the workings of history and politics can be a part of your fate and mine.★

★Jonathan Kozol came out with a book in the mid-1960s called *Death at an Early Age,* which treads similar ground. Kozol was a schoolteacher, having gone to Harvard, written a novel, been published in the *Advocate.* He then ended up teaching in Roxbury, Massachusetts, where he saw rather quickly how institutions do not always smile on those who belong to them—indeed, sometimes hurt them all too significantly.

As we enter the written text in *Let Us Now Praise Famous Men,* we meet confessional assaults—an unnerving thing for us to consider, to the point that we're tempted to wonder about Agee's purposes and, yes, about *him.* What does this guy want of us? Who is he? What is his problem (as it's put in the clinical cultural language of our time)? If something troubles you, then by definition *it* is troubled. If you read challenging words and can't get them out of your head and you take offense at them or, on the other side, if you are enraptured by them, then you have a "problem" and need to go and "see someone." Thereby we move ourselves from intellectual and emotional confrontation to the language of psychopathology.

Here is Agee addressing his future publisher and, of course, his future readers, those puzzled editors who, like you and me, strain over these pages and say, "What is this? Categorize it. Figure it out. Tell us, define it, A, B, C, or none of the above." He uses a technological kind of thinking, which we all have absorbed: "So does the whole subsequent course and fate of the work: the causes for its nonpublication . . . ; the problems which confronted the maker of the photographs; and those which confront me as I try to write of it: the question, Who are you who will read these words and study these photographs, and through what cause, by what chance, and for what purpose, and by what right do you qualify to, and what will you do about it." Every time he is posing these questions at you, he is also posing them at the "you" in him, sitting there in New Jersey, whiskey not too far away from him (he was his own kind of whiskey priest), sweating it out, living with his privileges, glad to have them. Glimpse and then picture with our camera what happens when one undertakes documentary work. We are asked to consider the disproportion of life between the haves and the have-nots, between those learning, observing, writing, reading, studying and those who don't feel they have a right to do anything but take one step after another, always with the feel of falling down on their faces, with stomachs that ache because they are not well fed, with bones that aren't strong, with who knows what diseases lurking right there in front of them from day to day. Those with futures that are constrained by fate and circumstance, bad luck, misfortune.

In the midst of their work, James Agee and Walker Evans would routinely get in their car and drive to Birmingham, check into the old Tutwiler hotel there and get smashed, and then return the next day. And go back for what? They are wondering about who these folks are and about what they are going to do with what they have seen and heard; they are wondering about their boss up there in the Chrysler Building who owns their work or their working days, and who is paying them well. Paying them more in one week than these people would see in a year, maybe five years. Many of these people lived on the old cash-and-barter economy. The cash went to the boss men, while the laborers bartered their labor for a place to live (if you want to call those shacks such a place) and for minimal food. Tenant farmers, sharecroppers—it was life in the thirties for some whites, and this is not even beginning to bring up the question of blacks, which Agee doesn't really do until he gets into the chapter "Education," and then only by indirection or in passing.

Nonetheless, Agee knew about the black and white issue, and he lets us know that he knew. He shows us this in "Near a Church," where there are two blacks, looking at Agee and Evans, and as you look at this you ask yourself, "What is this about and why is he doing this, this picture of people seeing others, frightened of them, trembling before them?" What do you and I do when we see fear in others and know that we are the source of that fear, not because we necessarily have animus or prejudice, but because we too are victims of those ghosts of the past and its estrangements and misunderstandings? Indeed, so much of *Let Us Now Praise Famous Men* has to do with misunderstanding, as it slowly moves toward understanding: fiction and nonfiction, poetry and essays, biography, autobiography— all of it reminding us that one can misunderstand oneself quite mightily. But imagine that scene in the book, and the kind of conversations Evans and Agee could have between themselves, and you can have right now with them and with yourself: "Hey, Walker, hey,

Jim, take it easy, you're getting those people more scared than they were initially by the way you are going to behave; and if you are going to go and do what you say you're gonna do, get down and beg their forgiveness, then what are they going to make of you, since they can't pick up a telephone and call the nearest doctor to have you carted off in a wagon? Don't make too much out of this, let this be." Or, on the other hand, we might wonder to ourselves: who knows what might have happened between these begging white folks, these two privileged outsiders, and those two black people—who knows what kind of moment of understanding, even intimacy, they might have had! How do we cross these divides of class and race? How do we get to know one another? You know that without directly experiencing Alabama in the 1930s—you know that in your own lives, within families, a neighborhood, a community as we look at one another and try to figure out how to behave with one another.

When I read *Let Us Now Praise Famous Men,* I think of Agee as singing in an opera—a sustained, passionate oratorio. I think of the long discourses of the poets of Greece and Rome, standing there on platforms with one another, with their rhetorical expressiveness. And note the language in this book, as lush and inviting and perplexing as the rural South can be, with its byways and its customs that can challenge so many of us. Here is Agee again: "All over Alabama, the lamps are out. Every leaf drenches the touch; the spider's net is heavy. The roads lie there, with nothing to use them. The fields lie there, with nothing at work in them, neither man nor beast." Here are the words of a young writer familiar with the Bible and its rhythms, Shakespeare and his rhythms, familiar with James Joyce and *Ulysses*—and here is a person of words making a huge effort to break out of simple sentences and the vernacular, to call upon language and all of its power and glory, and the King James Bible and all that it's come to mean to many of us. Agee continues,

The plow handles are wet, and the rails and the frogplates and the weeds between the ties: and not even the hurryings and

hoarse sorrows of a distant train, on other roads, is heard. The little towns, the county seats, house by house white-painted and
elaborately sawn among their heavy and dark-lighted leaves, in
the spaced protections of their mineral light they stand so prim,
so voided, so undefended upon starlight, that it is inconceivable
to despise or scorn a white man, an owner of land; even in Birmingham, mile on mile, save for the sudden frightful streaming,
almost instantly diminished and silent, of a closed black car, and
save stone lonesome sinister heelbeats, that show never a face
and enter, soon, a frame door flush with the pavement, and as-
cend the immediate lightless staircase, mile and mile, stone, stone,
smooth charted streams of stone, the streets under their lifted
lamps lie void before eternity.

Agee's poetic mind was dazzled and was drunk not only with language, but with a situation that has intoxicated him, maddened him,
morally awakened him, frightened him, jolted him out of the
rhythms of journalism and success as he struggled within himself for
expression and coherence.

Agee is a writer singing, stirred to song by the scene, as were
Homer and Shakespeare, as were Walt Whitman and William Carlos
Williams, both of whom sang of America: its beauty and its ugliness,
its land and its people. Their songs stir us free of interstates, and exam
pedantry, and regulations and technology and multiple-choice questions, stirring our hearts as well as our heads.

Agee offers something for anyone interested in individual children, in the human particularity that defies all the conceptualizations and formulations of the social sciences—those who want to
define, define, define: "All that each person is and experiences, and
shall never experience, in body and in mind, all these things are dif-
fering expressions of himself and of one root, and are identical: and
not one of these things nor one of these persons is ever quite to be
duplicated, nor replaced, nor has it ever quite had precedent."

All these "duplications" that make our careers, as we try to add

From *Let Us Now Praise Famous Men* by James Agee. Photograph by Walker Evans.

our various categorizations: *this* kind of person, *that* kind of person—the classifications of race, of class, of genre, of nationality, of regionality, all the definitions! You and I (again, as in Whitman, as in Williams), you and I can become sovereign, to some extent, you'll see this right through this book, culminating in George Eliot's statement that I'll read to you during the last lecture—when she echoes this or, rather, this echoes her. (Both of them would laugh at my momentary chronological effort to place them. They would say: "Don't do that to us, we are *together,* we can speak to one another without you letting them know that I, George Eliot, am before him, Jim Agee. We are kindred souls; don't let time be your definition, or chronology, which is just another way of pigeonholing.")

Continuing with Agee on human individuality: ". . . nor has it ever quite had precedent [this is quite something]: but each is a new and incommunicably tender life [as you and I were when we first came here that moment of the first breath, struggling to be], wounded in every breath, and almost as hardly killed as easily wounded." Note how Agee is careful in the way he defines, uses adjectives and adverbs, which are such easy weapons for us to use, in order to take full control of whatever it is that we want to describe. He modifies, and modifies, and modifies, and drives us crazy. He continues: "sustaining, for a while, without defense, the enormous assaults of the universe." "What's the use?" Agee asks this on page 64, trying to say what he felt, but then he goes on; he asks that rhetorical question, but he keeps making an effort in long, long paragraphs worthy of Henry James—not wanting to interrupt himself with a new paragraph, but wanting to connect and connect, to link, in one huge breath: to get to himself and what he is trying to assert and, of course, to get to you, his comrades.

There are those moments when Agee can be long-winded, can be exasperating and pejorative in his long-windedness. What do you do with a chapter called "Money," with an epigraph underneath in italics—and this is not him speaking: "You are farmers; I am a farmer myself"? Those words were spoken by FDR in 1936, when he was running for a second term. He was out in the Midlands, as the English would put it; he was in Nebraska and Kansas, and he was exhorting some farmers, whom he called "fellow farmers." Why would James Agee want to take that quote and stick it there before we start reading about this particular aspect of the American economy, the sharecropper life? Why? Ask yourself that.

We are offered an unsettling irony. Here is an American president who went to the preparatory school Groton and then Harvard College, and who went on to become an assistant secretary of the navy and governor of New York and who was exhorting people when he said, in essence, "You know, we're all farmers." Agee is saying, without saying anything but quoting him: "Oh yeah?" By implication Agee is saying, "Hey you, FDR, watch your language. It may get you votes and it may sound wonderful, and if at the time they had some 'focus groups' (God save us) it might have worked well; but for crying out loud, who the hell do you think you are, coming up with that stuff! And who the hell do *I* think *I* am—even though I am from the

From *Let Us Now Praise Famous Men* by James Agee. Photograph by
Walker Evans.

same background, as was my father, who was a yeoman farmer, as was
his father before him! Are we really all in this together?"

A demanding writer, observer, posing this to himself, says that he
will challenge a kind of rhetoric wherever it comes from. He'll challenge it mostly in himself because the temptation is strong to say,
"Well, here we are, all of us." Having just told us that in a sense we
all share certain similarities, he now slams that door in his own face
and our faces: yes, we all may have certain similarities (FDR and the
voters he addressed). Actually, FDR *was* a hurt, vulnerable man, a
powerful political leader who couldn't walk, who knew pain and
disappointment and terrible crippling disease. So there it goes, the

zig and zag, the back-and-forth—the tradition of the humanities: not literary criticism, by the way, but the humanities as they are given to us by those who write or paint or take pictures, who use complexity, irony, ambiguity, contradictions, all not to be resolved by compartmentalization or conceptualization, but to be greeted as an approach, of sorts, to truth.

In the chapter "Shelter," attend the careful, exquisitely careful, attention given to details of the documentary tradition: how cotton grows and is harvested; the nature of the buildings; the material conditions of life; the clothes worn—the dungarees, used pants, overalls, jeans, all those words to describe clothing—and then suddenly the break with an outsider's, a visitor's, observation. Now we receive a kind of interior sharing, how Agee feels in the company of the people he is with, and how—which is very important—he feels toward a particular young girl. Some may be scandalized that Agee, in our contemporary language, could be "turned on" (aroused?) by a young girl there. If you stop and think of social science literature, read the articles in anthropology and sociology journals, the writing is academic, usually written in the passive voice: "a selection of such and such people were observed." Then come the charts, the interpretations of others (not self-interpretations!), and, of course, a theoretical discussion.

Does it occur to us even to ask about someone who is doing this work, this research? What about the goings-on in his or her gut, or groin, or heart? Did the person maybe get infatuated with someone? Did she or he like someone and not like someone else? Do "they" ever tell us about that? Well, of course not. There is a chart of sorts, an abstract notion of what one expects in such descriptions, and it doesn't include an acknowledgment of these kinds of feelings. Maybe the people have so distanced themselves that they don't have feelings at all? I would wonder about that, and maybe you would too. You spend a year or so in a particular locale: How do you feel? And how does that affect what you are writing? These are subjects not often discussed in so-called methodological seminars: the anthropologist or the sociologist-observer as someone who may be struggling with being excited, provoked, or, God forbid, enamored. It was the genius of Freud to comprehend such matters; and it took him a lot of time to affirm what he came to realize; and he was very circumspect about the language he used, because he was very clever as a communicator and very aware of what the world would do with his writing. It was his genius to understand that even as he observed his patients and made sense of them, they were doing the same with him; and indeed, even as they began to realize that they were getting taken with him, he was also getting taken with them (and realizing that).

These emotions go back and forth in documentary work, as in clinical work: one surrenders one's power and authority, as an outsider, to some extent—maybe not explicitly, but subjectively. Maybe Agee didn't think about all this, and I'm sure he didn't tell this young woman what he felt, but he wants us to know about such a kind of human subjectivity (his as an observer). Why? Not so he'll get you and me wondering about him, but so that he'll get you and me, I think, wondering about ourselves. What do we do with our emotions, we observers? How do we deal with our emotions of affection, concern, compassion, fear, outrage, disagreement, disapproval? How do we handle all that? As Agee cannot write in a vacuum, nor can we read, relate, reflect, learn, *know* in one.

I remember the third year of medical school—the first patient I had a conversation with after all those years of taking organic chemistry and then anatomy and bacteriology and histology, and on and on. I still remember this particular patient; I remember talking with this patient and thinking to myself the questions that I ought to ask, and thinking of the teacher to whom I would be presenting this patient. But I also remember two other things: the look of this patient, her manner and her speech. They had nothing to do, really, with her illness but everything to do with the way my mind was working, maybe fighting, against that knowledge, but also connected to it as I struggled to understand another human being. To do her justice I had, in a sense, to come to terms with my own mind and its won-derings, yearnings, frustrations, needs, hopes, worries—all of which are the background against which my more cognitive, intellectual mind was working as it was trying to document the nature of the disease whose consequences I was observing: "lupus erythematosus," it was called. (We'll come to that disease in a different way when we get to Flannery O'Connor and her struggle with it.) In sum, I had to "study" a "patient," yet also deal with my own personal resistance to her—a mind of objectivity and subjectivity, which Agee aims to render for us, his readers, helping us see how we connect and un-derstand (and understand one another).

Agee is saying (to paraphrase): "Come with me, I'll take you there into the frontier of social observation but also of human connected-ness; and I'll do so calling upon the tradition of the novelist and poet and playwright and the musician and the artist and the photogra-pher, for whom ambiguity and contradictions are givens, and for whom disagreement within oneself is naturally part of the story, so

From *Let Us Now Praise Famous Men* by James Agee. Photograph by Walker Evans.

that when you are in discussions you can say *this,* and someone else says *that,* and one is not right or wrong, it's not either-or, it's *both* and then there is always more and more." The "moreness," of course, accounts, to some extent, for the very length of this book, over three hundred pages, but also for its demanding style. Indeed, when Agee is finished, you know and I know, we all know, it's not finished; this is a mere beginning. There is so much more that could be said and he also knows that, and so do we, his readers, his students: that human particularity holds, that each of us would have another kind of book to offer, because through our eyes and ears, connected as they are to our experience, there would be a different take on what is out there.

I remember a supervisor of mine, when I was a resident in psychiatry, saying to me, "You know, there are as many kinds of psychotherapy as there are psychiatrists." This I then found extremely confusing, puzzling, frustrating to hear, because I knew exactly the take I had accomplished on this patient and what I wanted from this supervisor (of course, seeking approval, validation, wanting an A). I wanted him to say, "That's right! You've got it!" What he was saying was "You got it, sure, but I might get something different, and then someone else is going to come into this room who is a fellow resident of yours and who (if he or she saw that same patient) might get quite another story from that patient." The back-and-forth of human interaction based on who one is—such goings-on are the heart and soul of the matter Agee wants to approach: the problems of human particularity and variation and the problems a writer ought to dare to address, directly or with an artist's knowing implication, in this powerful documentary account of the humanities as they got going, that get recorded for a book.

How Was It
We Were Caught?

The chapter called "Education," in *Let Us Now Praise Famous Men*, is part of a long tradition going back to Plato and, certainly, to Ignatius of Loyola, to Rousseau, to Thoreau and Emerson, to Sigmund Freud and Anna Freud, to William James, William Carlos Williams, Walt Whitman, all of whom concerned themselves with what you and all of us do in our various schools and classrooms—pursuing what gets called an "education." They push us to ask, "With what in mind? Why are we here?" You and I, very practical, respond and think, "Hey, buddy, I'm going to school because it will help me to make a living. I have a certain career in mind, or I'm looking to sharpen my mind, so that it will have the capacity to choose a career someday." But if you read the people who are called the great thinkers and writers, the novelists and poets, the historians, philosophers, and, more recently, some social scientists, you will see that they are not satisfied with that practicality; they have other thoughts in mind: these are moral thoughts, spiritual thoughts, and, certainly, psychological thoughts. What happens to you when you read these books, what should be happening, not only to your mind as a cognitive instrument, but with respect to your conscience and even your yearning, if not also your lusts?

Plato was perhaps the first and one of the most influential of the deep-thinking philosophers who tried to figure out how children ought to be educated—who tried not only in terms of knowledge acquired but as a civil matter for the Greek city-state: the educator as a responsible citizen, helping a coming generation to be itself a future member in good standing of a particular community. The Hebrew prophets Isaiah and Jeremiah worried about what the children of Israel were learning and about what they had already learned. Jesus taught and preached on mountains and on the plains, exhorting, remonstrating, insisting, pleading, and warning, sometimes in tears. The Sermon on the Mount, the Golden Rule, all of those exercises in moral instruction, perhaps self-instruction, on the part of the person who authored such lessons. It is a well-known aphorism of the Catholic Church, going back to Ignatius of Loyola: "Give me a child until he is seven, and I will give you the man." Jesuit education is based on values transmitted through teachers, who in turn have their own explicit values. Preservation of a religion, of a spiritual tradition, and more depends upon that. In our secular time, Rousseau, in his declaration of innocence on behalf of children, was perhaps the first prophet to remind us, or insist for us, that we are good and made bad by society—yes, among others, by teachers and schools.

I remember, as an undergraduate student at Harvard, reading Rousseau and wondering who this "child" was that he was telling us about, who seemed so perfect (having my own distant memories of not being so perfect). You can push this matter back with Rousseau's help, and pretty soon you have a beautiful and innocent child, which many parents know is more a fantasy than a reality. Indeed, the Bible tells us that we are capable even at very early ages of being difficult and demanding, if not evil (all too self-preoccupied), long before language arrives. Nevertheless, Rousseau's message was carefully attended, and persisted among some educational theorists, who embraced Rousseauesque notions of human nature. For that matter, Thoreau and Whitman argued in that vein: an insistence that society can be a kind of evil, even within a family—as against a child's intrinsic goodness, purity, and innocence, all of which get tarnished by events. Then we come, more recently, to Marx, who in his own way offers this version: society and its outright evils, capitalism and competitiveness fostered by economics and political power, make us what we are as against the possibilities of a more utopian inherited nature. In that sense, Marx and Rousseau meet, although they arrive there differently: one argues for goodness as innate; the other emphasizes society as an instrument of injustice (as if once we were rather decent, until the bad world around us came to bear upon us).

Next arrives Freud, who gives us an instinct, an id, an unconscious that has about it a biblical notion of original sin. There is for us who follow Freud, as psychoanalysts, no denying the grabbing, demanding, self-preoccupied side of human nature. Although Freud insisted that he was an atheist, some of his skepticism about human nature (his realism, we might say) connects well with the Bible's writers, their emphasis on our errant side.

What are our educational theorists today, in the last decade of the twentieth century (Jonathan Kozol, Herbert Kohl, before them Edgar Z. Friedenberg, Paul Goodman), doing with all of this? Kozol is not quite in the tradition of Rousseau, but his faith is that if we can make our schools better, then a deep goodness in our children will assert itself more freely. How does Agee connect to all of this? Agee starts out: "In every child who is born, under no matter what circumstances [that is an important qualification or lack thereof], and of no matter what parents, the potentiality of the human race is born again: and in him [and her], too, once more, and of each of us, our terrific responsibility towards human life; towards the utmost idea of goodness, of the horror of error, and of God." Now, there is a version of Rousseau. Certainly, this isn't a clinician or a psychoanalyst who has plenty of doubts about our motives, our lusts become manipulative expression on occasion, meant to further self-enhancement, or, for that matter, a skeptical religious critic, mindful of the Old Testament story of Adam and Eve's fall in the Garden of

Eden, their willful curiosity and self-affirmation (now, of course, a great virtue in our society) and their paying for it with the "wages of sin," that is, the certainty of death.

For Agee, here, the point is hope; but such hope, such regard for the possibilities of decency that so many possess, is betrayed—by white schoolteachers, by black schoolteachers, by social and economic systems. You may feel that in its scattershot way this sort of betrayal is outrageous. Here is a Harvard graduate telling us "a Harvard education is by no means an unqualified advantage." Well, you and I can skeptically say, "Look, Agee, you're tucking that diploma in your rear pocket. But it got you the job that enabled you ultimately to write this book telling us that the thing, the piece of Cambridge parchment, isn't so valuable after all."

The British psychiatrist R. D. Laing has told us that a neurosis can be a wonderful thing, compared to "adjustment," which, of course, can be the worst sin possible, leading to all kinds of conformity.

Before Laing, Agee insisted: "As a whole part of 'psychological education' it needs to be remembered that a neurosis can be valuable; also that 'adjustment' to a sick and insane environment is of itself not 'health' but sickness and insanity." He puts the words "psychological education" in quotation marks, thereby distancing himself from that way of thinking, as if to say, These people are going to tell you through psychology how to behave, but who are they? Under what moral and intellectual authority do they speak? "Adjustment" is another word he wants to distance himself from. Adjustment to what, and at whose behest? What is the fallout? What are the ramifications? Adjustment to the Nazis? Adjustment to the Gulag? Adjustment to power that is evil and wrongly intentioned— that is the fearful subtext of all of this. A psychiatrist, for example, told Dietrich Bonhoeffer (who later died challenging Hitler) not to go back home to Germany to fight the Nazis but to stay in New York City, where he was studying. Indeed, the doctor said he had "problems" and needed "help." This is challenging, troubling—the use of psychiatric terminology to encourage or discourage essentially moral courses of action, such as Bonhoeffer's wish to take on the Nazis, no matter the risk (an aspect of his "depression"!).

In *Childhood and Society,* his important book on psychoanalytical thinking, Erik Erikson describes the qualities that will make for a good psychiatrist or psychoanalyst. After cataloging various attributes, he concludes with an interesting quality that he considers the most important of all: "judicious indignation, without which a cure is but a straw in the changeable wind of history." Arguing for this kind of indignation that takes on injustice and that kind of even-handed neutral posture that has become, unfortunately, connected to people like me who sit in rooms supposedly listening to people and saying, "Uh-hum, uh-hum, that's interesting, very interesting" (if you can get those words out of us, by the way). Or that kind of neutrality that has its uses but that can become a caricature of itself.

I remember seeing *Let Us Now Praise Famous Men* in the South during the civil rights movement in those "Freedom Houses" in Mississippi, carried by students who went south in 1964 hoping to help register African-Americans to vote in the courthouses of the various counties in the Delta of Mississippi. This book was there, a huge presence, and was being republished with a new life. I remember when Dr. King marched at the head of thousands, from Selma to Montgomery. This book was carried by people, white and black, in their knapsacks. As we walked through that area, we were not far from where Agee and Evans were twenty-five years earlier. Some of the people there had come to the roadside not to praise famous men marching, but to heckle and scorn and use language of calumny and insult. I remember Dr. King saying to Bob Moses, who led that whole Mississippi project, "These are the 'famous men'—who would kill us!"

What does one do with that? Turn on the white yeomanly folks of the South and call them racists? Well they *were* then racists, even as some of us are in our private moments or thoughts and lives are, or may have been. The people we saw as we marched knew hate, and during that march it was directed on outsiders—white and black—

marching through their countryside. It is interesting in that regard to see how Agee doesn't mention any part of this racism in his book—the attitudes of the white families he held in such high esteem.

Note the limits of his generosity; note the limits of the generosity of all of us. He can be very generous to those three families, but does he ever really see their fears, their humanity? They are "praised" rather than given careful scrutiny, their inevitable flaws put down for us to consider. He presents them, rather, as good and fine people, and their work as honorable. They are exploited, so our sympathies are asked on their behalf, by Agee. He can be generous, you and I might say, to a fault. His investigative nature is flawed for reasons that we would have to think about in connection with his personal life: his racial background, the times (1936 was not the same as the 1960s, when even racists were forced by historical change and political activity to stop and think about race, about social change becoming inevitable).

That generosity of Agee's stops, however, when it comes to talking about schoolteachers, especially white schoolteachers. He pulls punches when he is talking about black schoolteachers because he doesn't want to be a racist. But he admits to us that he has never met the poor white schoolteachers, never even gone to a class in that county because he came during the summer. And yet there is a sweeping broadside leveled at the teachers, the classrooms. Here was an observer's mind, filled with idealism and generosity—but also able to find targets: local schoolteachers and a far-off president, even as he is sensitive and tender about those he aims as a writer to describe. It's harder to be objective, even in referencing the failings of others whom we are supposed to pity—namely, the "them" called the blacks or the poor whites—so a far-off political leader or a nearby teacher gets a punch or two. Agee exhorts, criticizes, becomes sardonic, affectionate, hopeful, very sad, and even melancholy; his moods tell of a writer going through moods as he circles a subject, and in a way circles himself, his subjectivity stirred by a particular Alabama objectivity.

Then come questions of rebelliousness and continuity. Here is a fighting rebel taking aim at conformity and constraint, continuity and the received tradition and saying, "Hey, listen, what does it give us? It gives us Tennyson: 'Ours is not to reason why, ours is but to do and die.' It gives us submission; it gives us rote compliance. Well, the hell with that. You who want to be free, who want to be your own person, are you going to let a bunch of teachers do that to you?" You say to yourself, I'm with Agee secretly (or I'm with Rousseau secretly), but I've got to go along with these authorities, so I'll just parrot those teachers in order to get an A out of them and then I'll be myself when I graduate, or I'll go along with the boss until I get promoted. This sort of false education puts us in a bind. The problem being that by the time we've done that long enough and often enough—you talk about the way things work in the mind—we are too much a part of it ourselves, so we pull back on our criticisms and we adjust, which is what bothers Agee. So he drinks that bourbon, and he says he is not going to give in. He quits *Fortune* magazine and he writes this book. But you see he came back to *Time* and wrote reviews, and to *Fortune* as well; he came back because he had to make a living. It hurt him and he was caught, just like we're caught, and he uses that image of being caught so many times, not only about these people who we know are caught, he reminds us, but about himself. The kinship, the companionship, the coming together of sensibilities is part of what informs the tension in this book and makes us so nervous and at times ready to get rid of him. At times we read him and say, "My God, I've never seen it put so beautifully, so lyrically, so compellingly, so powerfully. He really gets to me." As you read Agee's words, you stumble, like he stumbles, over moments of outrageous exaggeration, distortion, inconsistency, all the sins of our humanity, structure and improvisation in all art, creativity, whether it be clinical creativity, legal creativity, creativity in the classroom, never mind composing a symphony or writing a novel or a poem. It all comes down to that tension between conformity and rebellion, and you can sort out the writers and the thinkers along that gradient too.

We're now coming right up to William Carlos Williams, a fellow iconoclast, and his stand against conventional poetry, which earned him nothing but scorn from the establishment. Those who have "rebelled," those who have taken a stand outside of convention, those who improvise, whether it be Stravinsky, or Picasso, or Ibsen, or Freud—and, as you know, Newton, Darwin, Galileo—they have all paid a price, haven't they? Disapproval, outrage, condemnation, excommunication: you and I grow up and are told this is what is accepted, and you and I have moments in which perhaps we say, "No, no, no." Some of us take those "no"s and make careers out of them. With talent, more than careers, some enter history. But that familiar tension—yet again following or breaking away—informs this essay on education, even as those stories, which I urge upon you, help us with this chapter and help us to think about the time we have spent in our various classrooms. To this end, I encourage you to read three stories: Charles Baxter's "Gryphon"; Richard Yates's "Doctor Jack-o'-Lantern"; and Tobias Wolff's "In the Garden of the North American Martyrs."

Baxter gives us "Gryphon," a story that dares to challenge all we know to be conventional knowledge, that we insist upon, call true, call factual. Does two plus two always have to be four? Can you make eight plus five equal not thirteen but, rather, one? Well, you can if you are looking at the clock. Baxter gives us Ms. Ferenczi, a teacher who amazes with her emotionality, with imagination run amok, not just extended, and the creator of the story is fully aware of that. She comes in with her willful glee and she risks—what? Private madness or private thoughts woefully misinterpreted and therefore harmful to some poor soul, who is saying, "What is all this about?" Ferenczi and her forensics, as in legality, right and wrong, and Ferenczi as in the foreigner. What is foreign and what is accepted? What is native to your thinking and mine, native to a particular school system or a particular discipline, and what is foreign to it and out of bounds? In another story all of us should read, "Doctor Jack-o'-Lantern," Richard Yates, through the character of Miss Price, gives us a woman who wonders about the price paid, as a kind of a literalism, even in the name of compassion and understanding. It may be politically correct to think of this story's child in a certain sense as "disadvantaged," as hurt and troubled; but you know you can pay the price she pays. *We* pay a price in various ways, at various times, in the name of getting an "education." Finally, Tobias Wolff give us the character of Mary and that "Garden of the North American Martyrs." We should all read that story, maybe once a week: tenure and its deceits, higher education and its betrayals and phoniness and hypocrisy.

THREE

Leaving and Returning

George Orwell was born in 1903 under the name Eric Arthur Blair; "Orwell" is a pseudonym. The name Orwell also belongs to a river in Suffolk, England, not far from his parents' home, and that is why he chose it. He also chose George, which is an archetypal English name. However, his family, including his parents, lived in that home by the river only occasionally, as they were part of the imperial English tradition. They were teak merchants; they were clergymen; they were entrepreneurs; and they were in the British military, in Burma and India. The British Empire once controlled over a quarter of the land on this planet—"controlled" in various senses: economic, political, military, cultural. India and Burma, countries we now know to be independent in one way or another, were a part of this empire tradition and of Orwell's family. That's important to remember because it's part of the larger background of exploitation and privilege he knew, and of which his family partook.

Orwell was sent away at the age of five to a private school (called a "public school" in England), and ultimately ended up at Eton, just about the fanciest school you'll get in England, or anywhere else for that matter. When he graduated from Eton, instead of going, as they put it, "down the road" to Oxford or Cambridge, he decided (he could have easily gone anywhere, as he was a very able student) that he had had enough of formal education and he returned to India to become a policeman in the Indian Imperial Police. This stint lasted for several years, and he witnessed firsthand, as a corpsman and then as an officer, power being exerted on people who had no power—and that power was wielded arbitrarily, insistently, sometimes brutally. This witness of sorts repelled him, and he quit and went back to England and decided that what he wanted to do was to write, but not as a newspaperman. He wanted to write as he pleased, about what struck his interest, his fancy. He had plots, fiction, poetry in mind. Orwell did such writing, but he decided that he lacked the kind of fire and ability that would sustain him, so he did not submit his work to publishers. He instead embarked upon what, in his diary, he called a "project." He would live as others who are poor live, and he would write about the experience. At one point he used the word "document"—his aim was to document lives, as in the documentary tradition that goes back well before the nineteenth century.

Orwell spent the first six months in a slum in London, living among the people, trying to eat as they ate, and to dress as they dressed, and to take note of their habits and language—that mattered a lot, their use of words, their thoughts as he ascertained them through informal conversations in pubs and grocery stores, getting himself some candy, chewing tobacco, or cigarettes. All the while he kept a notebook. Then he went to Paris and did the same, spending some time with his aunt. He would repair occasionally to her apartment in one of the fancier neighborhoods, but the rest of the time, as in London, he made his way among poor people. He had a limited amount of money from an inheritance from one of his great-aunts, but it served to keep him fed and clothed. If you have read *A Tale of Two Cities,* you may recognize Orwell drawing on that book's imagery and reality. He loved Dickens, and if you want to look up his essay writing that came later in his career, he writes beautifully about Dickens. Indeed, Orwell would eventually title his first book *Down and Out in Paris and London,* much in the spirit of Dickens's *A*

Tale of Two Cities. However, the contrast was not as Dickens gave it to us—a novelist rendering past historical change. Instead, Orwell's writing is a powerful evocation of poverty by someone who lived in the midst of it.

Orwell went on to do other such writing. He worked for a number of summers as a hop picker in England (our equivalent would be a migrant farmworker), harvesting the crop that would be processed into beer. He lived among the indigent people and followed them into hospitals—and wrote a memorable essay called "How the Poor Die." He got himself hospitalized so that he could watch others ailing and dying. You and I might call this "participant observation," and it sure was—a contrast, really, to what Agee did. Although Agee lived among those people for a month, it was never with the kind of intimacy and personal intensity that Orwell felt and described.

In *The Road to Wigan Pier,* Orwell continued such observations, living among coal miners. The book begins by noting, "The first sound in the mornings was the clumping of the mill-girls' clogs down the cobbled street. Earlier than that, I suppose, there were factory whistles which I was never awake to hear." Already we have privilege, as against utter necessity. He can sleep; they have to go to work. The whistle sounds and they are there, or they lose their jobs, very precious jobs in the midst of an unemployment rate that was up to 25 and 30 percent. So it's *them* and *me,* and there he is in the lodging house, observing in those first pages what happens between him and the Brookers, the owners of the house. He talks about them, critiques them, their food, the cleanliness of the chamber pot, which they don't empty; indeed, take note of all that—Orwell uses words such as "pig-like" and "disgusting." "On the day when there was a full chamber-pot under the breakfast table, I decided to leave. The place was beginning to depress me," he writes. Contrast the way he is with the Brookers versus the miners—although the Brookers, after all, were miners until they retired and got a little imperial energy on themselves. Do the miners get this kind of treatment? When he talks about the miners eating, does he use the word "disgusting"?

Does he talk about them as being "pig-like"? Does he express the kind of vehemence and antagonism toward them that comes so readily to him as he thinks of his moments with the Brookers?

Eventually Orwell departs this particular situation, and there is a very important moment: the train boarding. He can leave and go on to the next spot, stay with some more people, decide whether he wants to live with them or move on—he has this privilege (one that you and I have) of aspiration, of accommodation, of choice, of dreaming and hoping. He writes, "As we moved slowly through the outskirts of the town, we passed row after row of little grey slum houses running at right angles to the embankment. At the back of one of the houses a young woman was kneeling on the stones, poking a stick up the leaden waste-pipe which ran from the sink inside and which I suppose was blocked." Here again is "I suppose": conjecture, and an effort at identification and empathy. Is it successful, valuable, or is it something else—someone *assuming,* not supposing, and for whose purposes? Maybe his own, as a writer, as one who wants a scenario, if not a story to publish. "I had time to see everything about her," we are told. Humility is thus thrown out of the window, since this moment is just a *second* as the train is going by. "I had time to see everything about her—her sacking apron, her clumsy clogs"—very wonderful language here, very descriptive writing—"her arms reddened by the cold." Orwell's sentences are not as flowery and lyrical as Agee's, but it's language that will get you through college with admiration and nice little comments from the teachers, such as "strong, vivid writing" or "terse, powerful and affecting."

Continuing with Orwell: "She looked up as the train passed, and I was almost near enough to catch her eye." Note his self-reference, perhaps objectionable in Agee because it is more flagrant, but it is subtler here. "She had a round pale face, the usual exhausted face of the slum girl who is twenty-five but looks forty"—the "usual" he claims to know and dares generalize—"thanks to miscarriages and drudgery; and it wore, for the second in which I saw it, the most desolate, hopeless expression I have ever seen. It struck me then that we are mistaken when we say that 'It isn't the same for them as it would be for us,' and that people bred in the slums can imagine nothing but the slums. For what I saw in her face"—tell yourself as a reader that what actually was in her face has to be distinguished from what he claims he saw in her face—"was not the ignorant suffering of an animal. She knew well enough what was happening to her—understood as well as I did how dreadful a destiny it was to be kneeling there in the bitter cold, on the slimy stones"—nice writing—"of a slum backyard, poking a stick up a foul drain-pipe."

Here is one of the book's most memorable passages; indeed, Orwell, when being interviewed by the BBC, referred to this passage as one of his favorites. His choice wasn't a vain or boastful one. He sincerely felt he had captured a moment there. But you and I have to look at that moment and wonder. What was actually happening to that woman? She could have been humming a song, smiling to herself about her children, or remembering a nice time with her husband, looking forward to a meal—all the range of human possibility that you and I know, surely she could have known also.

We don't know the entirety of what was happening at that moment. Nor does Orwell, although we read this and are convinced that we do know, because he has told us, told us with verve and clarity, and he has entered history—we don't even have to use his first name: he is Orwell, a great writer who has so very much to tell us.

Even then, before *1984* and *Animal Farm* catapulted him, on the backs of anti-communism, into the universality of well-known writers, even then he was writing under the auspices of the Left Book Club. He was a graduate of Eton; he was well educated; he had written a handful of books that had been published; he had written essays that had been published; he was a writer. He worked in a library; he thought of becoming a teacher. He *knows*. He tells us a lot, and does so tellingly. Yet we can have a conversation with Orwell, with Agee. You and I are here as readers with our own authority, and we may assert that authority with the writers we read and, too, with professors at a university. We may want to respond to Orwell, to say, "Hey, wait a minute: there is the life of that woman, and there is the life of this guy on the train passing her in one second. What is going on here?" Talk about impositions of sensibility and a writer's hopes, if not out-and-out psychological projection. Yes, there is empathy too, and empathy is part of projection, or projection is part of empathy. (On and on this goes: attribution in what name, for what purpose?) A writer was at work on a book, picking up dramatic moments, and was ready to "use" them, not in the pejorative sense, but let's summon the accusing (and maybe unfair) word and say that he was thereby "exploiting" people for his own purposes, out of his preferences, which is also a subject to write about, his ideological convictions.

All of this is part of your conversation and mine with the writers we read, and that is why Agee uses the phrase "conversation in the lobby." That is why we are carrying on a conversation here with these writers: neither to exalt them nor to pillory them but to bring them to us as *companions*. What they went through and what I am pointing out in this chapter is what you and I experience all the time as we try to understand one another, quickly but not so quickly. How exactly and quickly are we capable of comprehending another human being? With what degree of knowledge do psychoanalysts like me spend years and years, five days a week, trying to find out what was really on a person's mind as she or he did work, went about life? Maybe the woman Orwell glimpsed didn't even know what was on her mind, and maybe she would say to Orwell or to someone like me, in a clinical office: "*Nothing* was on my mind, and anyways, what is on *your* mind that is bothering you so much that it makes you want to figure out what was on my mind?" *There's* a good defense; as we know, the best defense is offense.

In any event, this is a section of Orwell's book that poses questions for you and me—ones to carry with us whether we are doing something called "community service" or we just go on the subway and watch others. What are those others like? What is on their minds? And then we might ask, Who is doing that kind of inquiry about us? Who is asking, "What are *they* like? What is life like for people who live on exclusive streets, and in fancy suburban towns, and who stay at fancy hotels like the Ritz-Carlton? What is on their minds, how do I understand them, what might someone write about them as they come out of these places or walk down those streets?" Might someone say they look heavy and self-preoccupied and smug, with their noses touching the sky, absorbed in their own vanity as they calculate how much money they have and whom they are going to use or abuse today in order to get their way? Is that a possibility—for that woman to leave that Orwellian situation, to go to some fancy part of the English Midlands, go up to Yorkshire, look around there and talk into a machine, describe those people in a certain way? Thomas Hardy, in *Jude the Obscure,* had, in 1895, a country bumpkin of sorts go to a city like Oxford and take a look at those people, and Hardy tried to see them through Jude's eyes—but that story is fiction. Orwell's account is supposedly factual. I am sure you and I could argue that what he saw was 100 percent correct: maybe she *was* sad, exploited. She was a member of the "proletariat"—there is an abstraction! You see how this can get at us, pose problems for us, move us into a more neutral posture on this platform as we ponder documentary work, its offerings, and its hazards.

Later Orwell says, "It is impossible to watch the 'fillers' [miners] at work without feeling a pang of envy for their toughness." Would *you* feel envy of miners going into a mine? Notice, further on, how he admires their bodies. He doesn't pull any punches about it. He gives them a sensuous dignity and charm and attractiveness. Is that romanticizing them? Is that patronizing them? After all, they *are* powerful men, muscular and strong, tested by everyday challenging experiences. What should your attitude and mine be toward them? Pity? A labor-organizing attitude? Social protest about their life? Generosity and kindness? How does one affiliate with others without risking being quite the snob? Most of the miners are small; big men are at a disadvantage in that job. But nearly all of them have sturdy bodies, and Orwell describes them well.

After Orwell gives us hell about the Brookers and their disgusting food, he goes on to tell us, in chapter 3: "From what I have seen I should say that a majority of miners prefer to eat their meals first and wash afterwards, as I should do in their circumstances." This is a complete switch. If it's the miners who are eating, he is not going to be repelled by the food or the way they eat it. There is a feeling of "I'm with them"; there is *solidarity*. And then you will notice, not too far on in this book, that he does start turning on people. First of all, he says, If anyone came and tried to do this to me, I'd tell them to go to hell. He writes, "Everyone was astonishingly patient and seemed to understand almost without explanation why I was questioning them and what I wanted to see." But Orwell wants us to wonder what we'd think or do if any unauthorized person walked into our house and began asking us whether the roof leaked or whether we are much troubled by bugs and what we think of the landlord; we would probably tell him to go to hell. We have that option, don't we: to tell others to go to hell; not to submit to the social inquiry of others.

Note, in particular, the way Orwell takes on his own kind in this book: the socialists, the Left Book Club people. He calls them every name fathomable within the polite parameters of discourse: "fruits," for example, a pretty tough and nasty word. He shows himself capable of being mean-spirited, unkind. He talks of "fruit-juice drinkers," people who do yoga. He parodies them; he caricatures them. He is unfair to those people. Someone who is bending over backward to understand miners and convey their situation so that you and I will reach out to them with compassion and human feeling not only gives a swift kick to the Brookers, but now indulges in widespread and outrageous social, cultural, and political generalizations. Just as outrageous as some of you might feel Agee's are—all of which then ought to prompt you and me to ask, Why does this happen, these two taking these swipes at those people? Why do they do this?

I remember when masses of students went to Mississippi as part of the Mississippi Summer Project (an effort to end segregation and initiate voting rights for African-American citizens). They got as far as that march from Selma before they were confronted with sudden thoughts of who was watching them and swearing bloody murder at them. When they returned home, they would come back here and some of them would talk about places like Harvard not unlike the way Agee did. They turned on the very world they'd left to go down to Mississippi in the summer of '64. What is that about? Why notice these things with such special intensity at certain moments in one's life? I am afraid of that word "guilt"; it's just not to the point, that word, and it's too easy to summon it. It's not about guilt, although in this culture we can have guilt about anything. It's about something else. What gets going in us is not necessarily guilt, because we didn't create what was going on in the Delta of Mississippi, and Orwell did not create those slums, and you and I are not responsible for what's happening in those parts of our hometowns that are called ghettos. Guilt is when you *do* something wrong and you know you've *done* it, and you lash out at yourself or are punished. . . . That is not what is happening here.

The issue is not guilt, but our responsibility as human beings to connect with others—and know of them, feel they're all right, if they live endangered lives. The scrutinizing is more outrage; the compassion and the compassionate effort that Orwell or Agee make help us link arms with others, far away. From Orwell we learn of Wigan Pier, from Agee of famous men, and begin to respect others, even admire them. Writers such as Agee and Orwell become part of the world they describe—they bring us to those worlds. This companionship, this gesture of affiliation, of understanding, is itself "noble"—as noble as the description of the coal miner's body; as noble as Agee's wonderful elevation of sharecroppers trying to survive against great odds. Isn't it "noble" for you and me to be encouraged to regard others with respect, consideration?

But there is, indeed, another conversation going on within the mind of an Agee or an Orwell: "I am doing this, and I am going to leave, and I'm going to write about this and I know it"—meaning that he understands that he will get something for himself for his altruistic or high-minded interest in others. So the guilt isn't as in "I did something wrong" but more like "I am going to do something with this that will also considerably, maybe mightily, enhance me." Then comes something that is more central to all this. A person of this kind of broadness of human feeling might have enough range of understanding to comprehend that those people might resent the kind of privileges that an Agee or Orwell has—resent these privileged outsiders who do "right well" by telling of others who've been so very unlucky in life. Such folks might say, "Look at you, look what you got out of this." In fact, it's true, because some of the people who are descendents of those whom Agee studied in Alabama were interviewed by a reporter, and they said that they resented the fact that Agee described their families as poor, when of course *they* had been rising on up and were doing much better than the way the book portrays their ancestors as living.

Why do some people say they don't like the idea that their ancestors were portrayed this way by Agee or that Orwell's effort became a source of profit? Imagine if it were you or me: we are doing a little bit better than those who came before us, and we don't want to look back, go back to the relative misery of our forebears, however extolled they were by an Agee or an Orwell. Perhaps those two savvy writers knew this in their bones and anticipated that the best way to deflect a later criticism or hostility was to find a scapegoat—another object to kick; thereby an Orwell or an Agee could continue their involvement with, their alliance with the people they were studying. Because together they could turn on others: Harvard, the intellectuals, the socialists in London who never dreamed of undertaking what Orwell did—namely, observing the poor in the midst of their lives. "If I can find some others to turn my anger on," they may have thought, "maybe I'll be more comfortable in my relationship with the people I'm observing and in my role as one writing about them." A little bit of complicated psychology going on here, but something to think about as you read this book of Orwell's and ask yourself why there has to be an introduction to it by the people who commissioned it, who say, "Hey, look at what we got going. We never dreamed that this guy would turn on us the way he did, and this isn't really fair." Well, it may not be fair, but it gives us a clue not only about Orwell but maybe a number of others.

I discuss moving from one world to another in the hope that you might ask yourselves, as you read these books, why people leave one world, go into another. Some people do so, as we know historically, to conquer, to rule in the name of commerce, to extract gold, diamonds, and coal. Empires are built by armies who leave one world and go to another—and huge profits are made. Then some people go to teach in schools, whether they are missionaries or involved in public education. Some go to improve their own life and circumstances, or those of others. They go to teach in "that" community, of the "disadvantaged." Some go to convert others (that is the story of the Western world, isn't it?): in the name of Jesus, military conquests, or cultural conquests. If Orwell or some social psychologist were handing out questionnaires to those who traveled to far-off places (the Jesuits, Columbus at the bidding of the king and queen of Spain in the fifteenth century), there would be quite a mixture of motives: to find gold or ports for commerce; in the name of Christianity; to convert, to heal. Remember Dr. Schweitzer in the so-called darkness of Africa, in Lambaréné, in French Equatorial Africa, during the 1930s and 1940s. Then there are those who go to study as anthropologists, bring back "data," not gold. And then comes the travel, whether it be Richard Halliburton traveling to get a book out of it or you and me traveling to see the world. We might think, "Let's go to India" or "Hey, I want to take in Appalachia; I'd like to see a mine." If you go and see how "they" live in Calcutta, you are a tourist, but you may also get a little nervous, and you think, "My God, this is awful—here I am seeing this, and I'm going to leave. Lucky me, who can come, see, depart, leave" though with a thought or two, when the juxtaposition is a little too dramatic, or too painful a reminder of "them" versus me, us—so we get to thinking in certain ways as we all take in what becomes called "scenery."

Then, too, there are some who go to get away. They go to live elsewhere, period, as I well remember from the time when one of my sons was working with me in Alaska among the indigenous Eskimo population and we met people called bush pilots, who flew us from one town to the next. They would tell us stories about their lives in the lower 48, and how they were so glad to be away from that lifestyle down in places like Chicago. Some of them would tell me they were alcoholics who were able to quit drinking and survived because they left the circumstances of their frailty and found a whole new world. All these different ways for us to leave one world, be part of another world, for varying lengths of time and varying motivations! All of that is what Agee and Orwell help us to see, to contemplate—travelers as those who left and returned, as those who became observers, seekers, witnesses.

FOUR

A Healing Poet

As you read Orwell, you might try to connect some of the matters that mean a lot to him to what Agee was trying to do. Notice Orwell's attention to education. It's interesting how these two writers keep going back to the question of education: how one ought to be educated, and what is good and bad about the schools. In *The Road to Wigan Pier,* as with Agee at certain times, Orwell talks about rubbish; he applies the word to both history and geography. He doesn't really mean that, not for himself; he himself was acutely sensitive to history, as well as the fate of socialism and communism. He was keenly aware of Stalin's murderous proclivities—long before a lot of other people on the left were. Why does he say "take the working-class attitude towards 'education' "—and declare that attitude "immensely sounder!"? (He puts quotes around the word "education" to distance himself, just the way Agee does, and believe me, they did not share notes; they were working at the same time but were strangers to each other, and their books were published without influencing each other, although they shared a sensibility perhaps born of the time.) "Working people often have a vague reverence for learning in others, but where 'education' touches their own lives they see through it and reject it by a healthy instinct." Why this animus? He talks of the rubbish (dispensable?) in history and geography and presents a romantic view. He says, "In a working-class home—I am not thinking at the moment of the unemployed, but of comparatively prosperous homes—you breathe a warm, decent, deeply human atmosphere which it is not so easy to find elsewhere. I should say that a manual worker, if he is in steady work and drawing good wages . . . has a better chance of being happy than an 'educated' man." You and I can immediately dismiss that and say that this is overwrought and overgeneralized. He says, "I have often been struck by the peculiar easy completeness, the perfect symmetry as it were, of a working-class interior at its best."

Why do some of us do this when we leave the world to which we belong and go to other worlds, where we claim to find such joy and happiness? Why do we exalt what we observe? To return to the Mississippi experience again: I remember college students living in Mississippi homes with people as their hosts, families a social psychologist or a sociologist or an anthropologist would have categorized as poor, culturally disadvantaged, culturally deprived, using all of that language of educational sociology that descended upon us, unfortunately, in the 1960s and '70s. Staying in those homes, the students from institutions like Harvard were taken with their hosts, grateful to them, admiring of them, and posed for all of us a considerable irony. If they are the "downtrodden" on whose behalf you are giving months of your life (and risking some jeopardy, as some students were hurt and three killed at the very beginning of that summer), and you are there to help rescue them, educate them, and encourage them to register to vote, the stated objectives of this project, and yet you admire them and keep saying that they are better than all the people you know in community X and community Y, from privileged academia, perhaps even the geography of your own home, then how do you deal with this, how do you understand that?

Maybe *they* should come up from the impoverished Mississippi Delta to places like Harvard, in order to help *us*. I have no explanation for such a paradox, but I think these college youths were picking up on courage under stress, as Orwell does in a moral nod toward those miners with whom he tried to identify, whose work he knew was so necessary, as he keeps reminding us: such labor allows writers to write and you and me to have a view of another world, as if we were living in the middle of England at that time. Gratitude, admiration for others based on identification with, or the effort of identification with, and understanding of them, soon results in a kind of admiration that isn't critical but is heart-driven and soul-driven, and that takes over one's sense of who others are, as one writes and dismisses from one's mind the kind of detail and careful, minutely qualified observation that the rational mind, left to itself, would insist upon. It's not that this gesture is irrational so much as that it is soulful and "emotional," and not necessarily in the pejorative sense of the word "emotional," although you could say that over the course of our many educations we learn to polarize rationality and subjectivity (emotionality) as good and bad.

Agee and Orwell became a bit estranged from the miners or sharecroppers they at first exalted, praised, observed; they were at a remove from the finicky, careful, methodologically correct psychology or sociology courses, or reading lists, or whatever it is that gets us to question Orwell and Agee. As readers, why do we need credentials? "Credentials"—are they what serve to introduce us to these authors? When you see such an outcome—works of "credentials"— in the work of two different people, of different temperaments and backgrounds, doing similar work, you are surely given pause, reason for thought.

I want to take up again the anger that Agee and Orwell share, recalling that the best *defense* of oneself may sometimes be *offense* directed at someone else. This rather human response is something we all know from various moments in our lives when we are enraged and yet we don't want to express our annoyance, our anger directly at someone, so we find a scapegoat either explicitly or implicitly, that may be wholly unrelated to the cause. Here is Orwell again: "In a way it is even humiliating to watch coalminers working. It raises in you a momentary doubt about your own status as an 'intellectual' and a superior person generally. For it is brought home to you, at least while you are watching, that it is only because miners sweat their guts out that superior persons can remain superior." Immediately comes the anger: "You and I and the editor of the *Times Lit. Supp.,* and the Nancy poets and the Archbishop of Canterbury and Comrade X, author of *Marxism for Infants"*—this is cutting parody— "all of us *really* owe the comparative decency of our lives to poor drudges underground, blackened to the eyes, with their throats full of coal dust, driving their shovels forward with arms and belly muscles of steel." Now, that is powerful writing, and the miners, their lives observed, are enabling him to do that—and, of course, they are enabling a writer's career. Such writing became one more step in the career of George Orwell: writer, social commentator, paid emissary of the Left Book Club. Speaking of irony: the letter that Victor Gollancz, as a representative for Orwell's sponsoring organization, writes for the Foreword is rather polite, given the kick that Orwell is giving him and his kind.

Such anger will come up in other writers who are connected in one way or another with poor people, vulnerable people, hurt people, as they try to understand them and maybe, so doing, get themselves into a bit of an intellectual and moral dilemma. You'll notice that Orwell, like Agee, uses at one point the word "spy"—a not so subtle kind of self-criticism. Orwell says: "I went in fully expecting a fight. The people would spot that I was not one of themselves and immediately infer that I had come to spy on them." That whole notion of peeking, looking for one's own purpose afflicts these two observers (as I think it does a lot of us who do this kind of fieldwork). Orwell and Agee are novelists and poets who take what they get out of this kind of social observation and then construct stories. They are masters of narrative presentation, with themselves as the main characters. Now contrast that kind of effort with the works of Studs Terkel, in *Voices of Our Time,* or the works of Oscar Lewis, the anthropologist, now gone, who pioneered a kind of oral history in anthropology. In their work, the central narrative voice is that of the person being observed—or, if you want, "spied on." True, the intermediary is Terkel or Oscar Lewis, because they with their tape recorders heard what was spoken and, out of it, assembled and edited and selected and arranged a kind of narration from behind the scenes. The uttered voice is that of the truck driver in Chicago, or that of the lawyers, businesspersons, janitors—the whole range of people in a book called *Working*. But Terkel has chosen these people, and we don't know about those people he met who he decided weren't useful, "good," for his purposes. What does "good" mean, using what criteria? He doesn't really get into this. He assumes that the reader reading him knows what is "good"—namely, someone who will talk.

Now let us move ahead by going back in time to 1883 in September, when William Carlos Williams was born in a house on 9 Ridge Road in Rutherford, New Jersey. He was born in the same house he would die in, eight decades later. He was delivered by a friend of his mother's; and he would die in a bed in that house in 1963. His father was a businessman of English Protestant background; his mother was of Catholic and Jewish background. He would be sent to the local schools, and then across the Hudson River to the Horace Mann School, where he put in a couple of years; thereafter, he went straight to the University of Pennsylvania Medical School. He didn't go to college; he didn't have to take any premed courses; and he didn't take the MCAT test, but went right to medical school. He was only eighteen years old.

While a medical student, Williams was also writing poems, and some of them were published in small, local literary publications in Philadelphia. He met in the course of this kind of activity a graduate student at the University of Pennsylvania whose name was Ezra Pound. They became lifelong friends, and although they also eventually became huge political and moral antagonists, they remained friends. When William Carlos Williams graduated from medical school he went up to New York and took an internship at a hospital called the old French Hospital. He then went on to a residency in what used to be called general practice medicine, specializing in obstetrics and pediatrics. In the middle of the residency he stumbled on a kickback scheme between one of the head doctors and a local drugstore and reported it. Furious at the disclosure, which tarnished the hospital's reputation, the hospital's administration did not ask him to stay on. He had hoped to remain in New York because he wanted to be part of the New York writers' world. He decided to go back home and went back literally to his home; his father had died by then, and his mother was ailing. Williams married a young woman named Florence Herman, whose father was one of the first labor organizers (one of the founders, actually) of the American Federation of Labor (the AFL would eventually merge with the CIO and become the AFL-CIO). Williams established a practice, not mainly in Rutherford, a relatively middle-class neighborhood at the time, but in Paterson, New Jersey.

Paterson was where one of the first American factories was built, the birthplace of this sector of American capitalism. It was also the home of wave after wave of Americans who had come here from abroad—from Europe, from the Caribbean, from Asia and Africa, to be part of the American scene. And his practice for fifty years would be with poor, vulnerable people, newly arrived Americans, many of whom couldn't afford to pay him. They tried to pay with meals or sewing, in a kind of barter economy with the physician who looked out for them. These people figure in his stories, many of which were collected in his book *Life Along the Passaic River,* and in *The Doctor Stories,* which contains most of his early work. Talk about documentary work: in 1937, just at the time that Agee and Orwell were doing theirs, this American physician, who by then had put in a couple of decades with these people, was writing their stories. He wanted to render their lives in fictional form, although clearly what we are getting is them; but we are also getting the doctor who visits them and tells of them. When I was a college student I wrote an essay on the first two books of *Paterson,* which was Williams's greatest accomplishment and which would ultimately be a five-volume extended lyrical examination of America, of its working American people. It was a populist poem, and a long one at that.

At that time, the work of William Carlos Williams was not taught at Harvard; the English department would have no part of him. His poetry was "anarchic"; he didn't use rhyme; he switched from poetry to prose; it was "irregular verse." My undergraduate adviser at Harvard was Perry Miller, who would go on to have a very distinguished career there. He had just moved from Chicago—a world not unlike Paterson. He was a professor, but he was quite willing at times to mock the very institution that housed him, as some of his predecessors whose work he specialized in had also done, such as William James, Emerson, and Thoreau. (His field was American literature, which was looked down upon then by some of his colleagues.) I was searching for what I should do and he said, "Why don't you write about William Carlos Williams?" I said, "Who's he?" He said, "But you should know! That's the problem with this blankety-blank place." I was startled. It was the first time I had heard a professor swear. I fell silent. He said, "All the more reason for you, young man, to get to know this writer." So, swept up by him and his authority, I purchased the first two volumes of *Paterson*. I wrote my thesis and was then subject to those people who quiz you with difficult and often pointed questions about matters unrelated to either your intent or your focus. I did very poorly. The board was appalled that I had even been allowed to write this, that this had "gone through"; I think Miller had pulled a fast one, using me as his lever, so this was not for me a nice accomplishment. At the time I thought that I would graduate soon enough and go on to get a job (I hoped then) teaching English in a high school.

Professor Miller said to me, "Why don't you send what you've written to Dr. Williams." I said, "What?" He said, "That, what you wrote." I said, "I can't do that." He said, "You don't have the postage? No, you're either shy or embarrassed." I said nothing. He continued: "It might mean something to him." This was not the William Carlos Williams we know of now; this was the fighter who had been defeated and "rebuked and scorned"—who won all the fancy prizes only after he died. Who is now considered a giant! So I got his address and mailed him my thesis, and a week or so later I found an envelope in my box; on the outside it said, "WCW, 9 Ridge Road, Rutherford, New Jersey." No zip codes then. I opened it up and there was a piece of paper from a doctor's small, square prescription pad: William C. Williams, M.D., 9 Ridge Road, Rutherford, New Jersey. The prescription said, "Dear Mr. Coles, thank you very much for sending your thesis to me. It's not bad for a Harvard student." In a new paragraph he added, "If you are ever in the neighborhood, please come see Flossie and Me. Bill."

A week later I was in New York, having gone down there to be "in the neighborhood," and I was trembling, but I got myself to a phone in Grand Central Station to call and hung up before I heard a voice. I called again, and I told myself this was crazy, and I hung up again, after letting it ring a couple of times, then deciding there was no one there, and that I was going to go back, after maybe doing something in New York, like going to a bar or a movie. But then I called again and I heard, "Hello." It was a woman's voice, so I started stumbling and stuttering and saying that I was told to call if I was in the neighborhood, so I was calling. I didn't say who I was. So she said, "Well, where in the neighborhood are you?" And I said, "I'm in Grand Central Station." There was a laugh and she said, "Well, I guess that's the neighborhood." I then explained that I had sent my paper to Dr. Williams, and she said that Bill had shown her my thesis. I was so proud that Bill had shown her what I'd written! She told me to get on a bus and I got on a bus and went down there.

When I arrived, he wasn't at his office, so I found my way to their main house and she asked me in and served me milk and cookies and told me that if I waited long enough he'd be back. Fidgeting and trying to make conversation, I waited. After about forty-five minutes the door opened and William Carlos Williams in the form and affect of a tornado arrived. He had on what he used to call his greatcoat and a fedora and he was carrying that black bag of his. He came in and Flossie was right there, ready to help him out and feed him, and she whispered something that had to do with the fact that I was there. He came in and bounded toward me and shook my hand and said, "So you took that trip down from Cambridge, Massachusetts?" I said, "Yes sir." He asked me not to "sir" him. He was so sensitive to language, and could catch in a moment like that so much. It would take me years to complete my studies and go into analysis and realize that there are people who do this for a living who are called psychoanalysts. But here he was doing it: listening, noticing, figuring out, but in such a nice, available, and friendly—if brusque—way, which scared me. He asked me if I wanted to come with him to meet his patients.

The next thing I knew I was in his 1939 red Pontiac, being driven over to Paterson. Then we were going up those tenement house stairs; he was knocking on the door and getting down on the floor with his patients, those kids. I remember him entering a room and talking very briefly with the parents and saying, "Now you have got to leave me alone here with this young man" (or lady). And the next thing I knew he would squat down and say to them, "Now, will you tell me why I am here for you today?" They would look at him knowingly, for some of them were quite aware that this was how he behaved. They also knew that in his pockets were Hershey Kisses—talk about an American tradition of sorts—and that eventually they were going to get some of them. Sometimes he would dispense them at the beginning, to, as he put it, whet their appetites and, of course, bribe them, and sometimes at the end, just to say thanks. He would have pockets full of them, and he'd conduct conversations with the children and with their parents; he would tend to their ailments, and then he would leave. Then we would get into the car, and on a clipboard of paper he kept there, he'd jot down a note or two. Sometimes he would say to me, "Did you hear what she"—or he or that father—"said?" Well, I hadn't heard it the way he'd heard it! In the car, he'd be writing those words and phrases down, the vernacular: the responses of his fellow citizens—people he regarded as his neighbors—to their illnesses, to their various suffering lives (and he wanted to know that response). Eventually, when he got home, he would take those responses and submit them to his typewriter, and today if you look at *Paterson* or, for that matter, these "doctor stories," you are brought to what he has heard, seen, listened to, remembered, and then set down for others to consider. "Attending" is a medical word, as in the attending doctor on a ward. Dr. Williams, the writer, attended to those lives he'd encountered, then gave them to us, for us to attend to.

In his early poems, before he wrote *The Doctor Stories* and *Paterson,* you see the sensibility at work in these arresting poems. Here is one called "The Young Housewife":

> At ten A.M. *the young housewife*
> *moves about in negligee behind*
> *the wooden walls of her husband's house.*
> *I pass solitary in my car.*
>
> *Then again she comes to the curb*
> *to call the ice-man, fish-man, and stands*
> *shy, uncorseted, tucking in*
> *stray ends of hair, and I compare her*
> *to a fallen leaf.*
>
> *The noiseless wheels of my car*
> *rush with a crackling sound over*
> *dried leaves as I bow and pass smiling.*

He saw life in New Jersey as a metaphor for all of us trying to take root in this country and prosper, so that we will find our "spring" and so that we will be sprung from poverty and oppression and all the pain of those earlier nations we have left, every one of us, sometime in our collective American history. The poets sings of this: the land itself, the humble plants and weeds. (We, the weeds—not fancy orchids, to the manner born, but earthy weeds with toughness and courage, asserting ourselves and trying to make do.) All this he saw and turned into song, into vivid, summarizing, applauding verse.

"To a Poor Old Woman," the poem goes,

> *munching a plum on*
> *the street a paper bag*
> *of them in her hand*
> *They taste good to her*
> *They taste good*
> *to her. They taste good to her.*
>
> *You can see it by*
> *the way she gives herself*
> *to the one half*
> *sucked out in her hand*
>
> *Comforted,*
> *a solace of ripe plums*
> *seeming to fill the air.*
> *They taste good to her*

At around the same time, Williams also wrote this poem:

THE POOR

> *It's the anarchy of poverty*
> *delights me, the old*
> *yellow wooden house indented*
> *among the new brick tenements*
>
> *Or a cast-iron balcony*
> *with panels showing oak branches*
> *in full leaf. It fits*
> *the dress of the children*

reflecting every stage and
custom of necessity—
Chimneys, roofs, fences of
wood and metal in an unfenced

age and enclosing next to
nothing at all: the old man
in a sweater and soft black
hat who sweeps the sidewalk—

"The old man in a sweater and soft black hat who sweeps the sidewalk." This is not "in the room [where] the women come and go, talking of Michelangelo"! This is not the art museum or high culture in England. This is the American Paterson: the muscles of working people as they desperately try to get on the first rung of the ladder. They are beheld by someone who appreciates them and respects them, who has worked with them, healed them, tasted their food, thanked them for the things they made for him, with their needles and threads.

the old man
in a sweater and soft black
hat who sweeps the sidewalk—

his own ten feet of it—
in a wind that fitfully
turning his corner has
overwhelmed the entire city

This is a kind of social observation and social reflection that was undertaken by a person who lived as a physician among the people he tried to understand—and who later offered it to you and me through language, as a "writing doc," as he once called himself. A doctor who put in his time with those who did not share the opportunities he'd had, going to the Horace Mann School, and the

University of Pennsylvania Medical School, living in a nice old Victorian house (which is now on the National Register of Historic Places). This is the doctor, the person we meet in these stories. Through these stories we also meet the patients, and in how he presents those patients, and the questions that he brings up for us about them, we learn of a nation, its people.

PART II

When Strangers Meet

*Meeting so-called ordinary American working-class
men and women: courage, challenge, kindness, and
complexity in everyday living.*

*Featured: The Old Ones of New Mexico, Raymond Carver,
Edward Hopper, Tillie Olsen, and Ruby Bridges*

FIVE

The Old Ones

You may notice that we now and then move inwardly, take up the subject of moral and spiritual reflection. These writers, out of their religious and spiritual concerns, took aim at whatever was happening in the world and tried to evoke it in their autobiographies, essays, novels. Anyone who interviews others, talks with them and tries to understand them, will eventually encounter religion in one way or another.

You might ask what that subject matter has to do with "social reflection." Yet, as we see, the very title of *Let Us Now Praise Famous Men* comes from the Apocrypha, which is a part of the Bible, part of the Hebrew prophetic tradition. We can hardly claim for Orwell conventional religious or spiritual interest, although you can stop and think of *1984* and *Animal Farm,* his musings after World War II, when he relentlessly, pointedly, and prophetically criticized secular religion. (He often preferred to call it state capitalism or communism, in which so many messianic aspirations and fates have been invested for the past couple of hundred years.)

Some of Williams's poems show the meditative side of him as he struggled for meaning both as a clinician and as a poet. Tillie Olsen, who we will encounter later in this section, in her story "O Yes" takes us to a church scene, knowing full well how many churches have housed so much that has to do with teaching and signifying, instructing, and reprimanding young people and their parents, too. This story is about sorting, about recognizing lines impossible to cross.

Raymond Carver, whom we will also meet in the pages ahead, reveals meditation in his celebration of laundromats and diners, the world of the lower-middle class—their struggles and his own struggles with himself and against himself at times—and he has his characters wonder about their lives in reflective moments. Ralph Ellison gives us reflection on the go in his stories, moving people around America, making light of a lot of pretension: an underground man looking for meaning, enlightenment.

We will also meet Dorothy Day: her autobiography, her soup kitchens, her struggle as a liberal activist—no, more of a radical activist—so invested in her fight for political and social causes that she ended up in jail. We encounter Ignazio Silone and his book *Bread and Wine*. A brave anti-Fascist of the twentieth century, he was born the very year the century began, and he took on Mussolini when so many other intellectuals compromised, accepting jobs in exchange for their tacit complicity. We also encounter Simone Weil and Georges Bernanos, two French intellectuals drawn to Catholicism but enraged by political Catholicism and the relationship of too many bishops to wealth and power—a travesty, they both felt, of Christianity as it originally was, and was meant to be. Of course, Flannery O'Connor is so clearly interested in religion and, at times, its betrayal; her stories and essays constantly touch upon spiritual challenges.

I remember watching faith play out in front of me during the mid-1970s, when my wife and our children and I lived in Albuquerque, New Mexico. We lived in the North Valley of Albuquerque. I was talking with Spanish-speaking children, Native American children, Pueblo, Hopi, and Navajo from Arizona. By this time, I had worked in the South and in Boston when school desegregation began. I'd ridden in a school bus from Roxbury to the so-called white parts of Boston with the children who were being bused, and I'd done some work in Appalachia with children who lived in the hollows. I soon learned that the people who were going to decide whether I might work in the homes in New Mexico were not the children's parents but the children's grandparents. I began to learn, in the small communities north of Santa Fe, of the authority of the elderly people. I found myself sidetracked (as a pediatrician and child psychiatrist) by my growing interest in interviewing them, talking to them, learning from these elderly people about life in these small villages of northern New Mexico.

The book that emerged from that period in my life, *The Old Ones of New Mexico,* consists of narrative portraits of elder, Spanish-speaking people of New Mexico, and the words are accompanied by pictures. Here are the words of a woman who lives in a small isolated mountain community north of Santa Fe. She had no schooling and speaks a mixture of English and Spanish, which I have translated into vernacular English:

Sometimes I have a moment to think. I look back and wonder where all the time has gone to—so many years; I cannot say I like to be reminded how many. My sister is three years older, eighty this May. She is glad to talk of her age. I don't like to mention mine. Maybe I have not her faith in God. She makes her way every day to church. I go only on Sundays. Enough is enough; besides, I don't like the priest. He points his finger too much. He likes to accuse us—each week it is a different sin he charges us with. My mother used to read me Christ's words when I was a girl—from the old Spanish Bible her grandmother gave to her on her deathbed. I learned that Christ was a kind man; He tried to think well of people, even the lowest of the low, even those at the very bottom who are in a swamp and don't know how to get out, let alone find for themselves some high, dry land.

It's interesting how landscape works its way into all of our lives. She continues:

But this priest of ours gives no one the benefit of the doubt. I have no right to find fault with him; I know that. Who am I to do so? I am simply an old lady, and I had better watch out: the Lord no doubt punishes those who disagree with His priests. But our old priest who died last year was so much finer, so much better to hear on a warm Sunday morning. Every once in a while he would even lead us outside to the courtyard and talk with us there, give us a second sermon. I felt so much better for listening to him. He was not in love with the sound of his own voice, as this new priest is. He did not stop and listen to the echo of his words. He did not brush away dust from his coat, or worry if the wind went through his hair. He was not always looking for a paper towel to wipe his shoes. My husband says he will buy this priest a dozen handkerchiefs and tell him they are to be used for his shoes only. Here when we get rain we are grateful, and it is not too high a price to pay, a little mud to walk through. Better mud that sticks than dust that blows away.

Well, I should not go on so long about a vain man. We all like to catch ourselves in the mirror and find ourselves good to look at. Here I am, speaking ill of him, and yet I won't let my family celebrate my birthdays anymore; and when I look at myself in the mirror a feeling of sadness comes over me. I pull at my skin and try to erase the lines, but no luck. I think back: all those years when my husband and I were young, and never worried about our health, our strength, our appearance. I don't say we always do now; but there are times when we look like ghosts of ourselves. I will see my husband noticing how weak and tired I have become, how hunched over. I pretend not to see, but once the eyes have caught something, one cannot shake the picture off. And I look at him, too; he will straighten up when he feels my glance strike him, and I quickly move away. Too late, though; he has been told by me, without a word spoken, that he is old, and I am old, and that is our fate, to live through these last few years.

But it is not only pity we feel for ourselves. A few drops of rain and I feel grateful; the air is so fresh afterwards. I love to sit in the sun. We have the sun so often here, a regular visitor, a friend one can expect to see and to trust. I like to make tea for my husband and me. At midday we take our tea outside and sit on our bench, our backs are against the wall of the house. Neither of us wants pillows; I tell my daughters and sons that they are soft—those beach chairs of theirs. Imagine beach chairs here in New Mexico, so far from any ocean! The bench feels strong to us, not uncomfortable. The tea warms us inside, the sun on the outside. I joke with my husband; I say we are part of the house. The adobe gets baked, and so do we. For the most part we say nothing, though. It is enough to sit and be part of God's world. We hear the birds talking to each other, and are grateful they come as close to us as they do; all the more reason to keep our tongues still and hold ourselves in one place. We listen to cars going by and wonder who is rushing off. A car to us is a mystery. The young understand a car. They cannot imagine themselves not driving. They have not the interest we had in horses. Who is to compare one lifetime with another, but a horse is alive, and one loves a horse and is loved by a horse.

Obviously I've strung this together with interruptions and questions and discursive moments. "Cars come and go so fast," she says. "One year they command all eyes." I love the way she puts it, especially "they command all eyes." "The next year," she continues,

they are a cause for shame. The third year they must be thrown away without the slightest regret. I may exaggerate, but not much!

My moods are like the church bell on Sunday: way up, then down, then up again—and often just as fast. I make noises, too;

my husband says he can hear me smiling and hear me turning sour. When I am sour, I am really sour—sweet milk turned bad. Nothing pleases me. I am more selfish than my sister. She bends with the wind. I push my heels into the ground and won't budge. I know enough to frown at myself, but not enough to change. There was a time when I tried hard. I would talk to my- self as if I was the priest. I would promise myself that tomorrow I would be different. I suppose only men and women can fool themselves that way; an animal knows better. Animals are them- selves. We are always trying to be better—and often we end up even worse than we were to start with.

But now, during the last moments of life, I think I have learned a little wisdom. I can go for days without an upset. I think I dislike our priest because he reminds me of myself.

Boy, if a lot of us could have that kind of intuitive insight, without paying a doctor for it, we'd be doing pretty well. And the self- medication she speaks about below—it's a little better than Prozac, don't you think?

I have his long forefinger, and I can clench my fist like him and pound the table and pour vinegar on people with my remarks. It is no good to be like that. A man is lucky; it is in his nature to fight or to preach. A woman should be peaceful. My mother used to say it all begins the day we are born: some are born on a clear, warm day; some when it is cloudy and stormy. So, it is a consolation to find myself easy to live with these days. And I have found an answer to the few moods I still get. When I have come back from giving the horses each a cube or two of sugar, I give myself the same. I am an old horse who needs something sweet to give her more faith in life!

The other day I thought I was going to say good-bye to this world. I was hanging up some clothes to dry. I love to do that, then stand back and watch and listen to the wind go through the socks or the pants or the dress, and see the sun warm them and make them smell fresh.

She went on and on, but I've condensed this. I should say that after hearing these words I went back home and told my wife about these remarks, and together we looked at our washing machine and its dryer, which we call progress. But her story doesn't end with that image:

I had dropped a few clothespins, and was picking them up, when suddenly I could not catch my breath, and a sharp pain seized me over my chest. I tried hard to stand up, but I couldn't. I wanted to scream, but I knew there was no one nearby to hear. My husband had gone to the store. I sat down on the ground and I waited. It was strong, the pain; and there was no one to tell about it. I felt as if someone had lassoed me and was pulling the rope tighter and tighter. Well here you are, an old cow, being taken in by the good Lord; that is what I thought.

I looked at myself, sitting on the ground. For a second I was my old self again—worrying about how I must have appeared there, worrying about my dress, how dirty it would get to be. This is no place for an old lady, I thought—only for one of my little grandchildren, who love to play out here, build their castles of dirt, wetted down with water I give to them. Then more pain; I thought I had about a minute of life left. I said my prayers. I said goodbye to the house.

To watch those children being very careful of water is to remind oneself that the mind is influenced by the social world, the landscape, and, yes, even the physical world, the landscape of our lives. And how many of us would say good-bye to our homes? This home, which had been handed down from generation to generation, gave her a sense of place and belonging.

I pictured my husband in my mind: fifty-seven years of marriage. Such a good man! I said to myself that I might not see him ever again; surely God would take him into Heaven, but as for me, I have no right to expect that outcome. Then I looked up to the sky and waited.

My eye caught sight of a cloud. It was darker than the rest. It was alone. It was coming my way. The hand of God, I was sure of it! So that is how one dies. All my life, in the spare moments a person has, I wondered how I would go. Now I knew. Now I was ready. I thought I would soon be taken up to the cloud and across the sky I would go, and that would be that. But the cloud kept moving, and soon it was no longer above me, but beyond me, and I was still on my own land, so dear to me, so familiar after all these years. I can't be dead, I thought to myself. . . . Maybe the next cloud—but by then I had decided God had other things to do. Perhaps my name had come up, but He had decided to call others before me, and get around to me later. Who can ever know His reasons? Then I spotted my neighbor walking down the road, and I said to myself that I would shout for him. I did, and he heard. But you know by the time he came I had sprung myself free. Yes, that is right, the pain was all gone.

In her own way, she described her condition as worthily as the *New England Journal of Medicine* would have. "Lassoed"—well, it's pushing it a little bit, that word, but I think we could persuade some editors to let it be used!

He helped me up, and he was ready to go find my husband and bring him back. No, I told him, no; I was all right, and I did not want to risk frightening my husband. He is excitable. He might get some kind of attack himself. I went inside and put myself down on our bed and waited. For an hour—it was that long, I am sure—my eyes stared at the ceiling, held on to it for dear life. I thought of what my life had been like: a simple life, not a very

important one, maybe an unnecessary one. I am sure there are
better people, men and women all over the world, who have
done more for their neighbors, and yet not lived as long as I
have.

Here she went into a long moral inquiry worthy of Job: where is
justice and what is it about? Then she returned to the personal:

I felt ashamed for a few minutes: all the complaints I'd made to
myself and to my family, when the truth has been that my fate
has been to live a long and healthy life, to have a good and loyal
husband and to bring two sons and three daughters into this
world. I thought of the five children we had lost, three before
they had a chance to take a breath. I wondered where in the universe they were. In the evening sometimes, when I go to close
loose doors that otherwise complain loudly all night, I am likely
to look at the stars and feel my long gone infants near at hand.
They are far off, I know; but in my mind they have become
those stars—very small, but shining there bravely, no matter how
cold it is so far up. If the stars have courage, we ought to have
courage; that is what I was thinking, as I so often have in the
past—and just then he was there, my husband, calling my name
and soon looking into my eyes with his. I'm all right, I told him.
He didn't know what had happened; our neighbor had sealed his
lips, as I told him to do. But my husband knows me, so he knew
I looked unusually tired; and he couldn't be easily tricked by me.
The more I told him I just worked too hard, that is all, the more
he knew I was holding something back. Finally, I pulled my ace
card. I pretended to be upset by his questions and by all the attention he was giving me. I accused him: why do you make me
want to cry, why do you wish me ill, with those terrible
thoughts of yours? I am not ill! If you cannot let me rest without thinking I am, then God have mercy on you for having such
an imagination! God have mercy! With a second plea to our

Lord, he was beaten and silent. He left me alone. I was about to beg him to come back, beg his forgiveness. But I did not want him to bear the burden of knowing; he would not rest easy by day or by night. This way he can say to himself: she has always been cranky, and she will always be cranky, so thank God her black moods come only now and then—a spell followed by the bright sun again.

I will say what I think happened: I came near going, then there was a change of heart up there in Heaven, so I have a few more days, or weeks, or months, or years—who knows? As for a doctor, I have never seen one, so why start now? Here we are so far away from a hospital. We have no money. Anglos don't like us, anyway: we are the poor ones, the lost ones. My son tells me the Anglos look down on us—old people without education and up in the hills, trying to scrape what we can from the land, and helped only by our animals. No matter; our son is proud of us. He is proud to stay here with us. He says that if he went to the city he would beg for work and be told no, no, no: eventually he might be permitted to sweep someone's floor. Better to hold on to one's land. Better to fight it out with the weather and the animals.

Again I say it: doctors are for others. My mother and my aunt delivered my children. I once went to see a nurse; she worked for the school and she told me about my children—the diseases they get. Thank you, I said. Imagine: she thought I knew nothing about bringing up children, or about the obstacles God puts in their way to test them and make them stronger for having gone through a fever, a rash, some pain. No, I will see no nurse and no doctor. They are as far from here as the stars. Oh, that is wrong; they are much farther. The stars I know and recognize and even call by name. They are my names, of course; I don't know what others call the stars. Is it wrong to do that? Perhaps I should ask the priest. Perhaps the stars are God's to name, not ours to treat like pets—by addressing them familiarly. But it is too late; my sins have been recorded, and I will soon enough pay for each and every one of them.

Of course I had to find out what her names for the stars were. To understand such a life—as I think you'll agree when you read *The Long Loneliness* or *The Diary of a Country Priest*—is to understand the search for meaning. We ought to aim to document that kind of effort too, as we document the factuality of poverty, of educational deficits, of medical inquiry. Let us learn to understand our fellow human beings in and on their own terrain—their moral and spiritual terrain, as well as the economic or educational. (The latter two are the kinds of landscape we are always surveying.)

When I was a resident at Boston Children's Hospital, in the pediatrics division, there was a girl who was dying of leukemia; I will never forget her and the conversations we had. At that time there was no real cure for this particular cancer (although now over 80 percent of the cases are curable through chemotherapy). Then all we had was blood, more and more blood transfusions, which gave a respite in this race between the blood-killing cells and the blood we could round up for these children, who at seven or eight or nine lay there dying! This particular girl, who was eleven or twelve, was a tough one. She noticed us noticing the cookies and the food by her bed and would say, "Take that." And we'd say, "No, no, no." She'd respond, "Well, you've been looking at it." "No, no, we weren't." "Oh yes, you were." Talk about a young, ailing patient becoming a social, psychological observer! We'd "transfuse her up"—that was the phrase. One day we got talking about what she'd do if she got a little better, and she said she'd like to go to the Red Sea. I said, "Why would you like to go to the Red Sea?" She said, "Because I know I would enjoy it there." I wondered what this was all about—a clinical reflex on my part.

I was interested in the art children created. One day she volunteered to draw me a picture of the Red Sea. I looked at the picture and I said, "That's the Red Sea?" She said, "Yes!" I figured out that the color red symbolized the Red Sea. I asked, "What's happening there?" She said, "Well, that is someone on the Red Sea, you know, and it can keep you afloat because of all the salt, I think." So I said, "What is going on there, to the right of the picture?" She said, "Well, that's an island and the person floating hopes to land there."

Meanwhile I was noticing, in her picture, those dark clouds in the sky that were preventing the sun from shining, and she'd given me a clue with an arrow; if only I'd looked a little closer I'd have realized the body was headed toward that island. I kept looking at that picture and was trying to figure out in my mind why she had chosen this subject matter. Suddenly, without saying a word, she looked up from the bed to her right, and I followed the trajectory of her eyes to a bottle standing beside her bedside, held up on a stand where a tube was waiting to be joined to her in a blood transfusion. Suddenly my mind clicked, and she saw it clicking and me staring at that bottle. She said, "You see?" And I did "see." I literally and figuratively "saw" what she saw literally and figuratively: that her only chance was that Red Sea and some respite on an island for a while.

This was a girl who used to talk to me about God and how He must be puzzled by children like her who were dying so young. Did He intend this to happen? She didn't think she deserved it, to die, but it was happening. And so, as she was dying, she was trying to figure out life: her parents' faith, and the biblical stories of Moses, his refuge in Egypt and the Sinai Desert, and her desert and the islands of safety we all try to find for ourselves from the various storms and threats in our lives! Soon enough she would go, she would die; and I would hold on to these drawings—through them, through listening and listening to her words, I've been helped to understand how life goes, just as through listening and listening to the elderly Spanish-speaking woman (*"una anciana,"* she called herself) I've also been helped to understand how life goes. Documentaries work as expressions of a kind of soul-searching for those being held up to scrutiny and often, even more so, for those doing the holding.

SIX

Really Something

William Carlos Williams was a New Jersey boy and in many ways looked up to another New Jersey boy: Walt Whitman. I think if he were alive today he'd want to shake the hand of another New Jersey boy (that's three balladeers in a row), namely Bruce Springsteen, who raises his voice for America and for the working class. A continuity, theirs, of a kind of insistent populism—a determination to break ranks with the academy, the intellectual tradition as it imposes itself on poets, as well as other kinds of writers. How far can you step off any professional platform (be it as a doctor, writer, or rock star) and yet remain part of the people who read you or hear you? That question, that determination was a big part of Williams's life. You will notice in Williams's *Doctor Stories* how he gets rid of punctuation marks and in the process gets rid of the various ways we distance ourselves from one another, including writers from readers. Nevertheless, he wrote those stories and submitted them to a publisher, to critics, and to readers, and the distance to some extent was there even as he struggled with the distance of his own background as it kept him, he felt, from understanding others, those whose language, customs, immediate circumstances were different from his.

Think of what we have covered so far in this book. We have had three writers, all of whom went to fancy private schools: Eton, Exeter, Horace Mann. Three men, three individuals privileged in background by virtue of their parents' circumstances, their own education, what they could summon for themselves and had been taught was available to them in their early years of growing up (that they could go here and go there and could have this and that). Their work was consequently affected.

Now we depart these circumstances and turn to Raymond Carver. He was born in 1938 and died in 1988: fifty years of life, only. Two packs a day of cigarettes starting when he was thirteen, fourteen, fifteen; lung cancer spread to his brain, leading to his death in August 1988 in Port Angeles, on the Strait of Juan de Fuca, west of Seattle. His father originally came from Arkansas, as in the Dust Bowl and *Grapes of Wrath* and John Steinbeck, and the migration of a predominately white, midwestern, and southern population across the continent to California, out of desperation and poverty and a weather-inflicted agricultural disaster that went on for years (as if it wasn't enough for America that the manufacturing aspect of American capitalism had by 1935 become almost moribund; hence the New Deal). The agricultural economy also fell apart because of the weather and one of the most prolonged droughts in the history of the nation. As Route 66 began its entrance into American apocrypha, that migration in a sense marked the rise of modern California; the California we know today began then. If you go to what are now the affluent parts of the area below Los Angeles and immediately north of it, you will find people whose family history goes back a couple of generations to Arkansas, Oklahoma, and Amarillo, in the panhandle of Texas.

Carver's father went out on his own first; later, he and his family ended up in Oregon and Washington. He had moved around, gotten jobs, worked on the Grand Coulee Dam as it was being constructed.

Raymond Carver was born in Oregon, and he went on to graduate from high school in Tacoma, Washington. By the time he was of college age, he was married, had a son and a daughter, and was working various jobs in factories, on farms, trying to eke out a living as a workingman moving about during the 1950s.

He was working as a janitor, as a matter of fact, when nearby he discovered one of the California state colleges, and he would drop in between shifts and listen in on lecturers' talks. One was given by the novelist John Gardner, and Carver was taken. He had always thought it was a wonderful thing to come up with stories, but he felt his life precluded such pursuits. Hearing Gardner and others talk about fiction and nonfiction, Carver started to do some creative writing himself, and then he began sending off submissions to various magazines. Although he unhappily got many rejection letters, he then started to get some letters of acceptance, and was eventually taken note of by an editor who thought there was something there, a compelling voice. On the strength of this, Carver headed east with his family, and was able to attend the Iowa Writers' Workshop—without a college degree or the test scores that now figure so prominently in the admissions process, alas. How ironic it is, given the life histories of some of our best writers, that multiple-choice tests bear such consequences for young, aspiring storytellers. But here he was in Iowa: a heavy smoker and drinker, an alcoholic, in and out of Alcoholics Anonymous meetings and sanatoriums of various kinds. A candidate for what we would call "counseling." I want to read part of an essay he wrote that can be found in a slim volume called *Fires,* which is a collection of his essays, poetry, and a few stories.

"In the mid 1960s," Carver begins, "I was in a busy laundromat in Iowa City trying to do five or six loads of clothes, kids' clothes, for the most part, but some of our own clothing, of course, my wife's and mine. My wife was working as a waitress for the University Athletic Club that Saturday afternoon. I was doing chores and being responsible for the kids. They were with some other kids that afternoon, a birthday party maybe. Something." Oh, does he love that word "something." Not the kind of word that figures to get you a good grade on a college writing-course paper. The essay continues:

But right then I was doing the laundry. I'd already had sharp words with an old harridan over the number of washers I'd had to use. Now I was waiting for the next round with her, or someone else like her. I was nervously keeping an eye on the dryers that were in operation in the crowded laundromat. When and if one of the dryers ever stopped, I planned to rush over to it with my shopping basket of damp clothes. Understand, I'd been hanging around in the laundromat for thirty minutes or so with this basketful of clothes, waiting my chance. I'd already missed out on a couple of dryers—somebody'd gotten there first. I was getting frantic. As I say, I'm not sure where our kids were that afternoon. Maybe I had to pick them up from some place, and it was getting late, and that contributed to my state of mind. I did know that even if I could get my clothes into a dryer it would still be another hour or more before the clothes would dry, and I could sack them up and go home with them, back to our apartment in married-student housing. Finally a dryer came to a stop. And I was right there when it did. The clothes inside quit tumbling and lay still. In thirty seconds or so, if no one showed up to claim them, I planned to get rid of the clothes and replace them with my own. That's the law of the laundromat. But at that minute a woman came over to the dryer and opened the door. I stood there waiting. This woman put her hand into the machine and took hold of some items of clothing. But they weren't dry enough, she decided. She closed the door and put two more dimes into the machine. In a daze I moved away with my shopping cart and went back to waiting. But I remember thinking at that moment, amidst the feelings of helpless frustration that had me close to tears, that nothing—and, brother, I mean nothing—that ever happened to me on this earth could come anywhere close, could possibly be as important to me, could make as much difference, as the fact that I had two children. And that I would always have them and always find myself in this position of unrelieved responsibility and permanent distraction.

I'm talking about real *influence* now. I'm talking about the moon and the tide. But like that it came to me. Like a sharp breeze when the window is thrown open. Up to that point in my life I'd gone along thinking, what exactly, I don't know, but that things would work out somehow—that everything in my life I'd hoped for or wanted to do, was possible. But at that moment, in the laundromat, I realized that this simply was not true. I realized—what had I been thinking before?—that my life was a small-change thing for the most part, chaotic, and without much light showing through. And at that moment I felt—I knew—that the life I was in was vastly different from the lives of the writers I most admired.

Well, I'm not so sure that, in fact, his life was all that different from the early life of Charles Dickens or Thomas Hardy, or Ralph Emerson, or Zora Neale Hurston, or Tillie Olsen. But there is no question that it was different from the lives of the three writers I have discussed at length. And, I guess, different from the lives of many of us who are able to attend college and who grew up in homes that had laundry machines, the washer and dryer, without any need to shove anyone aside or wonder when someone is going to get out of the way. To have and have not—it can come down to that: to a lousy machine and all that it implies about freedom and possibility and opportunity and time that is yours, belongs to you, that you can do something without having to look here and there, and wait and watch and grab.

The story "Where I'm Calling From" tells of someone who's "calling" from a situation where he is drying out in a sanatorium with others who have been drinking themselves toward extinction. And we would not have this book if, after getting out of that sanatorium, one more time, in 1977, he hadn't gone to a writers' conference in Dallas the following year and met the American poet and short-story writer Tess Gallagher. Nine or ten years of love and connection made up their life together (Tess and Ray), a ways west of

Seattle, and the writing of a lot of these stories; so that by the time that Raymond Carver died, the *Times Literary Supplement,* in London, could call him the American Chekhov. That is not a bad title to have in an obituary. Carver had wanted to go to Chekhov's grave and Tolstoy's grave, as he lay dying himself there in the state of Washington, going into the University of Washington Medical Center, being pounded with radiation to slow down a metastatic tumor of the lung. And he dreamed of going east to see Williams's house on 9 Ridge Road. He loved Williams's poetry and his stories and novels. He wrote a poem to Williams and to Hemingway, another one of his heroes: "Poem for Hemingway and W. C. Williams":

> *3 fat trout hang*
> 　　*in the still pool*
> *below the new*
> 　　*steel bridge.*
> *two friends*
> 　　*come slowly up*
> *the track.*
> 　　*one of them*
> *ex-heavyweight,*
> 　　*wears an old*
> *hunting cap.*
> 　　*he wants to kill,*
> *that is catch & eat,*
> 　　*the fish.*
> *the other,*
> 　　*medical man,*
> *he knows the chances*
> 　　*of that.*
> *he thinks it fine*
> 　　*that they should*
> *simply hang there*
> 　　*always*

in the clear water.
    the two keep going
but they
    discuss it as
they disappear
    into the fading trees
& fields & light,
    upstream.

Carver was a great fisherman and hunter. Note also the bridge; bridges figure in his stories, and kids going over them. In the middle of the poem, he brings Williams and Hemingway together.

For Carver, those W. C. Williams poems in the previous chapter—about the old lady eating plums, the poor person—addressed the kind of vulnerability he felt, lived out, died with. Carver knew that Anton Chekhov grew up in a humble home, with much distress and, indeed, pain and hurt and violence, and escaped to Moscow to become a doctor at a time when such professions were open to only a few. And as a medical student, Chekhov began to take note of all the hurt people he saw and with whom he identified so strongly. And these hurt and perplexed people, aching out of their past, wondering with respect to their future, these are the people that Carver wanted to offer us in his various short fictions.

At the end, he turned to poetry—oh, did he! In his last book, which was published posthumously, called *A New Path to the Waterfall,* he described, in a way, his last decade, a decade of blessedness and love that became possible for him. These poems are of rare beauty. For years I have asked medical students to read this one, called "What the Doctor Said"; it's about someone, during a medical visit, being told he is going to die of cancer.

He said it doesn't look good
he said it looks bad in fact real bad
he said I counted thirty-two of them on one lung before

I quit counting them
I said I'm glad I wouldn't want to know
about any more being there than that
he said are you a religious man do you kneel down
in forest groves and let yourself ask for help
when you come to a waterfall
mist blowing against your face and arms
do you stop and ask for understanding at those moments
I said not yet but I intend to start today
he said I'm real sorry he said
I wish I had some other kind of news to give you
I said Amen and he said something else
I didn't catch and not knowing what else to do
and not wanting him to have to repeat it
and me to have to fully digest it
I just looked at him
for a minute and he looked back it was then
I jumped up and shook hands with this man who'd just given me
something no one else on earth had ever given me
I may even have thanked him habit being so strong

This next poem, "Gravy," was published in the *New Yorker* posthumously:

No other word will do. For that's what it was. Gravy.
Gravy, these past ten years.
Alive, sober, working, loving and
being loved by a good woman. Eleven years
ago he was told he had six months to live
at the rate he was going. And he was going
nowhere but down. So he changed his ways
somehow. He quit drinking! And the rest?
After that, it was all gravy, every minute

of it, up to and including when he was told about,
well, some things that were breaking down and
building up inside his head. "Don't weep for me,"
he said to his friends. "I'm a lucky man.
I've had ten years longer than I or anyone
expected. Pure gravy. And don't forget it.

In Carver country, we meet a waitress; people who clean up motel rooms; bus drivers; mechanics; people who work in the post office; ordinary, humble housewives; children of working people who are off trying to earn a living; people who sell things; people who bake bread and try to make a go of life—the working people of America whom he knew so well. In most of Carver's stories, we go from misunderstanding toward understanding. "A Small Good Thing" gives us a baker and the rather well-to-do woman whose son is having a birthday; she goes in to order a cake for the boy, but in the meantime, fate knocks the child down: he is hit by a car. He is taken to the hospital and then, almost like out of one of those old Hitchcock movies, a kind of terror, in two different locations, gets going. The baker wants someone to come and pick that cake up, pay for it; he keeps calling the house—and calling and calling. The parents, who occasionally stop into this house, are coming home from their watch over their badly injured son, their night-and-day watch in the hospital, and they hear that phone. We are given the agitation of someone who wants his money, who doesn't understand why people don't come and pick up their cake, and the despair of people who don't understand why anyone would do this, call and call and call. And then there is the gap between this pair of parents and a doctor. Gradually, the tension builds up; the boy, we begin to realize, is dying. We have various kinds of misunderstandings: between the parents and the doctor and, not least, the parents and the baker, as well as between the two parents themselves. Tragedy hurts; there is suffering, there are consequences, and then a kind of redemption, as Carver brings them together: the grieving parents and the baker, who cooks for them and feeds them. A communion, as in bread and wine.

This is interesting, because that story as it was initially written didn't have the ending I just described. The earlier Carver didn't have it within him to offer that ending. The ending tells a lot about what happened to him as a short-story writer and as a human being who wrote short stories. (They are not mutually exclusive phenomena.) The story is itself "a small, good thing."

Then there is "Cathedral," where a blind man comes to a house, an ordinary house, to visit a woman he used to know, whom he's been corresponding with, and her husband. And what Carver gets going in that story, between those three people and then two people, trading them off, breaking off the triangle, is pure magic.

A husband gets annoyed with a blind man because his wife is obviously getting along with him in ways that they together don't seem to be able to muster for themselves. There is a certain tenderness and understanding that the woman and blind man seem to have. The husband gets funny about it. He talks about taking the blind man bowling and other such things. Then they feed, they all sit down to eat. Here is a description of an eating scene:

> We dug in. We ate everything there was to eat on the table. We ate like there was no tomorrow. We didn't talk. We ate. We scarfed. We grazed that table. We were into serious eating. The blind man had right away located his foods, he knew just where everything was on his plate. I watched with admiration as he used his knife and fork on the meat. He'd cut two pieces of meat, fork the meat into his mouth, and then go all out for the scalloped potatoes, the beans next, and then he'd tear off a hunk of buttered bread and eat that. He'd follow this up with a big drink of milk. It didn't seem to bother him to use his fingers once in a while, either.

We finished everything, including half a strawberry pie. For a few moments, we sat as if stunned. Sweat beaded on our faces. Finally, we got up from the table and left the dirty plates. We didn't look back. We took ourselves to the living room and sank into our places again. Robert and my wife sat on the sofa. I took the big chair. We had us two or three more drinks while they talked about the major things that had come to pass for them in the past ten years. For the most part, I just listened. Now and then I joined in. I didn't want him to think I'd left the room, and I didn't want her to think I was feeling left out. . . .

I got our drinks and sat down on the sofa with him. Then I rolled us two fat numbers. I lit one and passed it. I brought it to his fingers. He took it and inhaled.

"Hold it as long as you can," I said. I could tell he didn't know the first thing.

My wife came back downstairs wearing her pink robe and her pink slippers.

"What do I smell?" she said.

"We thought we'd have us some cannabis," I said.

My wife gave me a savage look. Then she looked at the blind man and said, "Robert, I didn't know you smoked."

He said, "I do now my dear. There is a first time for everything. But I don't feel anything, yet."

"This stuff is pretty mellow," I said. "This stuff is mild. It's dope you can reason with," I said. "It doesn't mess you up."

"Not much it doesn't, bub," he said and laughed.

My wife sat on the sofa between the blind man and me. I passed her the number. She took it and toked and then passed it back to me. "Which way is this going?" she said. Then she said, "I shouldn't be smoking this. I can hardly keep my eyes open as it is. That dinner did me in. I shouldn't have eaten so much."

"It was the strawberry pie," the blind man said. "That's what did it."

Well, this line of narrative goes on and on, wonderfully, and she goes up to bed, and the two men sit there, and pretty soon they are watching on public television the story of the building of a cathedral. The one man and the other try to respond to that television pictorial presentation of cathedral building. Then the sighted husband gets thoughtful; in his own way he reaches out to his blind guest:

Then something occurred to me, and I said, "Something has oc-curred to me. Do you have any idea what a cathedral is? What they look like, that is? Do you follow me? If somebody says cathedral to you, do you have any notion what they're talking about? Do you know the difference between that and a Baptist church, say?"

He let the smoke dribble from his mouth. "I know they took hundreds of workers fifty or a hundred years to build," he said. "I just heard the man say that, of course. I know generations of the same families worked on a cathedral. . . . But maybe you could describe one to me? I wish you'd do it. I'd like that. If you want to know, I really don't have a good idea."

Soon enough, the guy who was feeling out of it, put down by his own wife and this visitor, turns into a teacher. The blind man asks him to get some paper, saying,

"We'll do something. We'll draw one together."

So I went upstairs. My legs felt like they didn't have any strength in them. . . . Downstairs, in the kitchen, I found a shop-ping bag with onion skins in the bottom of the bag. I emptied the bag and shook it. I brought it into the living room and sat down with it near his legs. I moved some things, smoothed the wrinkles from the shopping bag, spread it out on the coffee table. . . .

"All right," he said. "All right, let's do her."

He found my hand, the hand with the pen. He closed his hand over my hand.

Note the details of this growing human connection, this trust between a story's twosome: a humble shopping bag, onions (as in something that gets to the eyes and makes us cry and quickly brings emotion to us), and the humility of not fancy drawing paper but, rather, an old crease-ridden shopping bag—these "things" become the stuff of touching, learning, telling, listening. A scene of two men with their hands on each other, as they begin to build a cathedral: the blind man "sees" a cathedral. The teacher, who can see, sees the cathedral through the help of (the need of) the blind man, as in the blind leading the blind. As in the blindness that we all have. Others can see what we can't, give us sight that can become more than sight—the insight that teachers help us find, and yes, that students help their teachers find. This was one of Carver's greatest stories, and may well be one of the great American stories of this century. Blind, we see with and through one another: we notice, understand our fellow human beings. A gift from Carver to us—he the storyteller trying to find his way, see his way, toward human affiliation, and we, his readers, becoming gratefully, knowingly, wide-eyed.

SEVEN

American Loneliness

Edward Hopper, *Nighthawks,* 1942, oil on canvas, 84.1 × 152.4 cm., Friends of American Art Collection, 1942.51, The Art Institute of Chicago. Photography © The Art Institute of Chicago.

Let us now be students of Edward Hopper's. A contemporary of Dr. Williams's, Hopper was a documentary artist intent on rendering vividly aspects of American life. We start with *Nighthawks,* perhaps his best-known painting; it is one of the great paintings Raymond Carver used to sit and stare at. We can see the light shining as light shines in some of those Carver stories, which take place, often, in the middle of the night, in city apartments or suburban homes, on lawns and in backyards, in parking lots and in diners and

restaurants, as people make do. Carver gives us characters that remember and shudder and wonder and wander on their search, as
they, and others, love and trust and hope, and hope.

The scene in this painting connects to the Carver story
"Menudo." It's four o'clock in the morning; Carver would want to
capture that light. Listen to this excerpt from "Menudo":

> I can't sleep, but when I'm sure my wife Vicky is asleep, I get up
> and look through our bedroom window, across the street, at
> Oliver and Amanda's house. Oliver has been gone for three days,
> but his wife Amanda is awake. She can't sleep either. It's four in
> the morning, and there's not a sound outside—no wind, no cars,
> no moon even—just Oliver and Amanda's place with the lights
> on, leaves heaped up under the front windows.

I taught for a while in a ninth-grade class in a school in Boston.
The kids were driving me crazy with their swearing, their throwing
of spitballs. I was in desperation one day; I didn't know what I was
going to do, but I guessed that I could always walk out, since I was a
volunteer. One day I told them I was going to walk out, and then I
started swearing away—and the more I swore, the more respect I
seemed to get from this class, to the point where they were so silent
that I couldn't believe my ears. I thought I had an educational mir-
acle on my hands. I didn't know what to do with the silence, but I
had some slides in my pockets, because I was on my way to give a
lecture "across the river," at Harvard. So I showed the class this Hopper painting, and I'll never forget how a girl raised her hand and said,
"You know, my mother works in Dunkin' Donuts on the eleven P.M.
to seven A.M. shift." She started telling the class about the people
who came into the store in the middle of the night for a cup of coffee, and how her mother talked to them and listened to them and
came home and said how hard a night it was, "a hard, hard night
with those folks," she would keep saying.

There it is, *Nighthawks,* now in the Art Institute of Chicago; my mother used to take my brother and me to see that picture. When were on our way to visit her family in Iowa, taking the train from Boston to Chicago, we'd get off and spend a day or so in the Windy City before going on to the farmlands. She'd have us look at that picture. I remember as a little boy wondering who they were and where they came from, those people Hopper presents to us, folks at a store's counter in the middle of the night, thinking, remembering, pausing, wondering. I can still hear my brother saying, "That guy has a girlfriend, but this one doesn't have anyone." He was about eight years old and I was about ten. He asked, "Why is that, Mama?"

Take a look, if you can, at a close-up *Nighthawks*. (One can be found at http://www.artsheaven.com/edward-hopper-nighthawks .html.) Note how the couple's eyes are clouded, windows drawn over their eyes. They are lost in themselves, even though they are sitting beside each other. You'll find this again if you read "They're Not Your Husband"—as in a woman working in a diner, feeling fat, serving a man tons of food, serving, listening, trying to figure out life while others eat and eat, and take from you and you give.

Hopper's *Night Shadows* is one of his etchings—a lithograph, actually. Talk about Camus and Sartre and existentialism and being dwarfed by the enormity of the metropolis, the anonymity. Or, as T. S. Eliot put it in *Four Quartets,* "Dark dark dark. They all go into the dark." It doesn't matter whether it be the subway station or the streets and the shadows ahead of us. Who knows what "shadow" means. From up there Hopper looks and has us look at a faceless man, an anonymous man, a hustling man, a striving man, a walking man.

Room in New York—that's another one my mom got us to see, back in Lincoln, Nebraska, where she had a cousin. There they are, together, lost to one another, lost in themselves, the man lost in the paper—oh, the many uses of a newspaper. And there is the piano, looking formal, set aside separate. There was a play that came out in the 1950s I think, called *Separate Tables.* Well, we only need one table for that kind of separation to exist here. We also have that huge

Hopper, Edward (1882–1967). *Night Shadows* from *Six American Etchings* (1921, published 1924). Etchings from a portfolio by various artists, plate: 6¹⁵⁄₁₆ × 8⅛ in. (17.6 × 20.7 cm.); sheet 9⁷⁄₁₆ × 11¼ in. (24 × 28.6 cm). Publisher: *The New Republic,* New York. Printer: Peter Platt, New York. Edition: approximately 500. Gift of Abby Aldrich Rockefeller. The Museum of Modern Art, New York, N.Y., U.S.A. Digital Image © The Museum of Modern Art/licensed by SCALA/Art Resource, N.Y.

door—a door that Ibsen could have taken and turned into a whole metaphor for the entire four or five acts of a play.

The next painting I'd like to address is called *Chop Suey.* The hats are from the 1920s, when some people wearing those hats would dance the Charleston. Those tables don't look very inviting, do they? Kind of stripped and bare in the shadows, and what are they suggesting about the life around them—also a bit humbled, not fulfilled. What are these physical things to one another? Hopper was a great one for putting people in the intimacy of a restaurant, but the question is, What kind of intimacy, if any?

Summer in the City takes us right into Carver's story "The Student's Wife," one of the stories I urge us all to read. You have a grad-

Edward Hopper, *Room in New York,* 1932, oil on canvas, 29½₂ × 36⅝ × 1¼ in. Sheldon Museum of Art, University of Nebraska–Lincoln, UNL-F. M. Hall Collection. Photo © Sheldon Museum of Art.

Hopper, Edward, *Chop Suey,* 1929, oil on canvas, 32 × 38 in. Collection of Barney A. Ebbsworth.

Summer in the City, 1950 (oil on canvas), by Edward Hopper (1882–1967). James Goodman Gallery, New York/The Bridgeman Art Library.

uate student who is reading Rilke, of all things. He's reading big-deal Rilke, but Lord knows he doesn't want to "read" his own wife. The two of them are sadly out of touch and out of kilter with each other. You just cry going through that, until finally, at the end of the story, she is on her knees in the middle of the night, praying to the Almighty, if there is an Almighty, for some kind of salvation from this estrangement. What a terrible thing for us to contemplate—that we can be so smart and have our scholarship but not necessarily be good and loving husbands, wives, parents, neighbors, or human beings, or doctors, or lawyers, or teachers, or whatever.

In *Night Windows,* we have a room with a view, but what view? What do we see around us now in this urban world of ours? This is not Wordsworth or an English countryside; it's the tops of roofs and maybe some flowers bought in a store, set in that vase. Perhaps it's a landscape of loneliness, and the woman in the painting might be Emily Dickinson with her back to us. Only this is not Amherst—though Dickinson's opening lines of a poem may apply: "I felt a funeral in my brain, / And mourners, to and fro . . ."

Hopper, Edward (1882–1967). *Night Windows,* 1928, oil on canvas, 29 × 34 in.
Gift of John Hay Whitney. (248.1940). The Museum of Modern Art, New York,
N.Y., U.S.A. Digital image © The Museum of Modern Art/licensed by SCALA/Art
Resource, N.Y.

Office at Night shows us the workplace. "Work and love are what's important," said Freud. If you get those two, you get an A and graduate with high honors from the Vienna Psychoanalytic Institute. Notice, in the painting, the contours of the woman's body: heightened by a dress, but harnessed to a filing cabinet. As for the man, all he knows is that there are records to go over, and the boss will want to see something from him in the morning. At times in life, we defer, defer, defer—it's called "sublimation." In any event, here is an office loaded with ambition and compliance, drudgery and obedience; and lust is about ready to be filed away. But lust does creep out. Anyway, Hopper has a lot going on in that office without writing a single word about it.

Let's take a look at *The Barber Shop.* Anyone know what that woman's occupation is? She's a manicurist. I can remember, as a boy,

Hopper, Edward, *Office at Night,* 1940, oil on canvas, 22³⁄₁₆ × 25⅛ in.,
collection Walker Art Center, Minneapolis, gift of the T. B. Walker
Foundation, Gilbert M. Walker Fund, 1948.

Collection Neuberger Museum of Art, Purchase College, State University
of New York, gift of Roy R. Neuberger. Photo credit: Jim Frank.

Edward Hopper (American, 1882–1967), *Automat,* 1927, oil on canvas, 36 × 28⅛ in. (91.4 × 71.4 cm.). Des Moines Art Center Permanent Collections. Purchased with funds from the Edmundson Art Foundation, Inc., 1958.2.

asking my father why there was a woman cleaning peoples' finger-nails and filing them down in the place he would take us for hair-cuts. My father would say there are some people who are so damn lazy they can't do it themselves. But there was more to it than that, I guess. In any event, she's waiting for her next customer while sit-ting in her own world, and the barber is doing the haircutting. That barbershop is flooded with a kind of interior, unnerving light.

Automat shows us one of these well-known scenes. The automat was a place where you used to stick coins into a machine, and you would get your food out of these little boxes. Again, I remember my mother telling me about this, and then she took me to an automat and my brother and I wondered where the people were. There were just these little boxes, and you'd put in a quarter and you'd get a piece of apple pie. Where were the people? You can ask that with Hopper. In a similar painting, *Sunlight in a Cafeteria,* there are two people, instead of *Automat*'s lone woman, but he's looking in one direction and she's looking in another. We hope they pick each other up and go off and have a long and happy life. But when you look at the revolving door, you just don't know. There they are looking and looking together and yet entranced by something that is beyond them, it seems, something that holds their attention.

Gas—this is a great one. I don't know why I like this one so much, except that I like to drive in the middle of the night. Look at the grass; it's inflamed. We see a Mobilgas sign; we long to be "on the road," as was Jack Kerouac in the 1950s. Here we have the call to be on the road, to be getting someplace, to keep moving to meet others unlike yourself: California, here I come. You got some pain, you got some trouble—well, you move on.

Hopper, Edward (1882–1967). *Gas,* 1940, oil on canvas, 26¼ × 40¼ in. Mrs. Simon Guggenheim Fund. The Museum of Modern Art, New York, N.Y., U.S.A. Digital image © The Museum of Modern Art/licensed by SCALA/Art Resource, N.Y.

That's the end of this collection of Hopper pictures I want to share—but remember what Eliot said: "In my end is my beginning." These Hopper pictures, taken as a group, express art and stories. They say, Come, America, you and me, let us consider our struggle to be, to find, to know, to trust, to love.

EIGHT

A Life's Moment of Irony

Dr. William Carlos Williams prompted me to think differently about what I wanted to do with my life. When I started taking premed courses, I complained to him, but he didn't have much sympathy, since he had never taken them; they weren't part of a doctor's education when he was a student. He found such courses utterly unnecessary for what he thought being a good doctor was about. He was not very sympathetic or understanding as he heard me recite my premed woes. He would brusquely say things like "Look, you have to do what you have to do." These oracular statements are not always what we want when we look to others for sympathy and compassion. On the other hand, I think a lot of us know that sometimes sympathy and compassion undermine us when we are called upon to have a certain kind of toughness of spirit.

As I got to know Dr. Williams, he would take me with him to visit some of his patients, and I would hear lectures from him. He told me about his friendship with Ezra Pound. I remember when he went to Washington to visit Pound at St. Elizabeths Hospital, where the government was keeping him, in lieu of sending him to prison for life. Ezra had been convicted of treason, having spent the war shouting out hate through radio broadcasts, speaking out against the

United States and against all kinds of people he hated. Ezra was a brilliant, accomplished poet living out what Williams would talk about as a life's moment of irony. There was a man who knew so much, who knew several languages, who knew the beauty of great writing, and yet he had become filled with hate.

One day Dr. Williams turned to me and asked if I knew who Joseph Goebbels was. I had this vague thought that he was someone who worked for Hitler. Indeed he did; he ran Hitler's hate machine. He was a "minister of propaganda and public enlightenment," as it was called, for the Nazi Party. Williams told me a biographical fact about Goebbels: that Goebbels had secured a PhD in comparative literature from the University of Heidelberg (Germany's Harvard). What does one do with that? I also later learned that Martin Heidegger, one of the great philosophers of the twentieth century, had also signed up with the Nazi Party. And there was Paul de Man, one of the great literary critics of recent times, who taught at Harvard when I was a student—on his way up the intellectual ladder in the comparative literature department. His history of Nazi affiliation and the writing he did to espouse Nazi philosophy also became known. And then, in my profession, there is the very dubious and suspect relationship of Jung to the Nazis. Jung allowed himself to run the German Psychiatric Association, as well as what was left of the German psychoanalytic societies, after Hitler "cleansed" them.

Even more horrible than a recitation of those well-known twentieth-century intellectual figures is the knowledge of what various German professors in fields such as medicine and law taught in the universities—and, yes, included in that list are members of the ministry. We have to wonder about the relationship of educated, even brilliant people to the brute evil and political power of Hitler and Stalin. Hundreds of psychologists and psychiatrists (people like me) were employed by the KGB to forcibly inject people with drugs, so that it would be easier to manage them. Years ago, the American Psychiatric Association had its annual meeting in Honolulu, Hawaii, and some of us American doctors went to talk with the Soviet doctors and ask them about that practice. What they shot back at us was: "What would you people do to spare your family if you were tested this way, if your country turned to this or that murderous political philosophy and carried it out?" Again and again, we were asked—and then we asked ourselves: What would we do? Who can know? Who can be sure? Who can take for granted one's moral nature when it is truly tested or threatened?

For Williams, the horror of Pound was that he did not have to be thus tested, morally challenged. He was an American. The horror for Williams was that, side by side with aesthetic genius, with poetic sensibility and accomplishment, could live this mean-spiritedness, arrogance, smugness. When I heard some of Dr. Williams's observations or comments, walking away from the car with him or walking toward it, I would get scared. I still am scared sometimes, remembering his words, his stories. Scared by his desire openly and publicly to confess—to wonder aloud about human nature, the moral challenges fate puts to it. Writers do not always confess. Sometimes they use their writing capacity to scorn others, to mock them, to caricaturize them, to connect with us readers so as to form a coalition that can then dump on this or that kind of person.

Williams's book *Paterson* goes back to my time as a college student, and the book starts out with a colon. This is his way of saying, "Look, whatever it is that I'm about, there are others. What I am doing is part of the human parade, and I want to acknowledge that right off." It's part of what he called "a local pride." He did not go to Prague or Paris or London; he is going to stay in his own backyard. He'll stay there through spring, summer, fall; he'll stay through the seasons and follow the descent of the river as it works its way across the land, toward the ocean.

Williams then pretty quickly takes on T. S. Eliot. You want to talk about hate, envy, and rivalry? he asks. Williams is challenging "Prufrock," and challenging *Four Quartets*. Eliot's well-known question, Do I dare to eat a peach? Well, Williams dares mightily. He rolls up his sleeves and eats away. Again and again he confesses or changes his tune; he'll be giving us beautiful poetry, or angry poetry, or dramatic poetry, and then he'll switch to prose. He'll evoke a scene in an office where he is a doctor and he's peeling the label off a mayonnaise jar. This comes after a long assault on intellectual arrogance, in the tradition of Agee and Orwell. Why do these people do this? What motivates these writers to do this?

Here is an excerpt from Book One of *Paterson*:

> *We go on living, we permit ourselves*
> *to continue—but certainly*
> *not for the university, what they publish*
> *severally or as a group: clerks*
> *got out of hand forgetting for the most part*
> *to whom they are beholden.*
> *spitted on fixed concepts like*
> *roasting hogs, sputtering, their drip sizzling*
> *in the fire*

"They" in the third line refers to intellectuals. This is not very nice, and as soon as he stops he switches to prose:

He was more concerned, much more concerned, with detaching the label from a discarded mayonnaise jar, the glass jar in which some patient had brought a specimen for examination, than to examine and treat the twenty or more infants taking their turn from the outer office, their mothers tormented and jabbering. He'd stand in the alcove pretending to wash, the jar at the bottom of the sink well out of sight and, as the rod of water came down, work with his fingernail in the splash at the edge of the colored label striving to loose the tightly glued paper. It must have been varnished over, he argued, to have it stick that way. One corner of it he'd got loose in spite of all and would get the rest presently: talking pleasantly the while and with great skill to the anxious parent.

A moment of a doctor's self-absorption, a distancing of the self from others who are needy and hurt and vulnerable. You and I have every right to insist that they are entitled to his complete and assisting attention. Why is it that what we read in *The Doctor Stories* bothers so many of us (maybe understandably)? What is it about these moments of an enraged doctor, almost tearing at a child's mouth to get a needed diagnostic swab? I could give you an intellectual explanation—about how the public health laws were written, and how diphtheria reigned at the time, and the need of this doctor to get the child's throat swabbed so that the law could continue its operation: namely, that a sign would be posted, to help others avoid getting diphtheria, a highly contagious disease that you and I will never know. But that is not what that story is about—it is about human subjectivity, its variations candidly given expression.

Think about this story, called "The Use of Force." Whose force is it, and against whom? And why do I so often find myself not able to recall the title of that story, even as you who read it will wonder what kind of a doctor this is. Certainly not the kind of doctor I want to be or see myself headed to being or, for that matter, the kind of lawyer or engineer or teacher or whatever you and I are or are going to be. Then we have to wonder about some of the other stories, even more offensive to some of us. We can go so far as to pick up particular sentences in them that sear our consciousness and our conscience.

Who is old Doc Rivers, from the story of the same title, this addict, this drunk? Does it help if I tell you that there are a lot of articles with abstract titles like "The Impaired Physician"? Will that, in your minds, condone what offends you when you get to know old Doc Rivers in that story? I hope not. Williams is not asking us to be "intellectual" with these stories, any more than he wanted to be an intellectual himself. These stories were written in response to a human being's confessional needs. These stories were written with hope against hope that you and I might be willing, occasionally, to remember or acknowledge to ourselves some of our tougher, blemished moments in life—when we strike out at people, dismiss people, or use people with our own kind of force. Sometimes it's not a hand with a swab going into a mouth; sometimes it's with language, or even with a look. Some of us who practice psychiatry can give that look to a patient coming in to see us. We give that hard, penetrating look, that look of: "I can see right through you and figure you out, and I can because I'm that smart. I can, and I will, and now I've done it, so I've *got* it—I've got *you*. I am powerful. I *know*. I will *find out*." *All of this even as we also get "turned on" by those we see.* What do I mean by that expression of your generation? I mean we are excited, amused, titillated, curious, and ready to probe with our questions, not our swabs. I can read to you about this kind of silent and not-so-silent prejudice, from "A Face of Stone":

> He was one of these fresh Jewish types you want to kill at sight, the presuming poor whose looks change the minute cash is mentioned. But they're insistent, trying to force attention, taking advantage of good nature at the first crack. You come when I call you, that type. He got me into a bad mood before he opened his mouth just by the half smiling, half insolent look in his eyes, a small, stoutish individual in a greasy black suit, a man in his middle twenties I should imagine.

For sure (I would hope), we are appalled: Who *is* this man? Isn't he the same guy who took on T. S. Eliot for his arrogance and snobbishness, and his not-so-subtle anti-Semitism? Isn't he the same guy who called his friend Ezra Pound crazy with hate? What is this story's outburst about? Every sleazy stereotype is available in one paragraph! Why?

I could give you a careful literary analysis of the story and we could safely work our way across that ocean of misunderstanding, as the story's doctor does with a family, to the safe and welcoming shores of compassion and awareness and charity and love and kindness. We could then put the book down and say Williams was the good guy after all, and that we now understand the story and what he was trying to get us to understand, about the gaps between some of us and others of us. But I think he is taking a bigger risk than that. What is he trying to tell us in those early paragraphs? He makes us contemplate a doctor who is hard-pressed, who knows he isn't going to get the money he wants or even needs, who is constrained by a conscience but also driven by selfishness, by his own imperatives.

In *Middlemarch,* George Eliot talks about "unreflecting egoism." You and I know that such a state of mind can come upon us. We know what we do in the privacy of our minds. We know what we do when we are rushed, or hard-pressed, or full of ourselves, or when we have our own agenda, period. That is not the whole truth about us, but it can become an important part of our lives, even if only for a few moments. And in those moments, certain truths leak out, descend upon minds: truths that we share with no one, not even our own roommates, friends, lovers, children, parents, husbands or wives—on and on the intimacy goes, and with it the limitations of intimacy for all of us (and the realization that in a second or two we can fall by the wayside morally).

The "heart of darkness" that Joseph Conrad described in his novella by the same name is not limited to one continent or class or race or nationality but is all over every life. In those dark moments we can make jumps toward that "darkness" with a little remark, a thought, that crosses our minds and is heard by no one. The point of this lecture is not to accuse anyone, but simply for us, with help, to understand how it goes when we struggle not only for knowledge of others but for knowledge of ourselves. What Williams understands about those people he describes is meant to help us understand what can happen to us. What we learn at the beginning of "A Face of Stone" is what some people have helped a doctor learn about himself, all of which he is then writing for you and me. He turns to the act of writing after coming to that knowledge, that experience of having those people come into his office, hearing them, and hearing some of those things as they cross his mind. If you can go from that, on the individual level, to the power of a state to institutionalize hate, then you can move on to the stories of ordinary Germans, and the ordinary people of any country, people faced with the excruciating moral dilemmas that twentieth-century totalitarianism posed.

When I was a medical student, I used to go to Union Theological Seminary to hear Reinhold Niebuhr talk—and sometimes he told us of Dietrich Bonhoeffer. Bonhoeffer, a German theologian, was regarded as out of his mind for leaving his native Germany (he was from the upper-class Aryan world) but then wanting to go back and take on Hitler. How many Bonhoeffers are there? Who among us can presume to have that kind of moral sensibility, including any among the persecuted group? There is the horror: the effects of brutal state power on everyone, the persecutors and the persecuted. The threat to life can cause people, even within those persecuted groups, to betray their fellow human beings. Not a few of us are capable, alas, of such a loss of self-respect, decency.

Williams lived during the first half of the twentieth century, the war-ridden decades of exalted poetry; he wanted so much to write beautiful words, but he knew that side by side with that beauty was the evident ugliness of this world. Going door-to-door and getting to know families firsthand was part of what a doctor's life was about: constant contact with patients' lives. Part of what these stories are about is the patient becoming a doctor. We can remember the girl who helped the man of brute force to see himself through her experiencing eyes, watching and taking note and feeling that fright and that horror; we can keep in mind the couple and their child, and their vulnerability as they call him to their side to help them, and thereupon see him and his second or two of coldness, calculation, lack of feeling; we can be impressed by the girl with the pimply face who could stand up to him, in a way give him the back of her hand and therefore egg him on all the more, so that he takes proper and careful note of the one he watches as an observer and a healer.

How much do we (or ought we or can we) extend ourselves for others? When do we decide that a life is so forlorn or shattered that it's not even worth our exalted time? These are terrible medical conundrums, and you and I struggle with them; they are pastoral conundrums—and those of others, practicing in any field, not only the so-called professions. One can be a "laboring man," as it was put in the nineteenth century, going to homes to help with the plumbing, the electricity, the leaky roof, and still be in that relationship of the helper to the needy, the person of knowledge (even power) to the person who is vulnerable and lacks that knowledge and the competence that the knowledge enables.

Those are the dilemmas Williams is getting at in this book. With what attitude, what movements of the heart, mind, and soul, if any, do we respond to various human beings, under the various circumstances of our privilege, our competence, our professional training—summoned or not? How do we evaluate one another? How does one present oneself to these people who have their own "faces of stone"? How do they respond to you? How does one in a short period of time find a shared truth? In something called psychotherapy, or in a diagnostic interview by a surgeon, what do we want to know of another human being? How do we ask? What do we learn? Might we think of our patients, our clients, our students as our sometime teachers? What might we, with a shift of words, of facial expressions, even of one's heart, have felt within oneself, have learned that we are missing? What do people truly want to tell us? What don't they at all want to tell us and why? How do we break out of these restraints? And do we even want to do so?

Doctors, teachers, lawyers, and business executives will likely face all of this. Doctors will be asking questions with a *chart* they have to fill out, or a *scale* on which they have to put a *rating,* because they have to go to a committee meeting where people will be judged— are they an 8 or a 9? Using what criteria and judgment for the decisions we make? Can one truly be "value-free"? Can one be "objective"? What do we do with the thoughts that cross our minds, our own memories or experiences that are brought into play by the particular people we meet, our students in the classroom, our patients, or our clients if we are in a courtroom? These are the struggles we all wage with ourselves. And can they be fairly or adequately resolved by multiple-choice exams, even when the issue is a matter of information or factuality, or intellectual capacity? This is the way so many are judged today: the numbers pinned on them, courtesy of those exams. What we are dealing with is human subjectivity in all its variations, in your life and in mine.

When I come to these books and remember Dr. Williams, I also remember the Adams House dormitory room I lived in as a college student. We were on the fourth floor; we watched cars coming and going, sometimes hitting one another, and we had a view of the other dorms. We saw the lights of the Lowell House dormitory across the street and knew that as long as they were blazing, the grading curve was going to go higher. We had come to the conclusion that the people in Lowell House were the "nerds." That is only one of many phrases we all know. We had "nerds" and "jocks" and "clubbies" and *Crimson* writers and *Lampoon* types and the people who chose to live in *this* house or *that* house. Well, amidst all this I was reading *Paterson* and getting to know Williams—a contrast to the learned snobbery that befell me and many others here and there.

I'm trying to tell you that it is quite possible to reenact sadly some of what Williams offers us in one's own life: to dismiss people by what buildings they go into, what houses they come from, what neighborhoods, what "backgrounds," how they dress, their intellectual competence, their athletic competence, their name, their skin color, what religion they favor, how they talk. Is there any end to this? Williams says to us: "You readers, let me reach out to you"—as in Michelangelo and the hands touching in the Sistine Chapel. "Let us touch in some way. Let me confess. Let me tell you that you may think this ugliness is beyond you, but I know that taking a hard look inside does matter—especially in a century that has seen a country like Germany turn so dark, a nation that I admired." As a boy, Williams went with his parents to Germany, learned the language, and loved the people.

I remember my father, who went to MIT and who had to learn

German (as all students who went there had to), hearing on the shortwave radio that voice of Hitler's coming out of Berlin, and telling kids that at that time Germany was the most educated nation on this planet. We are talking these days of "cultural disadvantage" and "cultural literacy," and we say, "Educate people and then we'll have a better country." Well, we should remember that at that time Germany had the highest rate of high school and college graduates on this planet. I remember my father listening to that voice and wondering how that great language, German, could come to be used for this craven, murderous purpose, and how these awful words could be heard with such adulation by the people who spoke it.

Williams faced the same questions—with his regard and deep friendship and love and affection not only for Pound but also for others. Such complex matters of mind and heart made him scratch his head, look into the mirror and worry and wonder. From that comes the doctor's, the writer's willingness to say something like this: "Please join me in this kind of moral introspection in the Augustinian manner. I make this request so that together we can begin with an acknowledgment of what we uphold, and why—and then one hopes we might walk away from all this, arms around one another, with our hearts more open to one another."

It took me years to realize that Williams's brusqueness, his toughness and manner of self-presentation, masked what his wife would eventually tell me was the vulnerability he felt, the tears that came to him all too quickly, that he hid even from her, but that you see falling to the ground in some of those poems. You may also find a kind of moral inwardness in these terribly unnerving, provocative stories, some meant to be confessional, which I urge you to take to heart and regard carefully. You must keep in mind that you are meant to be vastly upset by them, and therefore moved to contemplate them not only in connection with the life of the writer, but also with the life of the reader.

NINE

Open Up These Windows

I want to begin with an extract from Carver's story "Nobody Said Anything": "I could hear them out in the kitchen." Now, these are children listening to their parents. "I couldn't hear what they were saying, but they were arguing. Then it got quiet and she started to cry. I elbowed George. I thought he would wake up and say something to them"—"Them": we are going to come to "them" with Tillie Olsen—"so they would feel guilty and stop. But George is such an asshole. He started kicking and hollering." Then the children speak to each other:

"Stop gouging me, you bastard," he said. "I'm going to tell!"

"You dumb chickenshit," I said. "Can't you wise up for once? They're fighting and Mom's crying. Listen."

He listened with his head off the pillow. "I don't care," he said and turned over toward the wall and went back to sleep. George is a royal asshole.

Later I heard Dad leave to catch his bus. He slammed the front door. She had told me before he wanted to tear up the family. I didn't want to listen.

After a while she came to call us for school. Her voice

sounded funny—I don't know. I said I felt sick in my stomach. It was the first week in October and I hadn't missed any school yet, so what could she say? She looked at me, but it was like she was thinking of something else. George was awake and listening. I could tell he was awake by the way he moved in the bed. He was waiting to see how it turned out so he could make his move.

"All right." She shook her head. "I just don't know. Stay home, then. But no TV, remember that."

George reared up. "I'm sick too," he said to her. "I have a headache. He gouged me and kicked me all night. I didn't get to sleep at all."

"That's enough!" she said. "You are going to school, George! You're not going to stay here and fight with your brother all day. Now get up and get dressed. I mean it. I don't feel like another battle this morning."

I don't know whether this is more "depressing" than Hamlet and his mother, or King Lear and his daughters, or what happens in *Macbeth,* or *Othello,* or in *Crime and Punishment,* the axing of the old lady, or in *The Brothers Karamazov,* or Anna Karenina throwing herself in front of a railway car as it comes down the tracks. My hunch, though, is that we are certainly moved when we read Melville or Hawthorne (talk about feeling "down"), or Shakespeare or Tolstoy, or Dostoyevsky, or Dickens's *Oliver Twist* or *Great Expectations.* But when we read them (another "them"), they don't get to us the way Carver does, not because they are not great writers, but because Carver is bringing us close to the bone marrow of the present day, of contemporary moments that you and I in this room live out in America—the genius of a Chekhovian talent that makes us sweat, tremble, and remember.

Now, it could be said that what Carver does is take the stuff of *Oprah* and elevate it to the highest kind of art, so that we are unnerved and, if we want to say it, "depressed"! But I would tell you that it's even more "depressing" not to read Carver: to be without that way of knowing about what is happening in our daily American lives—to miss out on what Carver lets us know with poignancy and pain. His stories put a certain light on all of this—a light that gives the reader some edge on things, some leeway that allows thought, and a light that isn't overworked into a lot of psychological or sociological reductive interpretations. Instead, it is a light that makes us shiver and makes us stop and think and wonder. This is a moral and aesthetic sensibility at work, helping us to understand ourselves in these last years of the twentieth century; in that sense, it is uplifting. Sure, some of his stories, like "What We Talk About When We Talk About Love," are a "downer" at times. But it's also funny the way he works over that language; even as you and I know what happens when we have one beer and then another beer, and the result is that our minds get into a delightful, exuberant state that lasts for a while and gives us a new view of life, a rush of thought and feeling—and on and on that goes.

In his story "Bicycles, Muscles, Cigarettes," Carver looks back on childhood, on parents, on having a fight, on being rescued by your parents. This is the stuff of your life and mine, how we grow up, the tension between wanting to be independent and wanting to hold on with all of our might to our families. Now I'm getting psychological and interpretive myself with these stories, which don't need that. What they need is for us to read them and feel that we are understanding something about how life goes, and getting at something, helped along by talent and energy and humor, a lot of humor—even in some of the grimmer moments, such as in the story "So Much Water So Close to Home." It's a very tough story. These guys out hunting come upon a body, and the wife of one of them reacts to her husband's response to what he saw and did. The story grows the way Hopper's pictures grow, from the inside out.

Tillie Olsen's life was not unlike Carver's, the same story of vulnerability and determination. Born Tillie Lerner, she grew up in Omaha, Nebraska, but was from an eastern European, Jewish, socialist-reformist tradition. She came from self-educated people, idealistic, hardworking, and honorable people. Perhaps the best way to begin understanding Olsen is to go back to the earlier years of the twentieth century, to the Lower East Side and all the struggles of Dorothy Day, who much appreciated the Jewish idealistic tradition. Dorothy stood for a kind of liberalism and progressive politics, deep reading in the classics of the Western tradition and the Bible and, of course, prophetic Judaism, the here-and-now Judaism that says we must change this world for the better and each day earn our honor with God through deeds in this one and only life we have.

Olsen gives us this in the first story in her collection *Tell Me a Riddle,* "I Stand Here Ironing," which is very personal. Personal because she knew of teenage pregnancy at a time when it was considered an occasion of scandal to be unmarried, to become pregnant, to bear a child, bring up that child alone, as she did with both her first and her second children. She eventually left the Midwest and became a labor organizer, along with her husband, in California and for many years worked in the labor movement with Harry Bridges, who helped strengthen the bargaining hand of the dockworkers in the earlier years of the twentieth century. She took a host of jobs to make a few dollars to get by while trying to raise and provide for her children.

Her story "I Stand Here Ironing" begins:

I stand here ironing, and what you ask me moves tormented back and forth with the iron.

Now, how you read the second paragraph will depend on your attitude toward the teacher, the guidance counselor, the principal, the expert who is calling her up who says,

"I wish you would manage the time to come in and talk with me about your daughter. I'm sure you can help me understand her. She's a youngster who needs help and whom I'm deeply interested in helping."

Does the narrator rankle at that? Does she find that talk patronizing, condescending? Are we confronted with, as Walker Percy once put it, "the mannerisms of the clinic"? Or is this a heartfelt interest on the part of someone speaking to someone else whom she knows to be in some kind of difficulty, evident from the way a child is behaving in a classroom? And here's the mother's answer:

> "Who needs help." . . . Even if I came, what good would it do? You think that because I am her mother I have a key, or that in some way you could use me as a key? She has lived for nineteen years. There is all that life that has happened outside of me, beyond me.

Pablo Picasso, *Woman Ironing,* Paris, spring 1904, oil on canvas, 45¾ × 28¾ in. (116.2 × 73 cm.), Solomon R. Guggenheim Museum, New York, Thannhauser Collection, gift, Justin K. Thannhauser, 1978, 78.2514.41.

Sometimes people like me need to be reminded of that. We have "schemas" in our mind, concepts, formulations, and they are not always as all-encompassing as they might seem to be. Later the mother says,

> I nursed her. They feel that's important nowadays. I nursed all the children, but with her, with all the fierce rigidity of first motherhood,

© National Museums Liverpool (Walker Art Gallery).

I did like the books then said. Though her cries battered me to trembling and my breasts ached with swollenness, I waited till the clock decreed.

We have come now, in this course, to a woman writing about what it means to be a woman at a time when expectations and denials extended to women were not as they are now. Olsen would go on to write about women writers and the obstacles they faced and how many of them disappeared into pseudoanonymity, if not total anonymity.

I now want to pick up later in the story:

And even without knowing, I knew. I knew the teacher that was evil because all these years it has curdled into my memory, the little boy hunched in the corner, her rasp, "why aren't you outside, because Alvin hits you? that's no reason, go out, scaredy."

Note the two uses of "they" when she continues later still:

They persuaded me at the clinic to send her away to a convalescent home in the country where "she can have the kind of food and care you can't manage for her, and you'll be free to concentrate on the new baby." . . . They never have a picture of the children so I do not know if the girls still wear those gigantic red bows and the ravaged looks on the every other Sunday when parents can come to visit "unless otherwise notified"—as we were notified the first six weeks.

This is a long, sustained aria of sorts, directed at some of us who have the privilege of advising, if not occasionally remonstrating with, others, telling them they ought to do this or that. You might say, and it might be argued in taking on this story, that she is "defensive." We have strategies for putting people down: "She is being 'defensive,' she has a 'problem.'" Well, you bet! She has many. The story reminds us that people who are hurt and vulnerable can also be feisty, and resourceful, and ultimately become in their own ways the owners of their fates, notwithstanding the observations of some of us who have not been able to put ourselves in their shoes. Olsen is struggling with us and herself and the difficulties of understanding others: a well-intentioned observer understanding a particular mother and her fate. "Let her be," the narrator says. It's a cry for independence and a cry for personal authority—your authority, my authority—against the imposition of a kind of secular authority, one that becomes oracular, buttressed by political might in the educational world, the clinical world.

The title story, "Tell Me a Riddle," echoes what Agee is getting at in *Let Us Now Praise Famous Men* when he presents us with *King Lear*: forty-seven years of marriage, children, grandchildren, and then what? How do we understand that long story of hers, about a woman dying, still together with her husband of half a century, and yet distinctly apart from him and distrustful, both of them with grudges and memories that won't let them be? If the mother in the first story wants her daughter to be granted a certain respect, one that some of us, out of our own ways of thinking (if not training), are reluctant to grant her, to allow—although we ask, Who is granting this authority? And maybe they're ill-equipped to offer it?—then in the last story we are presented with a haunting paradox of a long-lived, solid marriage that has produced people who are strangers to each other. Later on, when we get to Tolstoy's "The Death of Ivan Ilych," think of "Tell Me a Riddle" and connect it with Tolstoy's version of a particular kind of death, where the same problem comes up but a different slant is given to it. In both instances, the subject concerns how people die and what dying can teach us about life. Yes, such a discussion can be "depressing"; or, quite to the contrary, it can provide a huge boost into ways of thinking, so that maybe we can be spared the same ending.

The husband and wife in "Tell Me a Riddle" grate on each other. He has his humor, which goes over like a lead balloon, and she won't forget or forgive. As we read, we wonder when this tension between them will somehow be figured out so that they can find resolution, so that there will be resolution for us. What is the riddle? The riddle is really the riddle of this marriage, and of your life and mine as we struggle for love and understanding, for self-respect, for a way of being with those we spend time with in college dormitories, in suburban homes, in workplaces. Some of those Hopper pictures are tough because there is no question that as we look at them we can feel either the tension that doesn't get resolved into some kind of affectionate touching (I mean that symbolically as well as physically) or the tension that means that these people are fundamentally enemies to one another.

You can say there is a lot of anger in Olsen's stories—for instance, the angry mother who feels put upon by people who don't understand her circumstances, or the angry grandmother and mother who feels put upon by her old husband when all she wants is to be left alone, even at a remove from her children and grandchildren. And what do we do with Whitey in "Hey Sailor, What Ship?" He's another outsider, an irritable one, we might aver, and yet, in that outsider there is a kind of generosity of spirit that maybe makes us nervous, maybe makes us wonder whether we are capable of even knowing what generosity is. The story's end is very hard, particularly when Whitey leaves: "By Jeannie, silent and shrunken into her coat. He passes no one in the streets. They are inside, each in his slab of house, watching the flickering light of television."

That's a scene that Hopper would have drawn or painted. If you do nothing else, please go to the moment in the story that begins "And in the kitchen." A mother is talking to her own daughter about Whitey, who is a part of this family and who has been a part of this family in the spiritual, and moral, and psychological sense for years and years, while this very daughter has been growing up. He has been wonderful to her, and now she turns on him and the mother is horrified.

"They don't hear the words," says the mother. In this story, Olsen does what Williams does: she doesn't use quotation marks. She wants us really to get into this and be part of it. The mother continues, alternating with the daughter:

They hear what's behind them. There are worse words than cuss words, there are words that hurt. When Whitey talks like that, it's everyday words; the men he lives with talk like that, that's all.

Well, not the kind of men I want to know. I don't go over to anybody's house and hear words like that.

Jeannie, who are you kidding? You kids use them all.

That's different, that's being grown-up, like smoking. And he's so drunk. Why didn't Daddy let me keep the ten dollars? It would mean a lot to me, and it doesn't mean anything to him.

It's his money. He worked for it, its the only power he has. We don't take Whitey's money.

Oh no. Except when he gives it to you.

When he was staying with us, when they were rocking chair, unemployment checks, it was different. He was sober. It was his share.

He's just a Howard Street wino now—why don't you and Daddy kick him out of the house? He doesn't belong here.

Of course he belongs here, he's a part of us, like family. . . . Jeannie, this is the only house in the world he can come into and be around people without having to pay.

Somebody who brings presents and whirls you around and expects you to jump for his old money.

Remember how good he's been to you. To us. Jeannie, he was only a few years older than you when he started going to sea.

That effort in moral education is one that all of us might remember from our own childhoods—and one that we, in turn, will offer to our children. It's the most important education in the world, even more important than getting high marks on the SAT, even more important than mental health. Back to the narrative, to Jeannie:

Now you're going to tell me the one about how he saved Daddy's life in the strike of 1934.

He knows more about people and places than almost anyone I've ever known. You can learn from him.

When's he like that any more? He's just a Howard Street wino, that's all.

And here's the clincher from the mother:

Jeannie, I care you should understand. You think Mr. Norris is a tragedy, you feel sorry for him because he talks intelligent and lives in a nice house and has quiet drunks. You've got to understand.

You read something like that and I'll tell you what goes through a mind like mine. Raising issues of class, access, attention, how resources are deployed. For years I have supervised psychiatric residents from the Cambridge Hospital here in child psychiatry. We did a study there years ago on who got outpatient care and who didn't, and what kind of care they got. (Another "they" or "them.") We tried to figure out how a hospital that was part of Harvard Medical School responded to cries for help. What we found out was that if the patient who came to that clinic was a student from any of the colleges around the area, or came from a certain social and economic background, that person was much more likely to get our individual and sustained attention in what is called psychotherapy than others coming from different backgrounds of the same age and same problems; those others got a briefer kind of attention from us and were quickly, if not immediately put on drugs.

Now, there is a long history for this kind of psychiatric investigation. When I was a resident in the late 1950s, a study came out called *Social Class and Mental Illness.* What they found out is what Tillie Olsen is trying to work over in this story: that how we see one another has to do with who we are, what we have experienced. The so-called objectivity of medicine is connected in daily life to the clinician's subjectivity.

At Cornell about five years later, a study called *Mental Health in the Metropolis: The Midtown Manhattan Study* showed that in a particular profession we were quite willing to respond to a particular kind of patient and rather unwilling to respond to another kind. To put it another way, we had our own hierarchy of who deserves what. I remember thinking, when I was a resident seeing patients at the emergency ward of the Massachusetts General Hospital, "Ah, what an interesting patient so-and-so is"—whereas others weren't so compelling, their presence regarded less intensely by us young doctors in training. Take alcoholism, as Olsen does in this story. There are the Mr. Norrises, who can go to our fancy hospitals and get a lot of attention, and then there are others to whom we give the back of our hands, and are termed "not good candidates for psychotherapy." Alas, I remember well those words on charts. Maybe what I might have been asked is, Are *you* a good candidate to be a psychiatrist? And by what "criteria" do you think this?

What ship will welcome Whitey? Saying yes is important for all of us, never mind for Whitey; it's important for us to connect with and understand and link arms with others; our lives are at stake, our honor, our decency, our self-respect.

Yes, we are "pulled down" by some of these questions posed by Tillie Olsen and Raymond Carver. They can be disheartening at times, but also, I plead, exhilarating. Open up these windows: the fresh air of truth will make us free. Truth, yes, but even more important (in Carver and Olsen) are the "movements of the heart," as Pascal put it: tugging at us so that we enlarge our view, achieve an elevation of perspective. We enlarge our view so that we do understand, so that we understand the urgent narrative passion of these two writers, who came to us (no matter the tough circumstances in their own lives). They were able to soar with language, with stories that take hold of us, stir our thoughts, give us hope—a promise of what can be, has been, and might be: that out of poverty and hard-

ship, suffering, struggle, impoverishment, and longing (including alcoholism in Carver's case and the so-called single-family life amidst
poverty that Tillie Olsen lived for many years) can come these extraordinarily moral and even spiritual intelligences at work, rendering stories that tug on our hearts and minds.

TEN

Don't You Think
They Need Praying For?

I'd like to tell you something about my life—how I happened to come to this point. What I'm going to tell you about shaped my life in a very big way, and led to a singular moment that still lives on in my head and heart. An incident transformed my life, my work, my perspective, the trajectory of my career.

I attended Harvard College, took premed courses, and then went on to medical school. I started out in pediatrics and shifted over to psychiatry and child psychiatry and then psychoanalysis. There was a law in this country during the 1960s that required every physician to go into the military for two years; it was called the doctors' draft. We went into the army, the navy, the air force, or the Public Health Service. I grew up in New England and had never been south of the Mason-Dixon Line. Though I had been to various foreign countries, I had not visited the South, which for many years was described as a nation within a nation. I signed up for the air force and was assigned to Keesler Air Force Base in Biloxi, Mississippi. Because I had some residency training in psychiatry, I was put in charge (in my late twenties) of an air force psychiatric unit, with forty-eight beds and a large outpatient service.

I first went to Montgomery, Alabama, where Gunter Air Force

Base was located. We had a month of basic training, modified for people who were going to be officers in various parts of the country and world. I hoped to be sent (as you can probably guess) to an air force base in a place like California or Japan or Germany or England. Instead, I was sent further south, to Mississippi. "Bad luck," I thought then, and the best luck in the world I now know.

I had to look up Biloxi in an atlas to see where it was. My brother, who teaches English literature, knew that F. Scott Fitzgerald had mentioned Biloxi in his stories. Well, this seemed like a connection to reality for someone brought up in a certain provincial way.

Back at Gunter, they had us marching in the hot July sun. They would give us guns and have us shoot at some targets. There was a target with another target above it, and we were supposed to hit one of the bull's-eyes. I remember that vividly; I had never had a gun in my hand. I pointed my gun at this bull's-eye and the sergeant said, "Hey, you know what you're doing." I said, "I do?" He said, "You hit the bull's-eye." I said, "I did?" He said, "Right there." I saw those hands pointing to the lower bull's-eye, but I had aimed at the higher one. But I thought, "Yup, I guess I do know what I'm doing."

We made it through basic training, and I remember driving down a state highway—there were no interstates then. I remember hitting the Gulf Coast and going on to Biloxi. I really wanted to go to New Orleans, of course. Pretty soon, though, I was running a psychiatric unit, admitting people, evaluating people, writing up reports, discharging people. I was getting more and more unhappy with this. I found myself fighting with the colonel over who should be admitted and who shouldn't. He wanted me to "get rid of" men who were brought in by the investigative branch of the air force, men who had been found in certain bars and immediately classified as homosexuals. I was told that they should be discharged on the spot with the equivalent of a dishonorable discharge.

One day the colonel decided to clean up the ward, and he started discharging some of our patients. So we fought these decisions, and soon found ourselves the subject of classifications: bleeding-heart liberals, sympathizers, "closet homos," and on it went. Words that had once been applied to some of the people who had been admitted were now increasingly being applied to us.

I tried to get away from this by going into New Orleans during my free time. As you can imagine, as soon as someone like me announces their intention to visit such a city, family, friends, and colleagues give him names often connected to the world of power and opportunity from which they come: psychiatrists, psychoanalysts, pediatricians, internists, surgeons, the names of artists and photographers, friends. I looked some of these people up, spent time in nice restaurants in New Orleans, went to the Garden District and was entertained. I frequented art galleries. There are two medical schools in New Orleans, Tulane and Louisiana State University. I used to go to some conferences there and at the New Orleans Psychoanalytic Institute, where I enrolled for a seminar. I quickly figured out various shortcuts to get through the eastern part of New Orleans and through the Gentilly neighborhood.

Driving to a meeting one day, I found myself completely stopped. There were a lot of cars in front of me; people were getting out, and there was no movement of traffic. I, too, got out of my car and overheard someone say they thought there was trouble in the city today and we weren't going to get very far. I forced my way through the gathering and asked a policeman why we weren't able to proceed. He said, "Buddy, there is no way you are going to get to where you are going if you need to get across this city today." He proceeded to tell me that the roads were blocked, that there were riots going on all through the city, and that I might as well turn around and go back to where I came from.

I said, "What are the riots about?" He gestured in the direction of the street where we were headed and pointed out the school a couple of blocks up. I then heard a stream of epithets—screams shouted near that school. I heard someone say, "Yeah, it's the Frantz School. I read they're going to send this blankety-blank kid into the Frantz School." I decided to park the car and walk a couple of blocks. As I approached the building, I heard a roar. I remember getting closer and hearing, "Two, four, six, eight, we don't want to integrate!" I remember thinking, Why wouldn't people want to integrate? Now, I'm not exactly totally dumb and I was a reasonably educated person, but I hope that what you are getting from my narration is that I was slow-witted about something that was happening around me. Why? Well, from reading magazines and the daily *New York Times,* I probably knew more about what was going on in New York, or London, or back in Cambridge—but I didn't then know what was going on in Biloxi, never mind New Orleans. Slowly I began to figure out that this had to do with race. Once I got within sight of the school, I saw, as well as heard, a large group of people, and all kinds of shouting and screaming. Then, almost suddenly, I saw some cars drive up, and if you have ever heard a noisy, foulmouthed mob suddenly fall silent, you will know the noise of silence, the presence of silence.

Men got out of the first car, all dressed alike in gray flannel suits, sunglasses, and carrying guns. A couple of men got out of the second car, but they didn't have guns at the ready—rather, they were holding on to a little girl, who was about four feet tall and had on a white

Reproduced by courtesy of the Norman Rockwell Family Agency, Inc.

dress, white shoes, a white bow in her hair and was carrying a lunch pail. After the silence came the noise again, the screams, the shouts, the threats: "We are going to kill you, you blankety-blankety-blank." All of this was happening because she was a black six-year-old girl and she was integrating the William Frantz Elementary School, and as a result there wasn't another child in attendance. The parents of the white children had instigated a boycott and had kept them home. This situation was worthy of Kafka. I stood there and watched this little girl go into that building. Only one teacher remained, because she'd been ordered to stay on the job by the same federal judge who had ordered the integration, J. Skelly Wright. (He himself eventually had to be removed from New Orleans by President Kennedy, and appointed to the Washington, D.C., Court of Appeals because mobs were forming in front of his office in the federal court building in downtown New Orleans. You can watch this moment on a video called *Eyes on the Prize,* in the second episode.)

Eventually, I got back to Mississippi and I couldn't get what I'd just seen out of my mind—my remembering head's particular picture of that little girl. Her name is Ruby Bridges. She went through that experience every day for the entire school year. The mob assembled each morning to heckle and threaten her. There were varying amounts of people, but always enough to pose a threat to her. The local police did not protect the safety of this child—only federal marshals did, the men I had seen. In fact, many New Orleans police officers and Louisiana police officers were part of that mob near the school. They were active in protecting businesses, but not in protecting either Ruby or the school. The white population maintained the total boycott for an entire year. It is hard but important to remember that this event took place only a few decades ago in the history of our country.

What crossed my mind as I witnessed Ruby going past a heckling, taunting, threatening mob (despite some cautions I'd received from my psychiatric colleagues, who felt that I was getting into too much trouble with my military superiors) was that maybe I should try to get to know some of these children, four girls in particular: Ruby, who was doing this all by herself in the Frantz School, and three other girls who were going to the McDonough No. 19 Elementary School, not too far away.

My preparation for this kind of observation went back to when I was a resident at Boston's Children's Hospital. We had the last polio epidemic, and I worked with children who were paralyzed. It was the last polio epidemic before the use of the Salk vaccine came into prominence. Another resident and I talked and talked with children facing the horrors of paralysis. Some of them were so affected by polio that they couldn't breathe and had to be put into what we used to call an "iron lung," a respirator. There was a certain type of polio that attacked the breathing center of the brain stem. We were stunned by the emotional, the psychological, the human resilience of these children in the face of their overwhelming medical crises. With a remarkable dignity and clear-sightedness, many of them were more concerned about their parents, siblings, and friends than their own situation. There was a kind of selflessness, even nobility to their response, which we, of course, alas, thought fit a psychological paradigm: we talked about their "denial" and how they needed some "help" with what they were going through. You may have noticed that there can be a certain reductive side to the language of people like me.

In New Orleans, I wanted to do a study similar to what I had done in Boston at the Children's Hospital. This is a kind of careerism that many of us know—I'm not saying this in a pejorative way. I wanted to do a second research project studying stress, only this time it would be social stress as opposed to medical stress; you can see the symmetry. When I started formulating this in my head and talked it over with one of my medical colleagues, he agreed that it could be worthwhile and perhaps even good for me: good for my career, good for me psychologically. But he questioned how I'd gain access to those children, me being a white Yankee doctor from the air force.

I started at Ruby Bridges's lawyer's office at the NAACP. I had never been to that part of New Orleans before. I remember what happened when I climbed those stairs and opened the door—the look on the faces of the people in that office. You could have thought I was concealing a bomb. One goes through this life and begins to learn some things one doesn't in educational institutions. You learn about who you are and what you can take for granted, about what other people are going through and what they cannot take for granted. At first, I was told there was no way I could meet those kids. "Who are you anyway?" I was asked. So I told them. I explained what I was hoping to investigate and learn. Finally, a man there told me that the only person who could clear this would be either Kenneth Clark or Mr. Marshall. "Who is Mr. Marshall?" I asked. "He's the lawyer who heads the NAACP Legal Defense Fund. He is arguing this case in the federal court," the man said. He was talking about Thurgood Marshall.

So I went up to New York and presented myself to the North Side Center for Child Development. I spent a couple of hours with the psychologists Kenneth Clark and his wife, Mamie, who had presented important testimony for the original 1954 Supreme Court decision in *Brown v. Board of Education,* which outlawed segregated schools. That case was also a landmark for its reliance upon social science in its legal briefs. The Clarks then sent me over to see Mr. Marshall, and after a day with him it was agreed that I could start my inquiry. They suggested that I tread lightly, carefully, protecting the children and perhaps, ultimately, myself. Clark said, "Young man, we're going to help you meet those families, and we think that when you have finished talking to them you will have learned more about yourself than you will have learned about them." I will never forget that moment—listening to Kenneth Clark speaking.

Soon enough my wife and I were brought to those four homes, including Ruby Bridges's. There are various categories for a medical interview. One of them is called the social history and the family history. In those interviews one tries to learn about the family of the patient and about the patient him- or herself. I remember learning from Ruby and her parents about their history—how they came from the Delta of Mississippi, how they came into New Orleans because of the collapsing agricultural economy, the mechanization of agriculture, so that hands were not needed. I remember learning that Ruby had been delivered not by an obstetrician but by her great-aunt, that she had never seen a doctor before in her life, that I was the first physician this family had ever met, and that they had several children. Ruby was six years old.

After the preliminary interviews were done, I prodded further, trying to figure out how these children were responding to the stress of their experiences, how their appetites were holding up, how they were sleeping, how they were studying, how they were getting on with their friends. I was asking the kinds of questions that we all know help indicate, through the answers, the presence or the relative absence of anxiety, fear, apprehension, nervousness.

The longer I talked with Ruby, the more solid she seemed to be, and the same thing was true for the other three children. I would ask Ruby how things were going, and she would say, "Fine." I would ask her how she was doing; she would say, "Fine." How's your appetite? "Fine." Sleeping okay? "Oh, fine." How are things going at school? "Fine." Well, you don't believe answers if you are trained like I am; you say she is saying that but there is something else going on, underneath—all truth lies "underneath."

I was repeatedly told by the schoolteacher, "I don't understand this little girl. She comes to me with a smile on her face; she seems to be doing so well. How do you explain that, given what she goes through every morning and afternoon?" Well, I gave her a mini psychological lecture. I said that sometimes when people are under tremendous strain they mobilize every fiber of psychological resourcefulness they have, but this will last only so long and then will fall apart. Of course, what I had on my mind was the American Psychiatric Association annual meeting; I wanted to write a paper chronicling "symptom formation," evidence of stress in children.

What evidence did I have? What was wrong with these children that they seemed to be doing so well?! If you catch a certain irony here, I hope you hold on to it.

One day I came to school and Ruby's teacher told me she'd been thinking of me. Someone in my line of work will always wonder what that means. She said, "We had a little trouble here a while ago. Ruby came to school at the usual time and the men escorted her, drove her up to the building, just as always happens. But this time she held up and she started talking to those people in the mob and the marshals tried to pull her away. But she kept on talking to them, until finally she stopped and walked in. The marshals got her in safely; they hurried her in, but not before the mob started surging toward her, so closely and threateningly that a couple of the federal marshals actually had to pull their guns."

Then Ruby came into the classroom and said good morning to the teacher. The teacher said, "Good morning, Ruby, what happened down there?" Ruby said nothing. The teacher said, "Ruby, something happened. I was looking out the window and saw it happen. You started talking to those people." Ruby said, "I wasn't talking to those people." The teacher said, "Ruby, I saw your lips moving." Ruby said, "I wasn't talking to those people." The teacher said, "Who were you talking to?" Ruby said, "I was talking to God." The teacher decided she wasn't going to pursue this any further with her sole student. She decided that she was going to defer to a higher authority. The teacher asked me, "What do you make of this?" I responded that as we were going to Ruby's house that evening, we'd talk to her about it. The teacher was quite pleased, relieved.

I used to sit around the kitchen table with Ruby and watch and converse as she drew pictures, and often I drew alongside her. I'm interested, and have been all my life, in "children and art"—how young people use drawings and paintings to communicate with others and with themselves. As we were sitting at the table that night, I thought very portentously in my mind that I should bring up the matter of the day's events. I said, "Ruby, I wanted to talk to you for a moment about something that happened this morning. The teacher told me there was some trouble before you went into the school." She said, "No." I said, "Well, apparently you talked to the people in the street and you got them shouting even louder." She said, "I told the teacher I didn't talk to those people." I said, "Well, Ruby, the teacher saw your lips moving, so as to say something." She said, "Well, I told the teacher I was talking to God." I asked if she did that often. She said, "I like to talk to God." I said, "You do a lot of that?" She said, "As often as I can. When I get up in the morning, go to school, get out of school, and in the evening." I observed, "That's four times," and she responded, "Sometimes more." I remarked that that was a lot of praying, and she looked at me and said, simply, "I like to pray." Thinking that she was praying for herself, I said, "Who are you praying for?" She replied, "I was praying for the people in the street."

I was surprised and unwilling to drop the matter. I said, "Why would you want to pray for those people in the street?" She looked at me and answered, "Well, don't you think they need praying for? I always say the same thing. I always say, 'Please God, try to forgive these people because they don't know what they are doing.' "

I remember leaning back in that chair and thinking to myself that this had a familiar ring to it; this had been said before in the history of mankind. "Ruby, why do you say that?" I asked. She said, "Because my mommy, daddy, and my grandma want me to say that. They told me that is the thing to say." I said, "Ruby, why would they want you to say that prayer?" She said, "Because Jesus said that when there was a mob in front of him. He prayed for those people, and that is what I am doing."

That evening my wife and I went to a bar in downtown New Orleans. We were drinking bourbon and listening to Brahms's Fourth Symphony—that's a nice combination in an American bar. My wife, Jane, who used to teach, turned to me and said, "Bob, what would you do if you had to go through a mob to get to the hospital?" I said,

"What do you mean?" She said, "What if you had to go to the hospital every day and before you could get in there was a mob, and after you got out there was a mob, and if it weren't for some marshals, the mob would take your life?" I said, "I'd call the cops—what else could I do?" Well, upon this my wife reminded me that the city cops were not there defending Ruby.

The next thing I would do would be to get a lawyer. Ruby had no personal lawyer and no telephone to make the call. The assumptions I had made about picking up the phone and getting a professional person to help were not available to this family. The third thing I would do would be to immediately mobilize my academic and intellectual medical resources and start thinking about who these people on the street were: they were "disturbed"; they came from this and that "socioeconomic background." I'd call these people sick, psychotic, say that they were "acting out" (that is a very grave accusation). I once went with my wife to the Waldorf-Astoria, where we spent a whole weekend at an American Psychoanalytic Association conference listening to discussions about "acting out." When we got out of there my wife said she had a question: "What is the difference between 'acting out' and living?" I thought, Well, she is "acting out" by asking the question! (If you really want to get someone angry, call them crazy.) The fourth thing I would do would be to write an article about what I had gone through, or maybe it would be a book.

None of this was Ruby inclined or able, really, to do—only prayer was available for her. We used to go to the church where Ruby and her family went. And for hours they used to pray; even though her mother and father and grandmother didn't know how to read or write, they knew how to pray. They remembered words of the Hebrew prophets and Jesus, and they wanted to apply them to their own lives. They had taught that little girl to pray for people who yelled at her and threatened to kill her and swore at her. I wonder how many of us, even those of us who have taken courses in ethics, philosophy, and moral reasoning (and who got A's in those courses)—how many of us would be inclined to pray, as Ruby did, and as her parents were doing, in the face of such an experience.

One last thought: Ruby's last name, Bridges, would catch the eye and ear of an American Charles Dickens, were he around for this. I am reminded of one time when Ruby's dad, Abon Bridges, now gone from us, gave some thought to his own name: "I guess the good Lord wanted to test us—He asked us to find the 'bridges' for our people to help carry us across to the whole of America."

ELEVEN

Pity: An Ignorant Anger

M onths after Ruby Bridges entered the Frantz School in New Orleans, a few white children started coming back to that school. Ruby had been in one room, next to the principal's office; these white children were kept in another room, away from her. To follow up on our conversations with Ruby, my wife, Jane, also began visiting the homes of some of the white children, in order to learn about their lives. The day after the first of the white kids showed up, the mob outside the school turned on them with a vengeance. So much so that Ruby mentioned to me, after a couple of days, that the crowd didn't seem to have much interest in her anymore. She was right. Now they had turned their anger toward those white children and their parents for breaking up the boycott.

Two of the children belonged to a family named Conner. The father worked in a brewery in downtown New Orleans. Their mother had initially been a part of the crowd, but she'd changed her mind, and one day brought her children to school, subjecting herself to the same scrutiny and scorn in which she had participated. Her children were so loudly threatened and insulted that Mrs. Conner began going from home to home in her white neighborhood, pleading with parents to stop the protests and return their children to the

Frantz School. She became a community organizer. Perhaps more than anyone else in the city of New Orleans, except for the federal judge who'd ordered the desegregation in the first place, she was responsible for the actual school desegregation. It goes without saying, perhaps, that her entire life changed.

I got to know the family pretty well, and one day at a party they were holding, celebrating their own wedding anniversary, I asked Mr. Conner what it was that had prompted him and Mrs. Conner to take such a stand, a step that put them in considerable jeopardy, isolation, and loneliness. I had guessed that it must have been their own ideological position—some kind of latent liberalism or goodwill. Mr. Conner said, "For all the questions you have asked my wife and my children, you haven't been thorough enough! You haven't really gotten to the heart of the matter." I said, "What's the heart of the matter?" He said, "Go over and ask my wife what happened that morning when she sent those boys back to school."

I then went over and said, "Mrs. Conner, your husband says I should ask you some more questions."

Without looking up she said, "Well, what kinds of questions?"

I pressed on: "I haven't asked you what actually happened that morning when you sent those boys off to school."

"Oh, well, I don't want to talk about that," she replied.

This made me even more curious. I said, "You've got to help me. I'm trying to learn about what happens to the children caught up in all of this."

She shot back at me, "Well, what were the motivations of Ruby's family?"

I explained to her that Ruby's parents had felt that it was their solemn responsibility to take this hardship on behalf of their people.

She said, "Well, that's not what was motivating me."

I kept pressing her: "Then what was?"

She simply said, "Nothing was motivating me."

So I asked, "Well, how did you happen to send them off to school?"

She finally offered this: "I never intended to send them off to school." She then confessed to me that she had been part of that original mob protesting Ruby's attendance at the Frantz School. She went on to say, "I just woke up one morning at six o'clock, a little earlier than usual, because I heard something break in the living room. I realized it must have been a lamp or some glass that had shattered. So I got out of bed and I found that two of my children, the two oldest boys (who were eight and nine at that time), were squabbling and had knocked over a lamp, a lamp I just bought. I was furious with them. I wanted to know why they were up in the first place and what had preceded this accident. They gave me the usual song and dance. So I shouted at them and told them to go back to bed. I cleaned up the mess and went back to bed myself. I knew that I couldn't go back to sleep, but at least I could get a little rest. But in about ten minutes they were up again, now fighting in the bathroom. It was a real bad day, already, because one of them had dropped the glass they used to rinse out their teeth, which one of them was still in the process of doing when the other said something to him that bothered him. So now I had to go in there and clean up some more glass. This time I screamed at them and told them to go into the kitchen and sit there at the kitchen table. Then I heard the younger children getting up, because they had heard all this noise. I told them to please stay in bed a little longer.

"I started preparing breakfast for my husband, for myself, and for the rest of them. As I was doing that, the two boys sitting there started in with the drone of 'You're this' and 'You're that.' One of the boys punched the other. While moving his hand away it somehow got into his eye so the boy's eye got teary and he claimed that he couldn't see. I was making French toast. I left the stove to attend to the boy with the hurt eye. I determined that it was all right and went back to cooking. They immediately started that squabbling again, whereupon I picked up the frying pan, slammed it down on the stove, turned to these boys, and said, 'That's it! I know what I'm going to do with you two. You are going back to school!'"

It takes someone like George Eliot to describe a moment like that, as she did in *Middlemarch*. One of those singular, often small and seemingly inconsequential moments in history that begin a change in a city's life. Eventually other families followed the lead set by Mrs. Conner and began to initiate a shift of behavior on the part of many whites in New Orleans. By returning to the Frantz School and by talking to others about their experience and those of their children, they helped others start to think about themselves—what they thought and wanted out of life and, yes, hate and mean-spiritedness, as they may have started to wonder about a little girl. Indeed, now they could identify with Ruby, because their own children were going through what she had gone through.

I remember Mrs. Conner once turning to my wife and saying, "I had the feeling that if this country was going to change, millions of people were going to have to go through what we had gone through. I don't know how that will ever take place." A mother was now thinking of other parents and their children. How might people learn to leave their own shoes, put themselves in the shoes of others, experience life as others experienced it? How do we understand people who are different from us? Ruby's parents and the Conner family were wondering about such matters, posing such questions. If we read "O Yes" and work our way into that story as Tillie Olsen wants us to do, we realize how much "sorting" (Olsen's word) takes place in an ordinary school, never mind a newly desegregated one. Children become estranged from one another, wonder how they might draw closer to others rather than pull away from others. Indeed, how much of ourselves are you and I willing to put into these stories, despite their willingness to receive us, so to speak, which is the beauty of fiction—it gives us such a welcome and doesn't put us off with distractions and generalizations.

Let us now move northeast from New Orleans, to Atlanta. In 1961 a federal judge in Atlanta (prodded by the Supreme Court and a new administration in Washington, which was taking a more active interest in what was happening in the South) ordered four high schools to desegregate and sent ten African-American students into those four high schools. In order to study what happened, Jane and I started commuting between New Orleans and Atlanta.

The first thing we were struck by was the difference between the two cities. Atlanta was the beneficiary of a particular mayor (William Hartsfield) and a particular governor and legislator who were shrewd enough to sense that these mobs meant real bad trouble. Thus the city was under the keen oversight of the U.S. attorney general, Robert Kennedy, who was in consistent communication with the city and its officials, letting them know that if they were to allow the mob mentality to continue, they could be sure that there would be federal troops there to stop it—and he meant troops, not just marshals.

When Jane and I came to Atlanta, what we saw was peace and quiet and the schools readily desegregated, with no mobs. President Eisenhower had repeatedly stated that you can't change the hearts of people through laws. This is a posture with enormous implications for education and, for that matter, psychotherapy. It sounds reasonable, in a way. He said that the hearts and minds of people can be changed only through individual actions, people interacting with one another. Yet what we had seen in New Orleans were mobs of people responding in such a way—people taking personal action! These mobs had become horrified and angry; with feelings of betrayal, they'd taken to the streets. Mind you, those feelings of betrayal were grounded in solid history; for centuries, these people and their ancestors had been led to believe in whites' dominance over blacks. For those of you who want to pursue this matter, I can think of no better book than C. Vann Woodward's *The Strange Career of Jim Crow*, as well as another book of his, *Tom Watson, Agrarian Rebel*, which is the story of the betrayal of a white politician by the very people who owned Georgia, the industrialists, the newspaper owners, the powers that be, so to speak. Such people have the ability to shape opinions, including yours and mine, through what we read, through employment practices, through the power of money and the media (especially radio and television).

I thought to myself that this was a different city. These people had a different attitude toward desegregation. Jane nudged me and jokingly said, "Good mental health in Atlanta?" I said, "Don't be sardonic." She said, "Well, better mental health!" Of course, what was going on in Atlanta, and all the time at the *Atlanta Constitution* and other newspapers and in the radio stations and on television screens, was a concerted effort to persuade people that there would be an enormous payoff if they abstained from protests. The slogan on the radio, in the papers, and on television was: "A city too busy to hate." The result was a more peaceful shift, which taught someone like me a lesson or two about the capacity people have to change, depending on their motivations and what leads them to begin to think differently (political leadership, jobs, and on and on those variables go).

There was tension in the schools, to be sure. The young men and women who desegregated the first schools in Atlanta did not have an easy time of it. In January, the superintendent rescinded the ban on extracurricular activities and sports, so I went with Lawrence Jefferson, one of the two African-American youths at Henry Grady High School, to the first basketball game held after desegregation. We arrived at the gym, and initially there was a lot of trouble. We sat up front, and the gym filled with students. The opposing team came from a high school that had not desegregated, and its supporters appeared to be looking for trouble. The police had underestimated what would take place, so they were not even there at first. As I sat beside Lawrence, we started being pelted with spitballs and chewing gum; paper planes bearing hateful messages floated down upon us. Pretty soon those students were throwing some tougher, harder objects, such as Coke bottles—an angry and explosive outburst. There were threats and swearwords and enraged voices rising.

It took me about a minute to nudge Lawrence and say, "Lawrence, I think we ought to leave." He looked at me and said, "No." I said, "I think it would be better if we got out of here." He said, "No." After another half a minute of this, I tried another tack; I pointed to an exit sign up top and said, "Why don't we go up there?" He said, "I'll stay here; you go up there." I suggested that if we moved up, we'd get a better view of the game. He said, "You can go home, and I'll see you tomorrow." I said, "I'm not going to go without you, Lawrence." He said, "You can." I said, "I can, but I won't." We sat back and this continued, and I was thinking to myself that I was doing my research here—learning how someone in Lawrence's position deals with anxiety and fear. Meanwhile, what my overwrought doctor's mind was thinking was that Lawrence couldn't really "face it"; he was pushing it out of his mind and he was resorting to "denial" and "reaction formations."

So I waited a little longer and then I tugged at him and said, "Come on, Lawrence, let's go." He looked at me again and said, "You go." Just as I was debating whether I was really going to get tough with him and try to drag him out of there or tell him enough is enough or, for that matter, go get the police myself, the police arrived. They cordoned us off and effectively protected us during the entire game. It was a new experience for someone like me, having the police watching me and watching over me as I, in turn, watched a basketball game.

When the game was over, they escorted us to my car and made sure that we got out of there. I drove Lawrence home, and he invited me in for a Coke.

As we sat there I said, "Lawrence, that was quite a game we went to." He said, "Yeah, wasn't it great how we won?" I said, "You could say that they lost." He laughed. I said, "What happened before that game, that was really tough." And he replied, "Not particularly."

I'm trained to pay very close attention to words. I protested, "It was an awful time there. That was an ugly situation." And again he said, "Not particularly." I said, "I think if the police hadn't come we would have had a really difficult time getting out of there in one piece, or even two. Have you ever been through anything like that

before?" He said, "Yes." I said, "You have?" He said, "Well, not exactly like that." I said, "It was pretty bad," repeating myself. He said,
"Not particularly," repeating himself.

After he had finished with his "not particularly," he did a very
ironic thing, given my inquiries, my pressing him. He said, "You
know, Doc, I remember when my mom took me to Rich's department store to see Santa Claus." I was following his "association,"
thinking how we'd been talking about the game and now we were
talking about Santa Claus. *You see,* I thought to myself, *he is always in
flight from what we are trying to talk about* (a little bit of psychiatric and
psychoanalytic evidence for my dreary mind). I said, "Santa Claus?"
He said, "Yeah." I said, "What were you doing in Rich's seeing Santa
Claus?" He said, "Well, it was Christmastime"—he looked at me
with a little bit of compassion—"and we could go and see Santa
Claus then." I said, "Who is 'we'?" He said, "All of us black people."
He meant that Rich's, for its own reasons, had desegregated its customers' line for Santa Claus before the Supreme Court had desegregated the schools.

He'd been six years old at the time, he told me, going on with his
story: "We were waiting in line to see Santa Claus and I just got a little fidgety. I didn't know what I was doing, and I guess I stepped on
the shoes of this little girl who was behind me. Boy, did her mother
get pissed off at me. She turned to my mom and said, 'You take that
boy out of here; you had better watch that boy. If he keeps behaving
like this, he's going to get himself in big trouble.' "That is what one
American mother said to another American mother. What
Lawrence's mother then proceeded to do, he also told me: "You
know, I never got to see Santa Claus. My mom took me home right
away. She was scared that that lady was going to get the police. She
gave me a talking to, and gave me a big, big ripping." She hit him
and she hit him. But before she started hitting him she shared stories
of her own childhood. To Lawrence's surprise, she was crying!

Lawrence's mother had been born in a small town in South Carolina, in the eastern part of the state, near Charleston. She remem-

bered as a girl being taught by her parents that when you are walking down the sidewalk and there are white people coming at you, you get off the sidewalk and let them keep on walking. She also remembered, out of her early memories, seeing a body hanging from a tree. Here was an American mother who remembered a lynching and was telling her son about that lynching. She was telling her son that if he didn't watch out, he was not going to live. This is a story for all of us to consider—how we learn about the world through our parents. We're either going to learn to look at the police as friendly, as benign and smiling people who are going to help us cross the street—as the children's story goes, help "make way for the ducklings"—or we are going to look at the police as potential compatriots of people who would murder us, *just like that,* if we step beyond certain socially defined boundaries. And it's not only the police; it's the schools, the whole world of shopkeepers and the post office and everything that is tied up with political authority and social authority and moral authority—even the churches, I regret to say, and the professors, the universities. Everything is "us and them."

Here was a boy who'd been "socialized," as millions of children are socialized all the time, into a particular understanding of this world. You can be sure that this kind of public experience is as powerful and influential as anything that goes on between children and their mothers and their fathers, the kind of emphasis that psychoanalytic psychiatry has reminded us is so important. In fact, if you want to get into social criticism with a skeptical eye, you may wonder why it is that people like me are so influential in promulgating our ways of seeing things—we who don't emphasize nearly as much certain ways children can be powerfully influenced: not only by parents and their behavior with their children, but by politics and class; those two also determine our dreams and our yearnings, our fears and our wishes and goals and hopes and ways of behaving. There is, indeed, the "Oedipal drama," as we in my profession call it, but there is also the political and cultural drama, and the drama of race as children learn it before they ever get to school. Such lessons were often, in the past, not in the schools' curricula? Children sometimes learn as Tillie Olsen tells us they learn: they learn lessons in the gut, by intuition, by systematic observation and reflection.

I didn't have the nerve or the presumption, after hearing Lawrence's story, to push him any further that evening. I listened to his story and thought that, alas, it was a little strange that he'd gone off on a childhood memory that had nothing to do with what we were talking about. As I said, I thought it was a "flight" in his mind, but in reality it was a "flight" in my mind. I went home and told my wife about this. She said, "You know if Lawrence really wanted to give it to you, he could have said something like this to you. He could have said, 'You know, Doc, you know what *your* problem is: you're so immersed in interpretive thinking, in your own way of thinking, that you can't leap out of yourself. You are *caught*. Don't you understand, Doc, that when I said "not particularly" I was giving you a big clue? I was telling you that you and I are different, hugely different. Just because we are sitting side by side watching the same performance, just because we are sitting there waiting for a basketball game to take place and the people are throwing things at both of us, and swearing at both of us, that does not mean we are going through the same kind of stress. You are sitting there and you can get up from that seat and walk out of there. What have you got to lose? Not a damn thing. You're you, and you're a shrink and you say that this is "inappropriate behavior" and you're not going to submit to this kind of "fear and trembling," so you get out. Isn't that in accordance with that "reality principle" of yours? But me, I'm sitting there. I've got everything at stake. I'm not going to leave. What you call a moment of stress I call a moment of opportunity. What you call a moment of people threatening you I call a confrontation in which I'm a protagonist and it's important for me to stand firm. Furthermore, I told you something important with those two words, "not particularly"—namely, that I've been going through this for years. You haven't, so you don't know. You're surprised. You're *shocked*. You call upon the privileges of your privileged life and you use your language. You look at me and in private you call me shrink names. You're in a position of privilege. I'll tell you what "not particularly" means: it means I've been going through this since I was six, as I tried to tell you by treading on your own territory, childhood memories. That should've impressed you. That's what you're supposed to be interested in.' "

Lawrence was saying to me by implication: "I have something to tell you, I hope. Maybe it's possible that you can understand— indeed, I'm worried about *you* that *you* cannot understand. In fact, that which makes you think you are so understanding is, in its own right, another irony, an obstacle to your understanding rather than a help, because you are so caught up in your search for a certain kind of understanding that has to do with threat, response to threat, to impulse, defenses against impulse, that you can't see a certain larger picture happening right before you. You can't even understand me, my overall life, the world that is mine to know and deal with, when I try to help you and educate you. So, I am concerned about *you*. And in some better world than we have now, I could deliver a paper to your colleagues about you and them, both."

It's ironic that at that time the single most influential book written by "my kind" about "Lawrence's kind" was called *The Mark of Oppression,* written by the psychoanalysts Abram Kardiner and Lionel Ovesey. If you pick up that book, you'll see that it goes back to the fifties. That book was actually a breakthrough for us in the social sciences because it tried to connect psychoanalysis to anthropology— namely, the study of the race problem by people like me.

What did that book study? Kardiner found certain patients in a hospital and decided that because of their race they bore a "mark of oppression," and all of us liberals were (and are) supposed to be terribly sympathetic. I don't mean to malign the purposes of the book or the book itself, but I want to remind us of the limited vision humans are capable of at various moments in history. Yes, there *was* a "mark of oppression," but there were also other marks: a sturdy, shrewd insistence on one's humanity. History itself is the great psychological variable that many of us ignore. What we can and cannot see depends greatly on the historical moment, never mind our repressions and anxieties and conflicts. Lawrence could have said: "All you people can do is call us names that have to do with psychopathology. You don't seem able or willing to work your way into *our lives,* so that you might then see us with our dignity, strength, resilience, and capacity to take on certain challenges—so we very well might be able to affirm ourselves."

A couple of years later, I sure did see those ironies tumbling out from young people in Mississippi, youths who were part of the Mississippi Summer Project of 1964, when people couldn't vote in this great democracy because of the color of their skin. We in this country had, in the 1930s and 1940s, gradually learned to recognize dictatorships in Europe for what they were and oppose them, but in our own country this terrible embarrassment—rather, a horror, a terror—continued.

Students in the Mississippi Summer Project were in the Delta of Mississippi, working with people to help them to vote. Students staying in the homes of African-American families began to admire the resourcefulness and the strength of these families as they got into the casual conversations that occur around the breakfast table, the dinner table. Indeed, I began to hear politically, socially, racially vulnerable people talked about in the same way our friend James Agee talked about the people of central Alabama: the students extolled them. And then one wry ironist in one of our discussions said, "Hey, if these people are the greatest people in the world, what are we doing down here, trying to make life better for them? Maybe *they* should come up north and try to help *us* become better people." Well, we were not about to overromanticize the great state of Mississippi, but there again you see what happens when you go beyond first impressions and begin to understand people who are different—to look into their assumptions, their ways of life, so that you penetrate to their goodness as well as their hurts, their strengths as well as their problems. It can be so easy for some of us well-intentioned people to emphasize the negatives, the problems, whether they are socioeconomic problems or psychological problems—"pity" is what that is called, and it is not necessarily one of the greatest emotions. Pity can be an ignorant anger, a kind of unknowing condescension; sorrow about the world, anger at its state—that's another kind of feeling.

The title of Ralph Ellison's book *Invisible Man* tells us to attend to invisibility. What is it that makes us blind? Let us not forget that for every invisible person there is a blind person. What are the roots of our blindness? What prompts our failure to understand and comprehend? Is it only our lack of good intentions, or is it the systematic ignorance and misunderstanding that we have experienced, making all of us victims, possessed of a "mark of oppression" ("us" being the so-called dominant folks)? Let's pay attention to these failures of connection that Tillie Olsen is talking about, even among children who have played together and known one another, like those kids in "O Yes." These distinctions inform our lives mightily. Let us try to understand how that takes place in our various lives.

PART III

A Storytelling Humanity

Ways of seeing race and identity—
encounters through the eyes of another.

Featured: Ralph Ellison, Flannery O'Connor

TWELVE

Visibility and Invisibility: A Struggle to See

Ralph Waldo Ellison (note that middle name) was born in Oklahoma City in 1914 and died in New York City at the age of eighty. The obituaries again and again told late-twentieth-century America about *Invisible Man,* surely one of the most important American novels (and certainly many of us would agree) in America, by an American-born novelist.

He grew up in "working-class America" and went off to the Tuskegee Institute for college. He eventually left—another college dropout. He was primarily a jazz musician but played classical music as well. Ellison headed for New York City and got a job for the WPA Writers' Project, doing some editing and then writing. He wrote some short stories and even a few poems. He then got an interesting job, working for a prominent American psychiatrist and psychoanalyst, the rebellious and brilliant Harry Stack Sullivan.

Sullivan worked in an office where he would serve his patients either tea or sherry or food, depending on who they were, what they wanted to have, and what they needed and could take. He would draw up a list of the patients' needs for Ellison, and Ellison would procure the items on the list.

Ellison had discussions with Sullivan about who should be getting what, why sherry for this one and tea for that, which food for whom, and thereby he learned a lot of Sullivan's thinking about his quite privileged white patients and how their power lived side by side with their uncomfortable vulnerability—rich, influential though they were, they were needy and troubled and hurt. This was a huge lesson for Ellison, as he would one day tell an audience at Princeton University. In a way it helped shape his genius as a novelist, because a novelist needs to be able to live comfortably with irony and paradox and inconsistency and contradiction, and to be able to render that in a story—and to have the capacity to create a story spacious enough to allow for ambiguity, rather than feeling the need to resolve it through theoretical formulations, pronouncements, insistences.

Invisible Man came out in the early 1950s, and gave us Ellison as a storyteller and a shrewd observer of both the American South and the North, of Alabama and Manhattan: a man who could remember every detail of Oklahoma City, Oklahoma, one of those border states that is basically southern but also has an opening to the North. He was able to pull all that together in this novel, which seized the day—the literary day, the social and cultural day, the psychological and educational day, not to mention the racial day—of the Eisenhower 1950s.

We can get abstract about this novel, call it a picaresque tale, the story of a young man's adventure—his journey from a certain kind of unawareness, if not ignorance, to an increasing sophistication about mind, heart, soul, environment, and a worldliness that is accumulated through experience. Many of you may have read *The Catcher in the Rye* and encountered Holden's insistence with respect to the phoniness of the world. Both Holden and the young, nameless invisible man didn't learn about how things go in life through textbooks, tests, and grades given; they learned through firsthand experiences that taught them lessons: about who owns what; about trustees; about corporations, which can be academic as well as commercial in nature; about power, be it academic, political, or cultural power (should he eat a yam and identify with this kind of person, or try to be that kind of person). Ellison's protagonist also encounters factory power, with the owners of that white-paint factory, and medical power, from doctors who extirpate part of the brain in the name of so-called therapy.

This novel came out in mid-century, after a period in which people had had to live with two world wars, and not in the "heart of darkness" that Conrad gave us in distant Africa, but amidst the murderous horrors of so-called civilized Europe. All of this, Ellison knew to connect. He met and repeatedly conversed with William Carlos Williams about the terrible paradox of brilliance and science and accomplishment being used for murder on a mass scale—all so humbling, admonishing, unsettling, for us to contemplate.

My father used to read *The Wall Street Journal,* and he sent me a clipping one day. He knew that as an assistant to Erik Erikson, for an undergraduate course he gave at Harvard in the late 1960s, I was teaching *Invisible Man.* I had come back from the South, where I'd tried to make sense of the lives of certain young children, Ruby Bridges and others, but also to make sense of my own education as a student here and, further on, as a doctor trying to deal with the human mind. My father spotted something in the *Journal* and wrote me a note: "Dear Bobby"—I always knew I was in trouble when he moved from Bob to Bobby—"Your mother and I thought you would be interested in the enclosed." The headline read: "In Boston Club Even Prize Fighting Can Be Very Proper."

The subtitle said, "A Formal Evening of Boxing Draws Capacity Crowd, Fun and Sometimes Blood." The article was written by David Gumpert in April 1979. As you read it, think of those first pages of *Invisible Man* and that boxing scene:

Cigar smoke fills the air. In the boxing ring two professional fighters punch away at each other, to wild cheers from the audience. Between rounds, rah-rah organ music plays and spectators place bets with one another on the outcome of the matches. The setting, however, isn't a local boxing club or sports arena. It's the ornate, wood-paneled dining room of the venerable and proper Harvard Club, a private social club where members are Harvard University alumni and faculty members. On this night about 350 Harvard Club members and their guests are enjoying what the club calls "a formal evening of boxing." The evening is a re-creating of an English private club custom, but is unique in this country. Once a year in late winter or early spring a boxing ring is assembled in the club's three-story-high main dining room, under silver chandeliers and in view of a portrait of Derek Bok, president of Harvard University. While the boxers battle, spectators in tuxedos and evening gowns sit at white-clothed tables enjoying a lavish meal of roast beef or steak and wine, followed by brandy and cigars. Sometimes blood from injured fighters splatters on nearby diners. But no matter; it's a very lighthearted, fun kind of evening, says a vice president of the Cambridge Trust Company, who each year buys ten tickets for himself, a fellow bank officer and eight bank customers. The cost, not including drinks, is 25 dollars a person, which is quickly forgotten before the evening is over. Almost everyone is half in the bag, he says. Indeed, at a club where bridge matches, travelogues and concerts are the dominant fare, the boxing evening eclipses everything else in popularity.

Then there is a long discussion about people who have been coming to the event for years. "The attraction isn't the gambling and it isn't the fights," says so-and-so (I'm not mentioning the names of the people quoted in the article), "it's the setting and the evening. It's a good man's night out. It's letting your hair down and yelling and screaming and doing things you haven't done since you were a kid." Others like the symbolism:

"It's a strange mixture of the civilized and uncivilized," says [so-and-so], a management consultant and one of only a few women who attend the boxing evening. "I wouldn't miss it for the world." Some members, however, find the evening distasteful. "It's very elitist," says [so-and-so], a management consultant, who attended the first boxing evening and never went back. "It reminds me of the Christians and the lions. What I would like to see is a couple of the members get up there and fight, instead of Puerto Rican and South Boston kids, who are the ones they have." Harvard club officials, however, say that opposition is minimal, consisting of only a few critical comments and perhaps only one critical letter a year.

Then Gumpert goes into a history of boxing in Great Britain in the eighteenth and nineteenth centuries, and we learn that the Harvard event is black-tie:

The evening starts at the club's subdued Massachusetts Room, which is adorned with portraits of famous Harvard University graduates, who became governors and senators and presidents. One of the least predicable parts of the evening is who the fighters will be. The club contracts with a local boxing promoter to arrange five or six fights of three to ten rounds each. Typically, though, the promoters don't know until the night of the fights which boxers will show up, and there is usually scrambling to put bodies in the ring. Most of the fighters aren't well trained in the fine art of boxing but are very scrappy, which has made them popular. There is only an occasional bum, observers say. Last year one boxer with a sizeable paunch was knocked out by a sizeable punch, they recall. "The first year I went there, in 1970, some of the fighters resented the audience and the surroundings," says [so-and-so], a construction worker who had managed several of the boxers and brought them to the club. "Since then, though, these boxers have come to enjoy the evening," he says. "The Harvard Club spectators have become more involved than any other crowd we have boxed before."

Near the end of the article, Gumpert notes, "a young Brockton, Massachusetts, welterweight says that he likes fighting in front of that caliber of people." Oh boy, the human mind! "He has hopes he might meet some influential people who might help his boxing career or help him along educationally."

All of this is a humiliation of sorts to consider, and yet enormously instructive: we learn not through the distant generalizations of *Das Kapital* by Karl Marx, but right here through the social history of our own beloved institution, which has done so much for so many of us—and yet, these shadows and clouds, these embarrassments, and worse.

Let us get back to *Invisible Man* and now connect it to Dostoyevsky's *Notes from the Underground* and the hope of more light. Perhaps the reason for hope of more light, as Milton said, is that the truth somehow will make us free, at least free to stop and think, and will shed further light not on a distant abstraction called "the race problem" or "the civil rights era" or even on those stories about some children in the 1960s, but on you and me, and here and now. I remember hearing Ralph Bunche give a talk in New York City. An African-American man who had risen to the highest reaches of political power, he had represented our nation at the United Nations, had advised presidents. I remember him describing his memories of when he'd been a graduate student: he couldn't find a place to live; many people wouldn't talk to him—ignored him, looked askance at him, to the point that he worried not only about their looks but about what that experience was doing to him as he looked inward. He worried about how their eyes became his eyes and how his invisibility to them made him feel worthless and invisible to himself.

There is a phrase I want to discuss: "identification with the aggressor." Haven't many of us known aggressors of one kind or another? You and I have our memories of elementary school, about how so-called innocent children can be filled with mischief and malice, and lots of fear—which, of course, energizes the mischief and malice, gets it going. Who recognizes whom? Whose eyes will settle on another with concern and justice and fairness? What and whom do we avoid looking at and how does that gesture on our part affect not only our view of them, but who we are? For every invisible man there is a blind man. Ellison's novel connects with Carver's story "Cathedral" and with Williams's stories about his own callousness, his candid stories about his smugness and impatience, which caused him to give the back of his hand, both literally and symbolically, to others—to not see them for who they were and what their lives had been and were like. We struggle with this, you and I, all the time, don't we? No matter what field we go into, whether we are going to be teachers, or businesspeople, or lawyers, or doctors, others can seem like stock characters or automatons to us as we hurry along, and as a result we become that way ourselves.

Does one gain knowledge of oneself, of others? How do we find, as Dr. King put it, the "beloved community"? Where and with whom? We must ask ourselves that as we meet an invisible man, a nameless man, an unnoticed man, a plucky yet frightened man, as he journeys through corridors of power and discovers hypocrisy and phoniness and duplicity, all masked with righteousness—no, self-righteousness parading as righteousness.

Sometimes the easiest way to handle a disappointment is to find someone to denigrate or insult or deny. If I feel hurt, threatened, or ignored, I'll find others to respond to similarly. What is it that prompts us to watch kids from South Boston beating the living daylights out of one another so that we can be entertained? Ellison asks that in *Invisible Man* as a novelist does, through a story. I'm talking not about honorable boxing (and we could have a long discussion about boxing per se), but boxing under these auspices, so that one can laugh and scorn. Just as painful is our desire, sometimes, to box (symbolically) for others—to go to any extent to perform for them. Maybe not in the ring with gloves but, regretfully, in classrooms, in law offices, in hospital rooms.

When do we end this kind of fearful activity? Those who get that ultimate power, what we think is ultimate power, those people who administer violence to other people's brains, those who own the white-paint factory, those who are college presidents or teachers— Ellison presents them as the blind leading the blind. He wants us to look at them, look at ourselves, look at our fear. Thereby, with his help, we can see part of ourselves through the nameless invisible man's observer's eyes—our squirming, adroitly grasping side.

Where would knowledge of race be without eyes? If race has to do with pigment, race ultimately has to do with vision. Without eyes, we'd get rid of the race problem, wouldn't we? The organ that enables us to be so much ourselves, to see, to become seers and to have visions and become visionaries, to encompass visually, is the same organ that enables us to scorn, to distinguish first and then scorn, in order to boost ourselves up. All this Ellison knew and wanted us to know as he takes himself and his memories, gives them expression in a novel; he takes you and me on an American pilgrimage of sorts, through places of secular worship: worship the people who give you a job; worship the doctors who say they can cure you; worship the people who tell you that if you follow them they'll change society; worship politicians, whether it be those who own politics now or those who want to own politics come their day; worship cultural arbiters, who tell us what to eat and what to wear and whom to look at and how to talk.

An invisible man is an existentialist man, a mid-twentieth-century man, a man cut off from many, one who yearns to see, wants more light, the kind we see Edward Hopper shedding on American scenes. Thereby, with an artist's help, a novelist's, we become less isolated from others; we can go out yet again and try to touch and be touched. Seeing with new eyes and a new vision, we can embrace the world with a little more awareness, kindness, humility. Humor— don't miss the humor in this novel; wry bemusement enables survival from the surgeon's knife, the employer's pink slip, the admissions officer's arbitrary grades, the college president's lying letter.

Yes, this is a novel about "race," but it is also a novel about you and me, no matter our skin color. It is about our lifelong education: how it takes place, what its consequences are in the hidden curriculum we have before us over the decades of our existence. By this I mean not a subject matter that is intellectual in nature but one experiential and moral in nature, one that has to do with how honest we are with one another (not to mention with ourselves), how open and willing we can be in that regard (as in Martin Buber's "I-Thou"). That is ultimately what this novel is about; it is a literary version of philosophical existentialism. The tradition for such goes back to Cervantes's Don Quixote and his journey, and Dostoyevsky's *The Idiot* and Myshkin's journey, and, in a terribly sad, humbling, and frightening way, Anna Karenina's journey, which Tolstoy gave us. At *Invisible Man*'s opening and closing we may be enlightened by those electric lightbulbs, of course, but also by the wry, knowing vision of this protagonist as he glimpses, gets to ponder others and himself, white and black, men and women, rich and poor, philanthropist and the most needy! On and on that human scene goes, that human parade goes, as we turn the pages of this extraordinarily complex, dense, figurative, highly charged, symbolic story.

Ellison's *Invisible Man* comes out of that underground situation now and then, as you and I do each time we seize the day. Every day we go back into ourselves, we withdraw to our private world, to our underground voices and visions. In dreams and daydreams, in solitary walks and sometimes in the midst of company when our mind leaves and we think and wonder and worry and wander and get carried here and there. This is what Ralph Waldo Ellison offers us, utterly loyal to his middle name, to his first name: he gives us an American novel worthy of Emerson, and, too, Hawthorne and Melville and Faulkner. For you and me here, it is a novel to give us some personal pause and some historical pause about our own time—about our leaders, about what they say, what we say, about our habits and our affiliations; about our visibility, our invisibility, our struggle to see without and within, and the sometime hope that we will become bigger in what we see, larger in our hearts, more generous in our souls, notwithstanding that cramped, hidden, isolated side of ourselves inside.

I didn't know what to do when I got that *Wall Street Journal* clipping from my dad. But I finally wrote back, "Dear Dad: Thanks a lot! Love, Bobby."

THIRTEEN

The Victim,
the Victimizer

To those we cannot or refuse to see we give enormous power, because they can look at us and understand us, even though we often do not look at them or we dismiss them out of hand. This is the essential metaphor of Ellison's *Invisible Man,* and in a strange way it makes an invisible man an invincible man. A kind of omnipotence and power go with lacking what so many people own, possess, wield—whatever the verbs are. Three of Flannery O'Connor's stories address this matter—as a kind of contrapuntal response to *Invisible Man.* Not that she wrote the stories for that purpose, but we can use that theme in our own kind of music making as we look at "The Displaced Person," "The Artificial Nigger," and "Everything That Rises Must Converge." They are a trio. I think they are her most powerful stories. In each of them there is a kind of invisibility of the other, of the black people and their role.

First, let me tell you something about Flannery O'Connor. She was born in Savannah in 1925, and she died in 1964—she was then only thirty-nine years old. If you ever go to her city of birth, you can find a plaque on the house where she was born. It is right across the street from the cathedral in downtown Savannah. Her parents were from old Catholic backgrounds—German Catholic on the mother's side. Her mother's name was Regina Cline, and the father was Edward O'Connor. They moved up to Milledgeville when Flannery was ten or eleven. Her father was ill and would soon be diagnosed with a disease called lupus erythematosus, from which he would die when Flannery was fifteen. This same disease would take her life. Lupus can be a mild disease, not seriously a threat to a person's health, or it can be a rapidly fatal disease. Both father and daughter had the rapidly fatal kind. It is a strange, weird disease, even a symbolic disease; she was well aware of that. *Lupus,* in Latin, means "wolf." In some of her letters she would talk about a wolf wreaking havoc in the house, meaning in her body. Lupus causes the immune system of the body, which protects us from disease, to go berserk, and the body develops a negative reaction to itself, and attacks various organs. It was devastating, but is now curable.

When O'Connor was young she was interested in cartoons and aspired to become a cartoonist. She went through the University System of Georgia, to a school at that time called the Georgia State College for Women, at Milledgeville. Milledgeville also had the largest hospital for the psychiatrically troubled patients in the state of Georgia and, in fact, was one of the largest mental hospitals in the nation. Flannery O'Connor and her mother and father were used to seeing psychiatric patients on leave, walking the streets of Milledgeville. Flannery was always interested in them; she struck up conversations with them as a young girl and as a teenager. In college, she majored in psychology and sociology. She quickly became appalled by the language of psychology and a certain pretentiousness that one can occasionally notice in the field and its brother disciplines: overwrought language; the claim that anything and everything can be explained through wordy formulations; and an insistence upon doing this at the expense of others, while reserving for oneself a kind of haughty immunity.

She took aim at pride, arrogance, and smugness in story after story, doing so in the biblical tradition of both the Hebrew Bible (which she much revered and refers to in her letters and the chapters of

Mystery and Manners, a collection of nonfiction) and, of course, the Christian Bible, where the sin of pride is the sin of sins.

She started writing stories when she was a junior in college, and she sent them off to editors. One of these editors wrote back and said, "There is talent here; learn how to nourish it." When she graduated from college, a friend of the family's who lived in Atlanta and taught in the English department at Emory told her that she ought to send some of her fiction off to the Iowa Writers' Workshop. She did, and Paul Engle, who was running the workshop at the time, wrote back on a postcard, "Come here anytime—you'll be more than welcome." No application, no essay, no multiple-choice tests, no recommendations required at that time. A couple of years after her graduation, she went to Iowa City to "learn" how to write—not that she didn't know already.

Soon enough, some of her writing started appearing in literary journals, and she started to forge a career. She went east and lived with Robert and Sally Fitzgerald. Robert Fitzgerald had been a Harvard professor, teaching in the English department, and was a distinguished poet and translator. She stayed with the Fitzgerald family for a couple of years—and then came the onset of the lupus, with weakness, dizziness, a sore throat, and a spreading rash. She was forced to return home and, once again, to her mother. If you read these stories carefully, you'll find in many of them strong, demanding, perplexing mothers—hard to deal with and yet strangely inspiring.

Mrs. O'Connor, Flannery's mother, died in 1995. She was ready to turn one hundred. My wife taught some Flannery O'Connor stories when she was teaching at the Shady Hill School in Cambridge. When we went south we carried the collection with us. Lawrence Jefferson's mother, Wilhelmina Jefferson, worked in the Emory hospital in Atlanta, as a ward helper. She came from South Carolina, and in chapter 11 I wrote about what she taught Lawrence when he was with her in Rich's department store, trying to see Santa Claus. One day she said to my wife, Jane, "You know, there is a writer I'm taking care of." She'd also told the patient that she knew someone who taught English; Wilhelmina beamed with pride as she told my wife that. "Well, what's the writer's name?" my wife asked. She said, "I don't know, but she has a funny first name." My wife said, "Why don't you ask her what her name is or look on the chart; I'd be curious to know." Next time we met up with Wilhelmina, she told us that the patient's name was Flannery. (In fact, O'Connor had been born Mary Flannery.) We figured out right away who that patient was.

About three months later, Flannery, having been discharged to her mother, was back in the hospital. She asked to see Mrs. Jefferson, with whom she had become friendly. She loved talking with her. She loved a certain toughness in her. One day we came to see Mrs. Jefferson and she told us she had lost her job. We wondered what had happened. She said, "Well, I lost my job because I lost my mind for a couple of minutes." I pushed for more detail, and she continued: "I was in Miss O'Connor's room and we were talking and a doctor came in. I hadn't emptied her bedpan because I was so busy talking to her, because she wanted to talk to me. The doctor said, 'Empty that!' I said, 'Yes sir, I will.' He said, 'Empty that now!' Then Flannery said, '*I'll* empty it.' The doctor looked back at me: '*You* empty that *now*.'" Flannery protested. The doctor, with his abrupt, demanding way, had gotten to Mrs. Jefferson's head, or maybe her friendship with Flannery had gotten to her as well, because she picked up the bedpan and threw it at the doctor. If that isn't a Flannery O'Connor moment, I don't know what is! Of course, Mrs. Jefferson was fired. Flannery O'Connor didn't know whether to laugh or to scream; one might laugh because the doctor had gotten his just deserts—had more than gotten what he'd deserved. At what price, though?

Here are some moments from "Mystery and Manners." The very title tells you what the author was about.

Of course, I have found that anything that comes out of the South is going to be called grotesque by the Northern reader, unless it is grotesque, in which case it is going to be called realistic.

Think about that comment! That's her mind at its absolute best—
no sociological study required!

The kind of written work I'm going to talk about is story-
writing, because that's the only kind I know anything about. I'll
call any length of fiction a story, whether it be a novel or a
shorter piece, and I'll call anything a story in which specific
characters and events influence each other to form a meaningful
narrative.

Yes, indeed.

It is the business of fiction to embody mystery through manners,
and mystery is a great embarrassment to the modern mind.

Alas, we are bent, occasionally, upon "resolving" mystery with
theory and explanations. Sometimes these theories become exalted;
we worship them. We forget that they are only conjecture, specula-
tion, or a way of thinking. They become engraved in stone and are
given life through our idolatrous desire for them—a kind of self-
worship, sometimes.

Not long ago a teacher told me that her best students feel that it
is no longer necessary to write anything. She said they think that
everything can be done with figures now, and that what can't be
done with figures isn't worth doing. I think that this is a natural
belief for a generation that can be made to feel that the aim of
learning is to eliminate mystery.

What are we going to do with that point of view: stand up, as
O'Connor did, for mystery? Or even develop a Department of Mys-
tery hereabouts?
Here she talks about poverty:

He begins to see in the depths of himself, and it seems to me that his position there rests on what must certainly be the bedrock of all human experience—the experience of limitation or, if you will, of poverty.

In her stories, again and again she is trying to remind us that whether we are rich or poor, black or white, Yankee or from the Dixie South, our humanity is not without vulnerability. Who is without one or another kind of weakness, or susceptibility to making errors? This is what we can share and link arms over. Through this we can understand one another—and the frailties, of one kind or another, we have. In a sense, class and race thereby get put into a context of our "limitations."

O'Connor said, "The mystery of existence is always showing through the texture of ordinary lives. I'm afraid this makes them irresistible to the novelist." She was talking about the ordinary people she observed in Milledgeville.

I want to share with you one of her letters collected under a wonderful title, *The Habit of Being*. The letters, in their sum, form a kind of epistolary novel from this hurt and hurting, brilliantly gifted writer. She was on crutches in her youth, and dying—and she knew she was. Yet as a writer, she shone with a kind of loving-kindness and a wonderful sense of humor—biting at times, but at other times charitable. She was impatient with a lot of cultural junk, but in her own way forgiving.

This letter was written to a professor of English at Rice University, a friend of hers. He had sent her some good papers from his students about one of her stories, "A Good Man Is Hard to Find," and she wrote this reply to him in March 1961:

The interpretation of your ninety students and three teachers is fantastic and about as far from my intentions as it could get to be. If it were a legitimate interpretation, the story would be little more than a trick and its interest would be simply for abnormal psychology. I am not interested in abnormal psychology.

There is a change of tension from the first part of the story to the second where the Misfit enters, but this is no lessening of reality. This story is, of course, not meant to be realistic in the sense that it portrays the everyday doings of people in Georgia. It is stylized and its conventions are comic even though its meaning is serious.

Bailey's only importance is as the Grandmother's boy and the driver of the car. It is the Grandmother who first recognizes the Misfit and who is most concerned with him throughout. The story is a duel of sorts between the Grandmother and her superficial beliefs and the Misfit's more profoundly felt involvement with Christ's action which set the world off balance for him.

The meaning of a story should go on expanding for the reader the more he thinks about it, but meaning cannot be captured in an interpretation.

Consider that statement. And, by the way, you could say that about psychotherapy and psychoanalysis, too. Some of us who do this work, in collusion with our patients, and get too anxious for such an outcome may start handing out interpretations, which are grabbed at hungrily—as the individuals called doctor and patient smile proudly, gratefully at one another. Liberation is achieved, well, for about five minutes. The motions of the heart, the motions of the soul that happen between two individuals and that heal are not going to be carried back and forth only with an interpretation. O'Connor continues in this vein:

If teachers are in the habit of approaching a story as if it were a research problem for which any answer is believable so long as it is not obvious, then I think students will never learn to enjoy fiction. Too much interpretation is certainly worse than too little, and where feeling for story is absent, theory will not supply it.

My tone is not meant to be obnoxious. I am in a state of shock.

We all know how exhilarating it is to be clever and to get an A or a raise, or just recognition for our cleverness. Clever stories become hyped up into the abstractions of this or that literary approach—and how sad for us, the storytelling creature who hungers for stories out of our need to know one another, to figure out this world.

As you may have gathered from that letter, there was in O'Connor a satirist. She wrote a spoof on a wedding announcement. Here it is:

Lyvidia Lucy LaPlant, the daughter of Mrs. Earle Splat Stuckburge of Hankoring Pines, Ohio and Frances Pantagenate LaPlant of Rust Hills, New Jersey was married yesterday to P. Pickering Pattoon, the son of Mrs. Potter Patton Pattoon and the late Mr. Pattoon of Pattoonaconsit, Massachusetts. The ceremony at the Shrine of Eternally Upward Mobility was performed by the bridegroom's uncle, the reverend Gasbard Pattoon. Present were a number of the board of Steers, Blight, and Smutch, Incorporated, as well as its executive chaplain. The bride's maid of honor was her sister Melony Melissa LaPlant, who is a junior partner of Palms, Petes, Fretes, Spang, Spaldien, and Escobar. The best man was Hilary Dark, heir to the huge mouse and clock toy empire based on the Hickory Dickory Clock Company, which was founded by his grandfather, the late Hector Dextor Doc. The bride is a senior project coordinator in the Alamantix division of Squexton. She is a certified corporate coordinator, licensed to coordinate projects in taxonomy, bifocals, quashing, esoterics, and group hysterics, as well as alamantics, quintonics, and luxurious weekends. She is a graduate of

Old Mum's Mosley's School for Girls in Foxy Crossroads, Virginia, and holds a degree in senior analysis, magna cum laude from the Massachusetts Institute of Degrees.

The bride's father, Mr. LaPlant, is almost entirely lacking in social distinction, but holds memberships in dozens of corporate boards. He is a former stock car racing driver who was later discovered to be the natural heir to the British Earldom of Fluvery, with immense holdings of slum properties in Birmingham, Alabama. Though the bride's mother, the former Countess, fluently divorced the lordship several years ago, the grounds specified in the suit did not discredit the peerage. Her subsequent marriage to the distinguished Stuckbridge family, whose business for three generations has made Hankoring Pines, Ohio synonymous with ball bearings, was followed almost immediately by induction into the Upper Hankoring Pines garden club.

O'Connor took note of language and silliness and self-importance and yearning. Yearning for what? If you read "The Displaced Person" you will get all kinds of aspiration, of self-satisfaction—the hierarchies that inform this kind of public announcement with respect to marriage. The title, "The Displaced Person," invites the topic of immigration: Who is to be let in where, and by whom? Whose America is it? Who is welcome and who is told to get out or stay away, and why? Who *belongs,* belongs in what is called "high society," belongs in the United States of America, belongs in your neighborhood and mine, belongs in this institution? Using what criteria? And, boy, do those criteria change over the generations. The "displaced person," whose name is Guizac, comes around after the Second World War to a small southern scene. Flannery O'Connor puts an outsider in the midst of us and shows us what is going on between us, because the outsider in a way tells us about what it means to be inside. All the levels, the heights and depths of power and influence and authority, are illuminated by this entrance. She has for us Mrs. McIntyre, who owns the setup, the farm. She has us meet white people called "Shortley"—as in shortly something is going to happen to them. We can sense the apprehension; the tension is palpable from the opening paragraph.

They are working-class white people. And then standing off on an elevation, looking down at them, are two figures called Astor and Sulk. These black men are set apart from the narrative. They are watching it—segregated, out of the picture totally, silent witnesses—yet they see it entirely. By being set apart this way, they are the only ones immune to the distrust and discordance that ultimately becomes murder. The displaced person immediately displaces the Shortley family, because he works so hard. He wants to get ahead. The harder he works, the more Mrs. McIntyre appreciates it. But all too soon there is a face-off between the new worker and old worker, and who's going to pick up the pieces? There is social unrest, and the boss becomes aware of the fact that she isn't going to get away with this herself.

As the story races to its denouement, a tractor driven by the worker who has lost his job backs into and over the displaced person and kills him. Mrs. McIntyre could have prevented this, could have shouted, spoken up, but in that moral second, the judgment eludes her. The story is really about how any of us can become displaced. Mrs. McIntyre becomes the ultimate displaced person. The Shortley family is displaced. The displaced person himself is displaced into eternity. Watching all this mayhem, this murderousness and competitiveness, are the people who are truly excluded, and by virtue of being excluded, they have an ironic authority and immunity from what is going on. As in: the last shall be first and the first shall be last. So we have Mrs. McIntyre reduced to babbling and a priest reduced to babbling with her—a not very friendly portrait of a priest by a devoted Catholic writer who knew how to laugh at the excesses of religion, including her own, as they accompany this kind of social, racial, and economic betrayal of Christianity. Historically, churches have often come to such ignominy; it is not a rare phenomenon.

Ralph Ellison, through an "invisible man," helps us see a lot about ourselves. Flannery O'Connor turns the coin over and says, I hope that when people read these stories they are not going to be reading them hoping the stories are going to illuminate the race problem per se. I'm afraid that such a way of categorizing a story might do an injustice to the story, and an injustice to you and me as readers, because we would be labeling it, and we would become blind to what I am really trying to do, which is to tell us how we behave as human beings with one another: the lapses to which we are heir through our humanity—through our various lusts, through the egoism that courses along our veins and coarsens us. How hard we struggle to single ourselves out, to puff ourselves up at the expense of others! We will find those others, won't we, when we need them? It is to that use that we turn to people different from us in various ways, turn on them, and ultimately, therefore, we become the victims. Attacking others, in response to our daily nervousness about ourselves (our worth, our "position," our reputation), we diminish ourselves. The victim sadly becomes an instrument of willful self-victimization.

FOURTEEN

The Humbling of Head

It can be unsettling for us to read James Agee's *Let Us Now Praise Famous Men,* to respond to what we can call an eloquent, highly articulate, and at times lyrical presentation of distress, pain, hurt in this world. At a certain point we may find that we are connected to that pain and hurt. The chapter on education turns out to be a tirade of sorts, directed at the privileged who know their James Joyce, as Agee did, and who know the poets, the playwrights, and the fellow novelists; who can pick up the subtleties he has directed at the reader and maybe even against the reader.

So, too, with George Orwell and his insistent denunciations of his own kind—the Oxford poets and writers, the intelligentsia of England. Dr. Williams also went after intellectuals, denounced the abstract mind, the conceptual mind, the mind of generalizations, of ready conclusions; "no ideas but in things," he said, thereby heralding the importance of human particularity, the concreteness of life. He went after the kinds of conceptualizations that you and I may lean on sometimes—that make us "smart" and distinguish us from others. Tillie Olsen also insisted that these so-called experts be confronted, that these know-it-alls be arraigned. It's a holding up of mirrors, of sorts, allowing us, through others, to see ourselves.

Raymond Carver, in "The Student's Wife," which really humbles us, presents a character who has read Rilke but isn't a kind, sensitive husband. Thereby we readers become nervous about how we are behaving with our wives, husbands, friends, lovers, and whatever; we may know so much that is so fine and yet be capable of behaving in a callous, indifferent, mean-spirited way, amidst our brilliant knowing. Then there is Ellison, who takes on, sardonically, higher education—for all of us this hurts, and it gets us very close to ourselves.

Now we have Flannery O'Connor—look at the way, in her letters, she spelled "intellectuals": "interleckchuls." Is this a kind of gratuitous, mean-spirited put-down, one we are not to take seriously? Or are we to take all of this seriously as it begins to accumulate from many writers? What are we to think? What are they, the writers, trying to do? It isn't as if this was a collection of people that gathered themselves together and formed some school or point of view. They are, as were those who contributed to *The Book of Common Prayer*, from "all sorts and conditions." Agee and Orwell were from two different countries; Williams, Tillie Olsen, Flannery O'Connor, Ralph Ellison—these were people operating on their own, not coming together in some courtyard, classroom, or university setting. But at different times and different places, their ideas come together.

Let us turn to "The Artificial Nigger." One day my wife gave me a summary of her take on the story: "the humbling of head," she said, meaning our "heads," in all their authority (the "heads" that brought us here to this university). This reminds me of how O'Connor was very fond of peacocks. She grew them, kept them, watched them, watched that strange mixture of beauty and pride, of excellence and a bit of strutting.

A member of my own profession, during the mid-1950s, a San Francisco psychoanalyst, Allen Wheelis, came out with an article in the *International Journal of Psychoanalysis* titled "The Vocational Hazards of Psychoanalysis." He went on to expand that article into a book called *The Quest for Identity*. He wrote at some length, in a confessional mode, about how dangerous it can be to be looked up to, to be needed by others. That warning would apply to teachers as well as doctors, lawyers, financial people, and, of course, to parents— maybe to all of us. But there are degrees, and when you are constantly being reacted to in such an intense way, either positively or negatively, beyond your own particular merits as a human being; when you are wearing some halo, dangerous or welcome (I repeat, teachers and doctors are especially vulnerable to this), there are hazards, as Flannery O'Connor wants us to remember. That mingling together of achievement and the honorable pride in that, along with something that goes beyond that pride—this can create a sort of danger that I think we all have known in our lives: a bit of satisfaction moving beyond accomplishment into self-satisfaction, a bit of smugness that enables us, sadly, not to have as much kindness directed at others who may lag behind in one or another way, and whose possibilities we choose not to notice because we can always notice that such folks are lagging behind us in our chosen way of measurement.

In these stories, in story after story, O'Connor unnerves us. "The Lame Shall Enter First" tells of a healer who so badly needs to be healed. I have used it for years with hospital residents in psychiatry and pediatrics, with medical students. People like me ought to read that story at least every year or so, and maybe every month or so, and sometimes when we are in real trouble. And we should read it when our families are picking up the tab, so to speak, when we are so intent on laying our hands on others, on interpreting for others, on getting them better, that someone close to us pays for it: a wife, a husband, children. The very brilliance that enables us to see others also allows us to be blind and maybe even pushes us toward blindness, because in our self-absorption and in drawing in ourselves to do that healing, we diminish ourselves and have much less of ourselves, ironically, left for those we are closest to. You see it in "The Student's Wife"; you see it in "The Lame Shall Enter First"—this theme, biblical in nature, as in "physician, heal thyself." These aphoristic statements that go back to the dawn of recorded and written history, writers like O'Connor repeat for you and me in their own particular and original and seductive ways; they draw us in, oh boy, do they.

"The Artificial Nigger"—the very title provokes. Then we enter the story: "Mr. Head awakened to discover that the room was full of moonlight"—moonlight, wisdom, seeing and knowing and understanding, enlightenment. "He sat up and stared at the floor boards— the color of silver—and then at the ticking on his pillow, which might have been brocade, and after a second, he saw half of the moon five feet away." The moon, light from the skies: this is going to be a journey of discovery, a teacher's journey, a healer's journey. Again, we should think of a classroom, a medical office, and a suggestion like "I will show you the way, tell you of the world." Let there be light and there was light, and there is light. The second paragraph begins with "Mr. Head could have said to it that age was a choice blessing"—you see a little bit of self-satisfaction there. Age, youth, middle age, early middle age, whatever age we are, we find it so wonderful, whatever aspect of ourselves we want to pat ourselves on the back for having—"and that only with years does a man enter into that calm understanding of life that makes him a suitable guide for the young." A guide for the young as Dante's Virgil was. ". . . He sat up and grasped the iron posts at the foot of his bed. . . .The hour was two in the morning." Two, as in those two who would set forth, as in intimacy and love and two. Not one but two, the number of closeness and trust, the number of human relatedness. They start off in this moonlight and this light, on this journey of promise. ". . . Nelson was hunched over on his side, his knee under his chin and his heels under his bottom. His new suit and hat were in the boxes that they had been sent in and these were on the floor. . . . Mr. Head lay back down, feeling entirely confident that he could carry out the moral mission of the coming day."

Pretty soon they are on that train, aren't they? And pretty soon the lesson starts being taught: " 'If you ain't been there in fifteen years, how you know you'll be able to find your way about?' Nelson had asked. 'How you know it hasn't changed some?' 'Have you ever,' Mr. Head had asked, 'seen me lost?' "

They are the lost, as in *Paradise Lost*. Then they go to the city, these country bumpkins. But one of them is not a country bumpkin. One of them knows, has been there. The boy is doubtful, but pretty soon that doubt will be squashed by the power and the authority of the teacher, Mr. Head.

So they go to the city, but even before they get to the city, on the train we have this: "A coarse-looking orange-colored sun coming up behind the east range of mountains was making the sky a dull red behind them, but in front of them it was still gray and they faced a gray transparent moon." O'Connor is playing with the light all through this story, almost as Hopper does in his paintings. ". . . Nelson jerked his hat on again and turned angrily to the window. 'He's never seen anything before,' Mr. Head continued, 'ignorant as the day he was born, but I mean for him to get his fill once and for all.' " Pretty soon, the teacher starts to work.

"Mr. Head's grip was tightening insistently on Nelson's arm. As the procession passed them, the light from a sapphire ring on the brown hand"—a little more light; that sapphire ring on the brown hand is going to give us the first glimmer of what is going to happen in this story—"that picked up the cane reflected in Mr. Head's eye, but he did not look up nor did the tremendous man look at him. The group proceeded up the rest of the aisle and out of the car. Mr. Head's grip on Nelson's arm loosened. 'What was that?' he asked." That's a teacher at work. " 'A man,' the boy said and gave him an indignant look as if he were tired of having his intelligence insulted . . . 'A fat man,' Nelson said. He was beginning to feel that he had better be cautious. 'You don't know what kind?' Mr. Head said in a final tone. 'An old man,' the boy said and had a sudden foreboding that he was not going to enjoy the day. 'That was a nigger,' Mr. Head said and sat back. . . . 'I'd of thought you'd know a nigger since you seen so many when you was in the city on your first visit,' Mr.

Head continued. 'That's his first nigger,' he said to the man across the aisle." Here Head is bringing someone else into this and humiliating this boy, the first in a series of humiliations at the hand of intellectual authority and political authority. Who wouldn't be made nervous by a story like this, wondering if someone is out to make you feel guilty? "The boy slid down into the seat. 'You said they were black,' he said in an angry voice. 'You never said they were tan. How do you expect me to know anything when you don't tell me right?' 'You're just ignorant is all,' Mr. Head said." It's great how O'Connor uses a southern vernacular and dialect.

Read this story closely if you want to understand what we call racism; if you want to understand something about people who wear white robes and scream at other people, as they've done in American history; if you want to understand how officers of the law murder; if you want to understand why we turn on people. We all have done it and we all do it in one way or another, turning on people different from us in one way or another, by virtue of race or class, hobbies or membership, vocations or wanted vocations, all the stereotypes.

"Nelson turned backward again and looked where the Negro had disappeared." He's been told he's ignorant; someone has criticized him. Haven't we all been criticized? How do you bring up children without criticizing them? So that they learn "no" as well as "yes," so that they learn that they cannot run out into the street and risk being hit by an automobile? Children learn "no" and that "no" can go from a deed to a sense of who they are, sometimes just like that. "He felt that the Negro had deliberately walked down the aisle in order to make a fool of him and he hated him with a fierce raw fresh hate; and also, he understood now why his grandfather disliked them." You see how he got swept into this, how we get swept into hate, out of fear and vulnerability, because there must be some way to stop this criticism and the best way is to join the critic. So we embrace the critic and we find someone to give a good swift kick to, scapegoating. It's easy to notice it in southern sheriffs and members of the KKK—a little harder to notice this kind of maneuvering in ourselves, in our offices, in our country clubs, in our classrooms, in our own lives and among families and friends. "He looked toward the window and the face there seemed to suggest that he might be inadequate to the day's exactions. He wondered if he would even recognize the city when they came to it." So Nelson is now doubtful and some of his childish cocky ways have been rubbed off and he is holding on to this teacher out of fear and trembling for dear life. This submission carries them away, but only for a bit.

"The train was in the station. Both he and Mr. Head jumped up and ran to the door. Neither noticed that they had left the paper sack with the lunch in it on the seat." This is not going to be a very happy time. The food is left behind and pretty soon, well, Nelson is connecting the sewer passages with the entrance to hell. They are descending into the darkness of human possibility. The demiurge, darkness, as Toni Morrison has reminded us in more intellectual and contrasting novelistic storytelling exercises, lies in this way that we use words like "black" and "white," and denounce what is part of us and attribute to others what we want to get rid of in ourselves. Pretty soon, in the city, they see some black people and the boy, watching them, is strangely drawn to them, almost in a Faulknerian moment, as if the black women is Dilsey, and would save him as Dilsey saved those others.

" 'You can go a block down yonder and catch you a car take you to the railroad station, Sugarpie,' she said." Despite that help, it is clear that they are both lost, but the grandfather doesn't know it. We are back to that metaphor of the blind leading the blind. And the grandfather is really blind because he doesn't know that he is blind. Talk about alienation and the loss of oneself. They go through the city streets, and then something happens. Meanwhile, of course, like all teachers, Mr. Head justified what he was going to do on the grounds that it is sometimes necessary to teach a child a lesson he won't forget, particularly when the child is always reasserting his position with some new impudence. "The boy was dozing fitfully, half conscious of vague noises and black forms moving up from some dark part of him into the light."

What has been happening here? It's that scene where groceries are strewn all over the sidewalk and the boy has inadvertently caused an accident, created a mess on the street. Then the world comes in, as you and I know it all the time: the crowd to judge. What does the grandfather do? He hides. What did Jesus say? "I will be denied by all of them." What did Isaiah and Jeremiah say? "Start talking like us, you are going to end up outside of the city's gates." So first the grandfather hides, and then he betrays his own kin. That's what he has to "teach" this child, in this moment of huge irony—Flannery O'Connor offers irony writ large; every one of her stories bustles and brims with it. The grandfather, the teacher, the heady one, in order to save his own reputation, in order to come off clean, in order to stay ahead, denies his own grandson, his own student, his own moral mission. He exposes himself as what? As a fraud with feet of clay—and when he does, it is all the more discomforting because we all know of these moments.

They continue on their way, but now they are estranged. We have moved from the pride of the mind in all of its glory, as promised by the introduction, to knowledge and confusion as they go through that city and the light is lost to denial. Then we move to despair. They are lost. Then we come to that title again. They are walking at a remove from one another and by chance they stumble on a ridiculous piece of plaster that you and I would be embarrassed to even think about possessing and we'd mobilize our language to put its owners down, the way Head puts down his grandson: ignorant people, superstitious people, coarse people, people who are not sophisticated the way we are. What kind of people socioeconomically (There is a nice compound expression!) would have something like that on their front lawn? What does this item possess? It possesses the mystery of being unknown to the boy, and even to his grandfather. They look at it—it's a piece of trash, you and I say—but they look at it, together.

The grandfather, who earlier had said, "This is not my boy. I never seen him before," and the boy, who was not of a forgiving nature, as you and I aren't when we are treated that way, are now wandering in the desert, as in the biblical story. "The sun dropped down behind a row of houses and hardly noticing, they passed into an elegant suburban section where mansions were set back from the road by lawns with birdbaths on them. Here everything was entirely deserted"— as in the desert. "For blocks they didn't pass even a dog. The big white houses were like partially submerged icebergs in the distance."

Eventually, in that neighborhood, they meet a man, and he gives them directions. Then Mr. Head sees something. "He had not walked five hundred yards down the road when he saw, within reach of him, the plaster figure of a Negro"—notice the shift in the authorial voice, the narrator's, and the contrast to that of the people working at her behest—"sitting bent over on a low yellow brick fence that curved around a wide lawn. The Negro was about Nelson's size and he was pitched forward at an unsteady angle because the putty that held him to the wall had cracked." Similarly, the putty in this story has cracked and they are at a very unstable angle, the two of them. "One of his eyes was entirely white and he held a piece of brown watermelon." Talk about clichés and stereotypes, which strangely, in the story, lead us to the truth, in contrast to very clever interpretations, which are notably missing. "Mr. Head stood looking at him silently until Nelson stopped at a little distance. Then as the two of them stood there, Mr. Head breathed, 'An artificial nigger.' It was not possible to tell if the artificial Negro were meant to be young or old; he looked too miserable to be either. He was meant to look happy because his mouth was stretched up at the corners but the chipped eye and the angle he was cocked at gave him a wild look of misery instead. 'An artificial nigger!' Nelson repeated in Mr. Head's exact tone." The two of them are coming together again. "The two of them stood there with their necks forward at almost the same angle and their shoulders curved in almost exactly the same way and their hands trembling identically in their pockets. Mr. Head looked like an ancient child and Nelson like a miniature old man." O'Connor goes on to talk about the common defeat and says, "They could both feel it dissolving their differences like an action of mercy."

So here comes, in the inevitable, accidental, arbitrary, unpredictable, gratuitous way of the grace of fate, this moment of reconciliation—mediated through what? Again, a piece of trash. This piece of lawn sculpture that you and I are embarrassed to think about, that was described in a title that was so provocative that even Flannery O'Connor's friends wouldn't publish this story in literary quarterlies, admiring the story but recoiling from the title. They insisted that she change the title, but she refused, probably smiling to herself and thinking that she was making a point even in her refusal. She probably thought to herself "They can get me to change the title, but if they think that's what's going to make them better people and will make them no longer racist, boy, it's too easy, all too easy for them. Let them concentrate on words—not the letter but the spirit."

So Mr. Head and Nelson come together by this accidental moment and they go back on that train. As they return home, "the action of mercy covered his pride like a flame"—here comes some light—"and consumed it. He had never thought himself a great sinner before but he saw now that his true depravity had been hidden from him lest it cause him despair. He realized that he was forgiven for sins from the beginning of time, when he had conceived in his own heart the sin of Adam, until the present, when he had denied poor Nelson"—a spiritual moment, indeed. "He saw that no sin was too monstrous for him to claim as his own, and since God loved in proportion as He forgave, he felt ready at that instant to enter Paradise."

Then this in the final paragraph: "Nelson, composing his expression under the shadow of his hat brim"—the darkness—"watched him with a mixture of fatigue and suspicion . . . as the train glided past them . . . like a frightened serpent into the woods."

That is, like a snake, as in the Garden of Eden, in the very beginning of mankind's story. Isn't that interesting. There is that whole question of knowledge and what that leads to. These storytellers, one after another, rail against Harvard and Oxford and T. S. Eliot (in the case of Williams) and the experts who counsel families with their dreary psychological gobbledygook (in the case of Tillie Olsen), and there's that devastating portrait that Ellison gives us of intellectual life, so called. And now we find this: the old story of eating that apple and what happens afterward. We become so smart that we think we know everything—Mr. and Mrs. Know-it-alls.

Now we return to the train with O'Connor's words: "But as the train glided past them and disappeared like a frightened serpent in the woods, even his face lightened"—there's that light again, like the light two paragraphs up—"just as the moon, restored to its full splendor, sprang from a cloud and flooded the clearing with light." In story after story she has light hiding behind trees, those trees that are lined up in her landscapes and then in a certain moment will either appear or disappear. Anyway, the humbling of "head," what are you and I to do with that? If we're going to go and observe others and be smart about it, write books and articles about it, if we are going to go into the classroom as a teacher, or into a clinic as a doctor, or into a law office, if we're going to be that smart and that knowing, we had better watch out, because the more clever we are, the bigger the fall.

I sat in a coffee shop with a friend recently and we discussed a news story in the Sunday *New York Times;* some executives had been talking and didn't know there was a tape recorder nearby, so their words became a major story in the *Times.* We readers thus learned how people behave who have tremendous power and authority and have achieved enormous success, become business leaders. What did they say behind those closed doors? They talked cheap, hateful talk—and now they are exposed. You and I, too, we have to watch ourselves, don't we: how we think and regard others, speak of them. We have to take care, try to live honorably with one another; with our children and grandchildren; in our lecture halls; in our medical offices; wherever our knowledge has taken us—lest we stumble badly, as Flannery O'Connor has Mr. Head doing: a warning to all of us, herself included.

PART IV

Bringing It Home

Intellectuals and the religious search—
finding meaning in the life given to us.

Featured: Dorothy Day, Ignazio Silone, Elie Wiesel,
John Cheever, Walker Percy, Zora Neale Hurston,
and a Potato Chip Truck

FIFTEEN

Teachers, Beakers, and Professed Ideals

All of these books, in various ways, treat these questions: How does one live a life? What kind of a life? And for what purpose? These books help us wonder how these questions might be addressed if one were a social activist, as Dorothy Day was; or if one were a priest, a young curé, as is the central figure in the *The Diary of a Country Priest,* struggling to find justice in the unjust, horrible world of the 1930s; or if one were Jewish, as Elie Wiesel is, educated, sensitive, thoughtful, and aware that in the third and fourth decades of the last century, murder, mass murder took place at the behest of those who controlled a nation more educated than any other on the planet; or if one were black, as Zora Neale Hurston was, bearing witness to the fate of black people in this nation, since its birth and before its birth (by birth I mean the Declaration of Independence and the Constitution). In each instance, we are asked to wonder, How does one go through a life? Ignazio Silone keeps asking this question, through the teacher and others in *Bread and Wine.*

Silone is a pseudonym for a man whose name as a child was Secondo Tranquilli; he was born the very year that the last century began, 1900. Silone grew up in a hardscrabble part of Italy where there were mines and miners, just like those Orwell observed in

England—scraping the earth to produce crops or digging the earth for coal. When Secondo was fourteen there was an earthquake that, within ten seconds, reportedly killed thirty thousand people, including his mother (his father had died a few years before) and five of his brothers. From that event also came a memory that haunted him for the rest of his life. During the aftermath of the earthquake, Secondo watched a carriage bearing away the local bishop, while most people were either headed for hospitals, if there were any rooms, or for morgues. The sight of the bishop disappearing in such a time of human suffering made Secondo forever wonder about the ongoing struggle of Christianity and those who profess its ideals.

In all of Silone's writing there is tension between holiness and social realism, not to mention political reality. In *Bread and Wine,* we are given Pietro, a man escaping murderous politics and ideology (what a personal story that proves to be, given Silone's own life) who dons a priest's garb to go into hiding, and in his own strange and ironic way becomes even more holy than many of the priests he encounters along the way. But the person Silone had in mind for the Pietro of his novel was a man of the thirteenth century named Pietro da Morrone, the only pope who resigned his office in the midst of a huge political struggle within the Vatican. Church officials had brought him out of his monkish contemplation, put him in charge of the Catholic Church. He lasted half a year before he quit, telling his fellow cardinals that he couldn't stand it: the greed, the ambition, the manipulations of power were not for him—not in Jesus's name. So he went back to his holy isolation at the monastery.

People like Silone had to make their choices—ask themselves if one should accommodate themselves to this or stand up to it. Does one fight evil and, if so, at what cost to oneself and one's family? You should know that Silone lived half of his adult life in exile, hunted by the Fascist thugs who took his only surviving brother hostage, locked him up, and killed him, hoping to get Silone back so that they could capture and probably kill him.

In 1937, James Agee had just left Alabama to try to struggle with what had happened to him when he'd spent the summer there. He struggled with a similar moral trembling within himself, with his own moral anxiety. Orwell, we know, had also recently returned from Lancashire and Yorkshire and was trying to figure out how to present to an intelligent, well-to-do audience his sense of things from what he'd glimpsed in those mines. That same year, Silone was working in a factory, by choice. He was the child of a doctor of considerable wealth and had chosen to work in a factory to try to find out for himself what it was like to be a working person. Meanwhile, Franco had recently taken possession of Spain, aided and abetted by his dictator cohorts from Berlin and Rome. Orwell, who had seen plenty at home, would go to Spain to fight on behalf of the Republic. In 1937, *The Diary of a Country Priest* was published and *Their Eyes Were Watching God* was published. *Bread and Wine* was published that same year, just after Roosevelt, going into a second term, talked about one-third of our nation being "ill-clothed, ill-housed, ill-fed."

Here is a teacher speaking to those he once taught in *Bread and Wine:*

"In several of you there seemed to me to be something vital and personal that coincided with the observations that I had been able to make of each one of you during the years of lower and upper school; and that something was by no means commonplace. Now, what happened to the something later, when you went out into the world? . . . You must be between thirty-two and thirty-five if my arithmetic is not at fault, and you already look like cynical and bored old men. Seriously, that makes me wonder what is the point of teaching. You realize that to me that is no idle question. When a poor man who has lived with the idea of making decent use of his life reaches an age such as I have reached today, he cannot avoid asking himself what has been the result of his efforts, what the fruits of his teaching have been."

"School is not life, my dear Don Benedetto," Concettino said. "At school you dream, in life you have to adapt yourself.

That is the reality. You never become what you would like to become."

What does happen to us as we go through this life and try to fig-ure out to what purpose it is being spent, or ought to be spent? I often get letters from lawyers and doctors and businessmen, as they struggle to make decisions. They wonder what these books have meant and ought to have meant to them, what this life holds and why we are all here and for what purpose. At a minimum, perhaps we are here to show the ironic tension between some kind of holi-ness that has to do with you and me as readers, seeking some kind of inspiration that will excite us morally and prompt us to have thoughts about what we are going to do with this time given to us on this planet, as against your desire and mine to "get ahead"—or just move forward, really.

I should share a story here. When I came back from meeting Dr. Williams, I started taking premed courses, including organic chem-istry. In that course we had to prepare substances every week in the lab. Why is it that now, all these years, even decades after I took that course, I can still remember a substance I believe was called triphenyl-carbonate? I can even remember the zinc oxide we had to put in as we were preparing the solution. I don't remember anything else about the class, but I do remember very well the preparation of triphenyl-carbonate. It took me almost a week to prepare it. I was not very good in the lab. I was breaking flasks left and right, and my father was getting the bills and was writing me notes. He never called me; he wrote me notes because they are harder to dismiss than a telephone call. He would write me a note that would say, "If these bills keep coming in, I'm going to have to take another job to pay them!"

My dad was an engineer, a chemical engineer. (A psychiatrist can enter the story at this point!) In any event, toward the end of mak-ing the preparation, I came down to two layers in a separation flask. You know what you do if you are "politic, cautious, and meticulous," as Mr. Eliot urged us to be (well, half-urged us to be): you save everything. You pour out the first layer and put it into a beaker, if you are after the second layer. But I knew this stuff cold, or so I thought, and I was in a rush. Plus, I had broken a couple of beakers, and I didn't have one handy, so I opened the separation flask, figuring it was the top layer I needed, and let the bottom layer just go down the drain. As I did it a teacher who was helping us started laughing. As he laughed, he said, "You're going to have to do it all over again," and he continued laughing. He had watched me do it and watched the stuff go down the drain. He didn't say, "Stop," he didn't say, "Wait." He didn't even give me a poor mark for bad lab technique, which he could have done, helping me save the stuff. He watched it happen, and he laughed.

So what did I do? I lost control of myself. I was fed up with the course anyway, fed up with memorizing stuff that I promptly forgot after the examination. I was fed up with the craziness of that lab, and with my own incompetence and stupidity, compared to the performance of the more competent students, who seemed to know exactly what to do and how to do it and were always days ahead of me, many days ahead of me, and whose grades were always much better. The whole business seemed futile—I was headed nowhere fast. At this point, life itself seemed problematic; my whole sense of what mattered in life was consumed by the notion that if I could only do a little better in preparing triphenyl-carbonate, life itself would be better. Yet I had begun to ask myself if this incompetence stopped in the organic chemistry labs. I was about ready to quit the whole premed routine and return to my initial plan of being a high school teacher of English or history.

I'm ashamed to say that I looked at the face of that laughing teacher, with its smile, heard the laugh yet again, looked at the drain where everything was gone, and I uttered two words. Short words, punchy words. Having said to a Harvard instructor, "Fuck you," I walked out of the lab. That wasn't a moment of holiness; it was a moment of desperation bordering on craziness. At that time, Harvard didn't have psychiatrists ready to pick up the pieces, and I sometimes wonder what would have happened if I had been sent to one. Probably not much, or maybe they would have filled out a commitment paper and sent me away for "observation." But all I could do was get out of that lab. It was early in February, and it was snowing, and I just walked around. Right across the street there was an organist playing—his name was E. Power Biggs. He was playing Bach in the museum near the old chemistry lab, and I heard that coming out of the building. I walked in and sat there all by myself and thought to myself, "What the hell is wrong with you, with doing this lab stuff? What's this got to do with being a doctor?" I dared not call my parents—who would have admonished and questioned me in ways I knew I would not receive well.

Anyway, at that moment the world seemed as if it had come to an end. I couldn't talk to my parents. My mother would have, predictably, told me to pray for the man who had just done this, who had laughed at my misfortune. Well, what do you do when someone tells you to pray for someone? You get angry at the person who tells you to pray, that's one thing you do. My father would have complained about yet another broken flask, because I had also smashed the flask on the floor while screaming those two words.

So I went to see Perry Miller, a professor of English, who would later guide me through my struggles to understand Williams's *Paterson*. Luckily, he was not reluctant to make his own sardonic remarks about the very academic world he inhabited. I went in there and I was all choked up, but knew that I must not cry. I came into his office and I couldn't speak. I could see that he was impatient and had work to do, and that he had just got off the phone. He looked at me, and I looked back, and then he realized there was something wrong here. He told me to sit down, which I did. I thought to myself that I had better start talking; otherwise I would fall apart. So I started talking and telling him that I thought I was going to have to leave the place, the college, or at least change majors, career paths, that I had done something I should not have done. He asked what I'd done, and I told him. I will never forget what he said after listening. He said, "Oh, for a moment I thought you'd done something wrong." I came back at him and insisted that I *had* done something wrong. He stood his ground and said, "I'm not so sure."

Well, truth be told, I wasn't interested in his opinion of whether this was right or wrong. As you can imagine, I was interested in getting out of this jam one way or another. I needed some help. I needed a teacher's power to be exerted. This is an unjust world, but hopefully someone has the power to remedy injustice. Isn't that what a teacher is supposed to do, remedy injustice? Professor Miller said that he thought "Louie Fieser should hear this story." Louie Fieser was the professor of chemistry in charge of that course (as in Fieser and Feiser, the organic chemistry textbook). Well, I'd never thought of Professor Fieser as "Louie Fieser"!

The next thing I knew Professor Miller was on the phone, trying to track his friend "Louie" down. When he got him on the phone, Miller simply said, "I have something you need to know. There is a student here you need to speak with." So I went to see Professor Fieser and told him what had happened. He summoned in the instructor, and I heard a lesson being given about what teaching means. He spoke about honor and integrity and hope and healing and guidance and humor, how one must be honorable. I stood there thinking that this was also a reminder about how *I* ought to be honorable with myself—never mind the desire simply to get out of a jam and fulfill a requirement. Present in me was the fear that in some way I was vulnerable, that my future was in jeopardy. But yes, I had seen a glimpse of something that means more than even an A in organic chemistry. I had watched a teacher give a moral lecture to a younger colleague, while I, the student, sat, listened. Out of this period of deterioration and collapse, the walk in the snow, the sitting there and listening to that music, this experience made it all worth it. It would stick with me, I well knew, and it has. I was told to go back to the lab and do my work. And carefully, watching every step, I did.

What I remember best is the release, for a moment, from that kind of drudgery and grind that you and I know are not so essential. I don't mean to say it's unpleasant, but it's not essential. Yes, we all have to go through life's hurdles, but how many do we *have* to go through, and how does an experience affect our lives? At what point does that daily experience become deeply moral and spiritual in nature, so that the kinds of adjustments and compromises we make, and that we think to be right or wrong, whether desirable or useful, turn out to be wrong—and consequently become a burden for which we pay a high price?

I survived my anger and frustration this time, because a teacher was ready to help me and others intervened to temper the situation in which I'd found myself. I heard, as I had never heard before (and would never hear again as an undergraduate), a teacher taking on the institution that paid, supported, and furthered his professional life, and this caught me by surprise. Miller knew that there was some realism involved, that another teacher had to be phoned, that I needed someone to get me out of a jam. That tension haunts us through this life and informs many of the works discussed here. It informs the life of that curé in *The Diary of a Country Priest* who spots hypocrisy and phoniness in the church he has joined and given his life to, who doesn't know how to fulfill his pastoral mission while at the same time distancing himself from the very institution that sponsors that mission. The same tension also informs what Elie Wiesel went through as a survivor of the Holocaust, to the point that on the one hand he survives at all costs—just as Rilke said, with those three words: "Survival is all." Don't we know that? I guess that is what Perry Miller and I were conjuring up in his office. The first thing was to get me through organic chemistry, to go over and talk to the professor, explain myself—yes, enlist him, call upon his authority, his power. But then what? To what personal effect, what moral cost?

I now want to jump to this passage from *Night*:

Another time we had to load diesel engines onto trains supervised by German soldiers. Idek's nerves were on edge. He was restraining himself with great difficulty. Suddenly, his frenzy broke out. The victim was my father.

"You lazy old devil!" Idek began to yell. "Do you call that work?"

I know it's wrong to leap from an organic chemistry lab to a concentration camp, but there was, in both instances, the matter of power, of authority as it is wielded on us—and what we do with it as it confronts all of us at various points in our lives. Back to *Night:*

And he began to beat him with an iron bar. At first my father crouched under the blows, then he broke in two, like a dry tree struck by lightning, and collapsed.

I had watched the whole scene without moving. I kept quiet. In fact I was thinking of how to get farther away so that I would not be hit myself.

So it was with O'Connor's Mr. Head, who wanted to be farther away from his grandson—his own pride mattering more than his nearby grandson's flesh. We distance ourselves from those we love, from our own selves at times, our moral selves, in order to adjust and accommodate and win.

The passage from *Night* continues: "What is more, any anger I felt at that moment was directed, not against the Kapo, but against my father. I was angry with him, for not knowing how to avoid Idek's outbreak. That is what concentration camp life had made of me."

My roommates and I once broke our glasses in the fireplace after having a drink, carelessly messing up the room. We felt free to do that because someone used to come and clean up after us. You know what her name was; her name was "the biddy." She was nameless—talk about invisible man, invisible woman, in the second half of the twentieth century: a woman, a fellow human being, called a "biddy." And we would smile to ourselves at the biddy because of the way she spoke, the way she dressed. We weren't being horrible and cruel and laughing in her face, but we snickered and gave one another looks. Then we would go down and eat in the dining room, where we were served. If they didn't give us the right kind of food we would complain and make comments to those around us. We weren't particularly mean-spirited, but we were wrapped up in ourselves and we didn't have much time or energy to think about other people, those who were caring for us and serving us and cleaning up after us. So it went; we were flunking morality!

A few years ago I had a seminar devoted to stories about "American life." We read Raymond Carver's short stories and we looked at Hopper's pictures. There was a young woman who took that course, a freshman—but a bit older than the other students. She came from South Bend, Indiana. She told me that the first week she was here people immediately assumed that her father taught at Notre Dame. But her father didn't teach at Notre Dame; her father worked at one of the factories to the south of Chicago. She got a job working in the dorms. Now, there are no more "biddies" at Harvard, and she was one of the students who got a job with the dorm crew as she started her Harvard career. In the morning she would clean up rooms. She got through that seminar, and the next thing I knew she came to see me in her sophomore year. She came to see me to tell me that she was leaving Harvard. I asked why.

She said that she was sick and tired of this place. I asked her why and my shrink head started to go into overdrive. She said that she was fed up with everything. I said, Everything or something?, trying to get her to focus a little bit on something. Then I heard from her a story about an experience she had had—when someone had made an unwanted pass at her. Well, who was this person who had put the make on her? He was a classmate of hers. He had also taken the seminar with her, with us. He was very bright and wrote for the newspaper, often denouncing in editorials apartheid in South Africa (very powerful editorials). They had taken a course in "moral reasoning" together. They both got A's in that course. She said she was sick of this. If someone can get an A in "moral reasoning" and behave in this way in the morning to someone like her, then she didn't want to be any part of that institution. I rallied to the institution's side and said, "Look, this is the way life is."

She was visibly upset with that kind of remark. She said, "It may be how life is here, but it is not the kind of life I want to be part of."

I said, "If you go to Notre Dame, that life will follow you there."

She said, "How do you know?"

I said, "Don't you think this is the way life is?" Here, again, we were negotiating reality, social realism, psychological realism.

Then she got angry with me and she said, "You're encouraging me to overlook something that I don't want to overlook."

Then, alas, I figured out a way of being clever and I said, "Look, if Harvard has done nothing else but teach you that you can get an A in 'moral reasoning' and not be a good person, that is a considerable achievement." She was taking courses that were devoted to ethics, and pointing out that one can get all A's in them but flunk ordinary living (a line that Percy has in one of his novels)—including getting an A, of all ironies, in a course devoted to moral analysis. Moral analysis is not the same as living a moral life, she was reminding me. She was insisting upon the limits of the intellect, to my nervous discomfort at the time.

I heard this: "You're the one who mentions Emerson, and what he said about character being higher than intellect. What do you think he would make of this situation?"

I came back with "Well, he'd probably tell you to stay here and fight—fight an injustice." I suggested she go see the dean; I offered to call him, go with her.

She said to me, "No!" As for Emerson, she wondered if he really would tell her to stay. She had to go soon thereafter—leaving me feeling pretty glum. Pretty soon she had left not only that office, but also this university, to go to Notre Dame. I still remember that brief encounter, and still regard myself as a student of hers, prompted by her, a teacher, to have second thoughts about what matters and what doesn't matter—prompted, I confess, to give himself a flunking grade. These novels are meant to do for us their own kind of prompting.

SIXTEEN

Purpose and Potato Chips

I went this morning to speak at a service in Appleton Chapel (the chapel in the center of Harvard Yard), which I do every year in the fall. Every once in a while, as a student, I'd go there, listen to those bells. I'd go there not really with any religious purpose in mind, often just to sit and listen to the music and hope that somehow, some exam that I thought I'd done poorly on hadn't gone as badly as I expected—praying for one's survival. I went there after the organic chemistry moment I described in the previous chapter. I told Perry Miller I'd been there and he said, "That's the heart of churchgoing for so many of us. We try to get something for ourselves." Nevertheless, when I go in and sit there now, it is to go full circle—a reminder of life's journey, its memories.

On certain occasions memories come flooding back to us, and in a strange way because of those memories we become more of ourselves and more real (in some sense). We spend so much time *not* remembering, and maybe even being in such a fog, that at the end of various days, even weeks, even months, we scratch our heads, wondering where so much of our life has gone to, and to what effect? Why am I here, and to what purpose, if any?

As I noted on the first page of this book, when I was teaching I played Billie Holiday before every lecture. When I was a medical student I used to leave the Columbia Presbyterian Medical Center to go downtown to hear her. She used to play in the Village, at a particularly good jazz bar called the Blue Note. I went to get away from the hospital, and medical school classrooms, and my whole life there, and listen to that music, listen to her crying her heart out and singing about love and disappointment, and yearning and melancholy, and to see her live it out—to see that voice redeeming a wounded body, and a terribly hurt heart, and the past, and childhood, and all those experiences that you and I could pore over with the modern weight of psychology. And doing so, maybe we would stifle that spirit which triumphs over sociology and psychiatry and politics.

In all these circular ways of life, I was in the fourth year of medical school, in the emergency ward, when they brought Billie Holiday in—she'd overdosed. I felt torn between the responsibility to help out and the inclination just to stare at her, as we want to stare at people who are very large, who inspire us or titillate us or make us wonder, people in politics and in the movies, in any realm of public life. All of us are looking, searching for people to look up to and, boy, are we often disappointed, but we keep looking, don't we? We keep hoping. As a medical student, I had a right to be there at the hospital. I had the obligation to be that resident who was questioning her. What did we find out? We found out that she was a fellow human being who had given herself too much of a badly needed, self-selected medicine to help her with all her pain. They locked her up. Eventually she would die too young, the voice increasingly husky, but still able. How might she put it? "I like to carry a tune. I like to carry a tune."

My point of reference was, and often remains, the chapel. In other words, there is no way Billie Holiday is being played at Appleton Chapel in the 1950s or even the 1970s. Who cannot think of her who has heard her, or who has read *Their Eyes Were Watching God,* or

"The Death of Ivan Ilych," or *The Moviegoer?* Those books are our companions—they sing as she sang: a chorus of her to them! She and the protagonists of those books eat and drink together of bread and wine—and we with them. I think of the lawyer in "The Death of Ivan Ilych"—successful, prominent, practical, and a stranger to his family, to the people he works with, and finally, most ironically of all, to himself. I also think of the stockbroker in *The Moviegoer,* Binx Bolling is his name, cleverly elusive, bowling, rolling, driving in that open sports car through Gentilly, through New Orleans streets with their pretentious names: Elysian Fields, Desire. Entranced by a movie marquis, seduced by secretaries, something sultry, by their appearance: attracted to possessions, an incomplete attempt at "success" and accomplishment, driving along, rolling along, and heading where and for what? Heading toward thirty? "Here I am," as Eliot (and Dante, before him) reminded us. "Here I am in the middle of this journey."

We encounter this same sense of journey in Zora Neale Hurston's *Their Eyes Were Watching God.* At four o'clock in the morning in Belle Glade, Florida, there is a place called the Publicit Zone, where hundreds of men and women, and sometimes children with them, assemble. People stand and are bid for by the cruel leaders of migrant farm crews. But before that, one can go into Belle Glade bars with names like Last Chance or Last Night or First Night or Here We Are (talk about existentialism!), "Here We Are" blazing in lights. Inside are the jukeboxes where Billie Holiday can be heard singing.

My wife and I, in the mid-sixties, had found our way to those places in certain cities, in part through Ruby Bridges, because of an uncle of hers. Instead of going into New Orleans or up to Chicago, the nomad that he was, the harvesting man that he was, he had found his way to that migrant-worker crew in Florida. That crew starts in Florida, moves its way up the Atlantic coast, and ends up in Maine.

Here is how Hurston describes such a scene:

Day by day now, the hordes of workers poured in. Some came limping in with their shoes and sore feet from walking. It's hard trying to follow your shoe instead of your shoe following you. They came in wagons from way up in Georgia and they came in truck loads from east, west, north and south. Permanent transients with no attachments and tired looking men with their families and dogs in flivvers. All night, all day, hurrying to pick beans. Skillets, beds, patched up spare inner tubes all hanging and dangling from the ancient cars on the outside and hopeful humanity, herded and hovered on the inside, chugging on to the muck. People ugly from ignorance and broken from being poor.

All night now the jooks clanged and clamored. Pianos living three lifetimes in one. Blues made and used right on the spot. Dancing, fighting, singing, crying, laughing, winning and losing love every hour. Work all day for money, fight all night for love. The rich black earth clinging to bodies and biting the skin like ants.

The narrator's voice distances itself from the language, which by now you and I have become so connected to—the language of Janie and her friends, those husbands, and the language, ultimately, of connectedness. "Only connect," said E. M. Forster; "I-Thou," said Martin Buber. All of this reminds us to trust, finally, someone else, and thereby finally find some self-respect that is more than one's own egoism.

Hurston gives us Janie and her search, which we can surely connect to Binx and his—but a search for what, the sight of what, of whom? Whether it be a movie's world, or a pear tree, or ultimately, God willing, a fellow human being. What do we seek? And what is it that Binx struggles with so much as he moves through time and loses so much of himself: a stranger to himself. Even as Janie can be married and have no idea of who this other person is, really. Then there are those moments in which we recover ourselves and suddenly realize who we are, and those moments when we recover ourselves collectively: *shared* moments of recognition and understanding.

I remember once driving home on Route 2 from Cambridge to my house in Concord. But Route 2 for those of us driving on it is often a period of aloneness, and often we forget who we are. Walker Percy wrote an essay that was published in the *Partisan Review* called "The Man on the Train." And what he describes, really, was a prophecy of what he would do later in his novel *The Moviegoer.* He describes a stockbroker coming in from the suburbs to Wall Street, and getting off the train and suddenly realizing that he has no memory of even getting on the train. Don't you and I know that experience from moments in our own lives—how we can go through a long swath of time and suddenly "come to," and become aware of how unaware we are? Those lost minutes may have turned into longer stretches, even hours. Is it forgetfulness? Is it what the Danish theologian Kierkegaard called "everydayness"—meaning that part of our existence that we don't look at very much? Some psychiatrists aver that we spend our time forgetting because we have "problems" or "issues" (those dreary words of our time). Yet maybe we forget because maybe not to forget is more than we can bear; we ourselves (no longer forgetful) take stock morally, spiritually, humanly—we confront the great existentialist questions that Camus and Sartre and Simone Weil and others have put to us.

In any event, driving along on Route 2, I suddenly found cars all over the place and no movement. It wasn't all that late in the day. The drive home should have been a breeze, but now there was a huge traffic jam, as far as the eye could see. There were cars everywhere, and people were getting out of them. I saw a bit of movement down the hill, and followed it. I also saw, soon enough, what had blocked all of us: a truck had overturned. Then I saw people picking things up from the road and walking away from this site, holding things. They all were clutching the same things, which as I got closer I realized were potato chip bags.

The truck was from the Tri-Sum potato chip company in Leominster, Massachusetts. Right there on Route 2 were hundreds of bags of potato chips! Pretty soon I had some in my hands, one for each of my three children and two for my wife and myself. That makes five. Greedily, I held on to five bags of potato chips. The truck driver, who had worked his way out of his cabin, and was clearly unhurt, was saying, "Take them all." We all were lingering, holding bags of potato chips, and we were talking to one another. We were noticing the day and the weather and one another, and thinking of how wonderful it would be to give those bags of potato chips to our families, how important and with meaning this all was. We were noticing the road and the houses and people who were coming out of those houses, and we were laughing! We were *with* one another—a veritable community. We went back to our cars after a few minutes, and finally we were able to get going. And it all ended. We moved on—having found a kind of purpose in a road's ample offering of potato chips.

I came home with these potato chips and went into the house and started offering them to my children and my wife, and they looked at me as if I had just escaped from a nearby psychiatric institution. My oldest son said, "Dad, did you take those from someplace?" He'd been tipped off by the lack of any shopping bag. He saw a strange look on my face that told him he was right: I *had* taken them "from someplace." I had found a "place" because, as you know, as you drive on this road, the same road every day, the same people passing you or you passing them, you are utterly anonymous, belong to no "place," don't know these fellow drivers, or the people who live in the houses along the road, and you do not take the time or energy to care.

Now, how does it go in the Bible? We looked at one another through a glass. Sometimes we see through it and sometimes we are face-to-face, and other times it is dark. But I still remember that moment with the potato chips and talking with and laughing with—meeting—the people on that public road; and sometimes when I am aware enough I think back to its magic. The magic of what, though?

Maybe it's the magic of human relatedness that somehow slips into an existence that can all too often deny it—a "rotation," Kierkegaard called it, when suddenly life exists for us, powerfully; we are aware, not in a haze or a fog, and this kind of reality, human reality, is ours. "Repetition" it is called in *The Moviegoer.*

I want to jump again, this time to lines given to us by Zora Neale Hurston: "The wind came back with triple fury, and put out the light for the last time. They sat in company with the others in other shanties." Shanties: you know what Kierkegaard said about Hegel and his big-shot elaborate philosophical system, his entire theory? He said that Hegel builds a huge castle and beside it you and I live in little shacks. Hegel tells us everything except how to get through an ordinary day. Often we learn everything except how to be halfway human to one another, to ourselves, and to others. More of Hurston: "They sat in company with the others in other shanties, their eyes straining against crude walls and their souls asking if He meant to measure their puny might against His. They seemed to be staring at the dark, but their eyes were watching God."

A hurricane, a truck that turns over, a mistake in an organic chemistry lab or a business meeting, a deadline missed, a disappointment for a parent or in a relationship that we have to leave behind, and the whole world comes crashing down—revealing what? Revealing ourselves and who we are. What if everything isn't handed to us and we don't get everything we want? We might shift our vision, let our eyes look elsewhere: yes, toward the God who is present for us in others, their lives such a big part of ours.

Pay attention, in *Their Eyes Were Watching God,* to the language, to the manner in which Hurston talks about people when she attends to the ways that people learn to turn on themselves by virtue of the shadings of their skin, the texture of their hair, their gender and status, and think and remember that this is not only Hurston's world of African-American agricultural workers; it's your world and it's my world. It's the world that we learn as we gauge one another, rank one another, the prestige of names, places, occupations: hierarchies

galore—all of this a kind of "sorting," as Tillie Olsen reminded us in
"O Yes." We are ever hungry for our own applause, and if we can get
others to join in, that is even more fulfilling.

Hurston writes about the high yellow and the darker shades of
people. As we read and understand "the mark of oppression" in
"them," please let us come back to ourselves: to the way we regard
others—how *they* write, what *they* say, how *they* dress, *their* accents,
their lineage. Percy and Hurston both show, in their stories, how social issues, concerns, considerations connected to class, to educational and social background become aspects of our lived lives, yours
and mine. We can be beaten down by life, but we can soar, too—
whether we are doctors, stockbrokers, or farmworkers. All of us have
eyes seeking, in some way, meaning in this world, seeking direction
and purpose.

You talk about Billie Holiday giving herself a shot of heroin; we
can do that without a needle. We can get high on ourselves; we can
get haughty about ourselves. I trained in *this* hospital and I had *this*
doctor for my mentor! You and I can fill in the blanks. We know this;
we talk about Percy's "malaise," the downside of things. But we have
moments of self-recognition and understanding about what we have
learned about ourselves, about others—about how fragile and vulnerable we feel. That emotion tells us that some sore moment has
been touched upon that struck a chord of truth. The more we laugh
at things such as the celebrity magazines that dot the landscapes of
our supermarkets, the more we reveal the pain of our striving.

Let us drive, then, in our cars through Percy's Gentilly or, in
Hurston, harvest those crops, and find love, and struggle mightily
against the hurricanes of this life as they reveal these truths:
Hurston's Vergible "Tea Cake" Woods, and the madness of fate and
life—rabies become God's will or fate's reckoning. The young antic-
ipate life's story, but love experienced and known, treasured, can
make for all of us a beloved community. No wonder, then, that you
and I can take the eyes Hurston gives us in that novel, can take her

story's eyes and make them our own, let them carry us across barriers and find in fellow readers a certain kind of recognition.

I remember watching some children playing in a park while an arborist was working on a tree; he was way up there. He was cutting some branches and the children were absolutely enthralled. We were walking by, not noticing. Some of the children started exclaiming, "He's great! He's great!" I thought to myself, Isn't *that* "great." Whether it be someone cutting tree limbs or reading from a book that we own because of a tree, whatever it is, our eyes are seeking those who can be, can do; our eyes are watching for accomplishments beyond us, and we are hoping against hope that we, too, can be part of what our eyes seek, what we find arresting.

SEVENTEEN

The Heart of Healing

Walker Percy struggles in all of his novels with the question of consciousness—with how close we come to both realizing and forsaking the very essence of what we are. He knows that we are creatures of language, and that through language, with a kind of awareness, we can communicate to ourselves, as we speak inwardly all the time. It was Freud's genius to understand how we do it at night in our dreams, while all of us work to understand how we communicate to others, and with others, during our waking hours. Language is the heart of being, and it is through language that we can search for a shared self, with others.

In his novel *The Moviegoer,* Percy began this kind of exploration of language with the character Binx Bolling, and he continues that theme in his novel *The Last Gentleman.* The central figure in the latter novel is named Will Barrett—or "will bear it." Bear what? Bear life? "I will bear it": those words come out, self-spoken, as you and I try to bear so much, or do more than bear it—try to transcend our times, our circumstances, our setbacks, or even our triumphs.

Many years ago, I was writing a biographical essay about Percy, and I would go down to New Orleans to visit him. As it turned out, he was a great aficionado of the various kinds of whiskey and bourbon that are indigenous to the southern bars we used to frequent. It was during a time when I was also talking with migrant farmworkers in Florida. Those conversations helped my wife, Jane, and me to connect to the Hurston novel *Their Eyes Were Watching God,* which we had stumbled onto at a time when it was out of print in the 1960s. That's a puzzle—the reasons certain novels go out of print and then come back into being, resurfacing not only on their own merits, but on the historical forces that make them either of little or of great consequence.

Originally, it was a public health nurse whom we knew in Belle Glade who gave us an old, weathered copy of the Hurston novel, which helped us to understand something about migrant farmworker women, which is one of the concerns of this novel. What does it mean to be a woman and to have to deal with men as they exert themselves and wield their power in a particular kind of a world? In a way, Percy shows us the flip side of that human scene: Binx and his girls and the way he is with them as a statement about his vulnerability, his hurt and pain, his almost pitiable side, and his search for redemption.

I remember one woman, a migrant farmworker, a Floridian who goes each year to Maine, but not on vacations, putting things this way: "I will feel tired and sick. I will feel mean. I don't like anyone, even my own children. I've been out picking. I have no strength left. I won't last the night. My lungs are bad, and I can't catch the air very good. Suddenly I'll see my youngest child and she'll be coming to me and I'll be different. It's not a second breath of air. I'm still struggling for the first breath." The reason she brought that up is because I said to her, "You mean you get a breath of fresh air?" She was wonderfully willing to criticize and reprimand me indirectly and politely, the person who had interrupted her train of thought. She went on: "I'm still struggling for the first breath. It's God giving me strength. It's me becoming a different me. I'm free of my old weary self. I ask the minister how it happens. He told me that it doesn't always happen, just sometimes. It happens when I see a certain look in my child's face. She needs me bad and I want so bad to be good to her." Obviously, a moral life is being expressed here, in all of its complexity.

She continued: "And I want so bad to be good for her, even if I have been out all day under that sun on my knees picking the beans. She is my last one, you know? I've made a lot of mistakes with the others." When I heard that, I thought of Tillie Olsen's story "I Stand Here Ironing." She said, "Some of them have turned out real bad, don't ask about them. I wish I could have been a better mother. I wish I could have offered my children a better life. I wish I had married a better man—instead of the one who would walk about and leave me and come back and leave me bearing a child. He's been married to the wine bottle all his life, to tell you the truth. The minister talks of the devil. Well, that devil must be the one who makes all that wine and sells it. The crew leader is the devil, too. He is a wicked man. There are a lot of times, though, when it's been me who is wicked. You mustn't always try to excuse yourself by pointing the finger at someone else." This is a leap into the highest realm of civilization. A leap that some of us don't always make with such ease as we find various people to put down.

She went on: "In church I look at myself and I know I've sinned. I don't stand up for what I believe. I let the crew leader push me around. I just do whatever everyone else does and I fight to breathe. But when I see my little child, the last one I'll ever have, smiling and coming toward me and the sun is going down, then I'm another person and I'm free and I feel like I could hold the whole world in my hands, just like we sing about in church. There she is, my child. I lift her up. Let me tell you, I've forgotten about my troubles breathing, and I've forgotten about my other troubles, and I'm a new person, tired as I was and late in the day though it is—a new person. For a few minutes I'm almost a stranger to myself. That's because I feel like this new person, almost like God has breathed His strength into me and I'd said, 'Yes, I'll use that strength; yes, I will.'"

Binx is also a stranger to himself in long swatches of this novel, as you and I occasionally are to ourselves, maybe more than occasionally. We forget moments and hours. We go through routines. We memorize, cram, crunch numbers, run errands, and make room for the next spell—of what? Of obligatory obedience, of saluting, of getting through a day and forgetting what the whole purpose of this life is, if it's of any purpose at all. Sometimes, in order not to acknowledge who we are, we summon labels and categories. When *The Moviegoer* was given the National Book Award, the judges brilliantly pointed out how it avoids what they call the "mannerisms of the clinic." What an incisive phrase that is and apt—those "mannerisms" that inhabit, if not infest, our daily lives. Percy and others who have read Kierkegaard and Gabriel Marcel know a certain phrase, "fact men." You can go very far these days by being a very successful fact person, with language to boot.

I remember talking once with a stockbroker, not Binx, who was telling me a lot about his own struggles with mannerisms and factuality: "When you are in bed and trying to catch a few hours of sleep, you have these thoughts. You wonder if there is anything bigger than you. Is there a God? How do I know? What should you do with your time here? I don't know. If you had another chance, how would you live your life? I don't have the answer to that one either, but it bothers me more than the other questions. Maybe some people know how to do things better than I do. I don't claim to know any secrets about life. Those ministers do, but I don't listen to them. I just try to get through the day. Is there anything else to do? In the middle of the night when you can't sleep, you think that maybe there is a better way to live a life. But in the morning there is no time for that kind of thinking. I have to get up and go to work. If I don't, well, I'll be wondering about a lot of things—namely, where the next meal is coming from."

The real-life version of Binx went on, telling me about his earlier life:

I was born in Arkansas and we were pretty well-off. My father lost everything in the Depression, though, and he was never the same. He got a lot back, but he never got back his self-confidence. He never really trusted anyone again. Then my mother died and he found out that she had been cheating on him. So he just made money and made money and he got himself a different girlfriend every year.

He was a smart man. He used to tell me not to be so nice to everyone, and I finally learned my lesson. A kid stole some of my money and my watch; a girl made out with me, and then went on to someone else the day after she told me I was her only one. My wife and I, we have an understanding: Don't ask too much of the other. She goes her way and I go mine. We've stayed together for the kids. We are not enemies. We have good times together, but if I have to go out of town for business, I don't get the third degree from her. I haven't been back to Arkansas in twenty years. I have a lot of property there. A lawyer handles everything for me. If you have a good lawyer you are in good shape. Without a lawyer, you are nothing.

Until I heard him say that, I had never realized the existentialist aspect of American law. He said, "Without a lawyer, you are nothing. You're in trouble. You are at the mercy of everyone. You have to watch yourself."

That is what we call an "interview," part of "research"—ironically, a person is talking indirectly of his "search." *The Moviegoer* is a story meant to help us comprehend this kind of narrative recitation, not unfamiliar in certain respects to all of us, as we attend the words of others. At times, however, there are interruptions, and Percy, getting a little didactic, tells us about "rotations" and "repetitions," those breakthrough experiences that stun us and stick with us and inform our lives, our reflective lives, and maybe give us moral, if not spiritual pause. You will notice in that novel the way war and illness bring people up short. You will notice all through literature the way novelists and playwrights and poets use these moments, these important moments of our lives, as a way to map our lives, psychologically, emotionally, and, again, to use that overworn word, existentially. Who does not remember the sudden moment of awareness when something disappointing, saddening, or surprising happened, or we got some good news or bad news—any news that takes us out of "everydayness," as Percy puts it? By that he means a level of un-awareness, if not unwitting boredom, that characterizes some as-pects of living for so many of us.

Stop and think about the Tolstoy story "The Death of Ivan Ilych." The story offers a lawyer facing death and wondering where his life was spent—not unlike Binx, the stockbroker. Who are these people and what are they struggling with? Who is Ivan Ilych, and what dies in him? What is Tolstoy getting at, through a story about a lawyer and his family and the arrival of cancer and a painful death? Such events are not exactly an extraordinary aspect of the annals of med-icine; every day thousands and thousands of people go through what Tolstoy describes. Why does Tolstoy tap into this, and what is he telling us with this kind of story? Why do I lump all these stories to-gether?

Please also read Tolstoy's "Master and Man"—about a business-man in a rush to make a deal despite a Russian winter, which will not be any obstacle to him. He'll let the others stop and spend the night in the Russian nineteenth-century equivalent of a motel. This businessman wants to win, so he pushes his servant and the horse to get there fast. The winter intervenes and they are going around and around in circles—courtesy of Tolstoy. The master, the man, the horse: round and round in circles they go, as some of us occasionally think maybe we are doing in our lives. Eventually, the master, spot-ting a really dangerous storm and getting nowhere, decides that he will continue to be an "entrepreneur"—that's not the word Tolstoy uses, but it's one that you and I know. Charged with assertiveness, he leaves behind the servant, and the sledge, and pushes on to his desti-nation to get there and to be first—top of the class.

But he continues to go around in circles. He finds his way back to the servant, who is sitting there obediently, and to the sledge. Then the master realizes that he is going to die, that this storm is going to get the better of him. Weakened, vulnerable, and suddenly aware of things as he has never been before, he looks at this man, this fellow human being, and at that horse, and is charged in his mind by the motions of his heart. He takes off his coat and gives it to his servant. He even offers what warmth is left in his body to that servant. You live, I will die. But I will die with honor. I will die as a moral human being. I will die decently. The way I die will be my only hope—now for you, not only for myself.

Percy read Tolstoy, read him again and again, and read Dostoyevsky, again and again. He knew their stories; he knew Ivan Ilych, the dying lawyer, self-absorbed, cut off even from his own family, his wife and children, and from his law partners. But something happens to this dying man and his servant—the servant, as in Jesus, who serves. And something happens, too, to Ivan Ilych. "The Death of Ivan Ilych"—the title itself is hugely ironic. It's really the story of the death of the kind of person who Ivan Ilych is. It is really the story of the birth of Ivan Ilych, the redemption of Ivan Ilych. That is the motion that is also going on all through *The Moviegoer*—the search for meaning.

My own mother died of cancer a few years ago, in Massachusetts General Hospital. She had lived a long and happy life, so far as one can judge. In any event, she had a comfortable life and a long and happy marriage. As she was dying, she was in a comfortable, airy room by herself with her books, the books she and my father used to read to each other: novels of Tolstoy, Dostoyevsky, works by Eliot and others, many of them now on the reading list for this course. In the hospital for the final time, she was accompanied by her beloved *Anna Karenina* and also some of Tolstoy's short fiction. My father called me up and said, "Your mother is sleeping with Tolstoy at Mass General." When I visited her I saw the stack of those books, with bookmarks tucked into various pages, denoting passages to which she returned again and again.

A few weeks after her admittance, I was called by the nursing station on her floor and told that I ought to come right away. They didn't say any more, just that. They didn't need to. I quickly raced in, stopping off at Mather House dormitory to pick up my son, and together we went to Mass General. My mother was still conscious, but going fast. She said good-bye to me, and to my son, her oldest grandchild, and asked him how he was doing on his hour exams. I was struck by the fact that she could have that kind of interest at that moment in her life. I realized that it was that kind of interest that probably got me through my own academic life, just as surely as you have parents who've helped you get through yours with that kind of interest and investment that never dies.

Then she died. This was not the first time I had seen someone die. Because I had been prepared for this for some time, I quickly left the room and started going through the procedures that relatives go through: signing papers, telling the doctors that they can perform an autopsy if they want to, and on and on and on. I was doing this and that, and then was ready to leave the hospital. I had been a bit detached from her illness, rather than overwhelmed by it, even as she was alive. I knew exactly what was happening to her and I knew this was the end. My son was considerably less detached, but I pulled him out of what, at the time, was a kind of emotionality that I just didn't want to have around me. I wanted to get out of there and go home and prepare for the next day's work.

So I signed everything, had my son Bobby at my side, and we were starting to leave when suddenly I felt a hand on my shoulder. I glanced around and down and I found myself looking at a rather short woman, whom I noticed was somewhat familiar to me. I realized that this was the woman who had been taking care of my mother—a "ward helper" we used to call them in hospitals. She was a short black woman, a little stout. She had on a uniform, and there she was with a hand on my shoulder. I asked if I had left something behind. She said: "Your mother." She paused. It was a jarring observation. Then she said, "Your mother—you should spend a little time with your mother before you leave." I looked at her and I wondered what she was trying to tell me. So she repeated herself: "Go back into the room and sit with your mother for a minute or two."

I felt annoyed and put upon and aggrieved—bothered to be upbraided in this fashion. But I went back and sat down, and once I was in that chair, which before I had not sat in—I'd stood during the last moments of my mother's life—once I sat down, my mind snapped, and I started having memories that went way back to my childhood, memories of being taken by her on the train to visit her family in Chicago, going to her beloved Chicago Art Institute to look at some of the Renoirs and the Hopper paintings that she adored. These moments connected me to my own life, as they had coursed through hers. And all of this was pushed upon me by a woman who hadn't studied psychiatry or psychoanalysis, who didn't know anything about Walker Percy and *The Moviegoer* or Leo Tolstoy and "The Death of Ivan Ilych" or "Master and Man." Maybe we can get her a degree and push her on to college. Maybe in college she'll major in psychology and will learn about "conditioning and learning" and "groups" and "cognitive life" and "defense mechanisms" and the "id and the ego" and the "superego" and "conflict resolution" and "childhood neurosis" and "transference phenomenon" and "countertransference." Words! Theories! Knowledge!

But here, her precious being was encompassed by a heart that worked, an inwardness of spirit that she wanted to connect with someone else's spirit: through her own few memories of a patient, one she'd bathed and fed and listened to so that she knew about the woman's children and grandchildren, her husband and his foibles and his achievements. A family's life, which she had attended and taken to heart, known and felt, and acknowledged. That kind of connection is what Percy had in mind as he struggled with this novel *The Moviegoer,* haunted by the specter that so often these days, in this contemporary world, solid and continuing connection is missing from our lives. So he tells us, at the end of his story in a beautiful moment:

> I shrug. There is only one thing I can do: listen to people, see how they stick themselves into the world, hand them along a ways in their dark journey and be handed along, and for good and selfish reasons. It only remains to decide whether this vocation is best pursued in a service station or—
> "Are you going to medical school?"
> "If she wants me to."

Percy himself lost his father when he was twelve years old, a prominent lawyer who committed suicide. His mother died two years later, in an automobile accident. When he got out of medical school, in 1941, and started a residency, he was looking forward to enlisting in the army and serving in World War II, as his brother had. But he contracted tuberculosis and for years lay on his back, expecting to die. If you have read Thomas Mann's *The Magic Mountain* and know about Kafka and his experiences with coughing up blood, and the way that was connected to the type of writing he did, you will know what Percy went through. Out of all those years of vulnerability and weakness and ill health came a kind of health that no amount of therapy can bring. A health that had to do with a mind that became directly wired to what this life means. Out of that illness came essays and novels, a distinguished career, a very odd career for a physician, but maybe exactly the kind of career that doctors need, that at least one of them needs to experience, for the sake of the rest of us: a career aimed at getting to the heart of what true healing is.

EIGHTEEN

Cheever Is Tough

I have read many papers in which students tell me about what they've worked through; they tell of their efforts to get into college, recount the costs as well as the achievements, and wonder to what effect and what purpose. Even some teachers who have been around for the long haul have some of the same questions go through their minds, not precipitated by the need to write a paper for a course but galvanized by an experience of another kind of course, called the course of life. We attend faculty meetings, see something that was written by oneself or one's colleagues, and wonder how it is that one ends up being the person one is. Sometimes success and achievement become not only habits but a personal self-belief, so that what you are left with, as poetic justice would demand, is yourself, large warts and all.

Facing yourself like that is tough, and John Cheever's writing, in helping us to do so, is tough. This toughest task, however, brings us close to what we are, or what we want to be.

Cheever grew up in Quincy, Massachusetts. He was of white, Anglo-Saxon Protestant background. It was a WASP background all right, but also one with poverty. His father had at one point been very well off but was ruined by the Great Depression. Cheever felt a kind of pain: to be in possession of privilege and yet to know poverty and vulnerability, to feel "in" and yet to be "out." He grew up near the end of the Boston subway's Red Line, and he never went to college. He was a "troubled" and troublesome man. He had, as they say in my line of work, "a problem with authority." He doused his pain in alcohol all his life, soaking it up. What an irony, because we know the pain that such self-medication brings, the suffering it causes families. Some in his family have written about it, including his father and his children. Not a nice fate to have family members who reflect on the costs they bore for one's achievement.

Cheever started writing when he was in his late teens, and by the time he was in his mid- to late twenties, stories started pouring forth. He lived on Manhattan's Upper East Side and had a home in Westchester, north of the city. Each morning he would leave his apartment and take the elevator downstairs. He rented a room in the basement, but he left the apartment in a Brooks Brothers suit, elaborately kept, so that he could feel like all those other people who were going to law, business, and financial offices. He would go down to the basement and write. His stories would chronicle a world that he witnessed and was part of and understood and embraced, even loved. They described environments and people and circumstances he knew so well that it can hurt for us to get to know this segment of life through him.

Here is the beginning of Cheever's "The Housebreaker of Shady Hill": "My name is Johnny Hake. I'm thirty-six years old, stand five feet eleven in my socks, weigh one hundred and forty-two pounds stripped, and am, so to speak, naked at the moment and talking into the dark."

Cheever is thereby tipping his hand as a storyteller. He strips Johnny bare, morally and psychologically, leaves him wondering in the dark, as Dante had his various protagonists wonder and wander in the dark. This darkness is much like the darkness we have been told about in this past century: the darkness of Hitler and Stalin; the darkness of the Great Depression; the darkness that these writers have given us from Alabama and Yorkshire, from Paterson, in New Jersey; the darkness in those motels and restaurants of Carver's, the darkness in the migrant-farmworker fields plowed by Hurston; and the darkness that accompanied, in several ways, an "invisible man" through his journey.

In "The Housebreaker of Shady Hill," Johnny Hake goes into his neighbor's house in the middle of the night and fetches a wallet for himself. This is a literal wallet, but it causes us to ask what we do, take, and/or covet. How many of us have taken things from our friends or from our neighbors? To what depths, to what degree— what will we sacrifice? Two Christmases ago, December 25, 1994, reading our paper of record, the *New York Times,* spread out on the floor, on page number 21, I saw this headline: "Friendliness May Have Been Ruse for Burglaries in Small Towns."You can't get much more American than that.

The article said, "Everyone in town knew that Roger Harlow, a friendly, talkative Sunday-school teacher and insurance agent, often dropped in at people's homes. But they may not have known how often, the police say. Mr. Harlow, 46,"—he is ten years older than Johnny Hake—"has been charged with 85 burglaries of the homes of acquaintances, including golfing buddies, family friends, employees and widows. The police say Mr. Harlow may have been so talkative so that he could learn when people planned to be away from home. Then, investigators say, he would drop by and take small valuables: coins, stamps, jewelry, baseball cards, cash." I used to tell my mother that if I could only save enough of those baseball cards, they would mean something someday. She used to ask what I meant. I said, "I could sell them." Then I got her second-level response: "You're interested in collecting things because you want to sell them." Trying to be clever, I eventually was verbally slapped down. Getting back to Roger Harlow: " 'On occasion, he would even manage to get them out of the house—for lunch or something— and while they were gone, he would burglarize the house, then show up late for lunch,' said Police Chief Joe Dagon." Pretty clever guy we've got here, as the article shows: Mr. Harlow has been accused of using these ruses:

- Showing up late for golf games so he could loot his partners' homes.

- Consoling a grieving widow, even crying with her, only to return to her home when she was gone and steal an heirloom ring.

- Going to dinner at a restaurant with a friend, then excusing himself and taking a pair of antique diamond earrings from her home before returning to the meal about 20 minutes later.

I hope you all feel free, as in a Hitchcock film, to laugh.

Looking back, people now say there were warning signs. Mr. Harlow seemed to go out of his way to ask about people's plans and where they would be. Then, later, he would be found in their homes, always with a quick explanation—he had noticed the front door open and was making sure everything was all right, or he had knocked on the door and thought he heard someone holler to come in.

But this is a small, trusting town of 13,000, northwest of Peoria. People do not often lock their doors, and they take a friend at his word—even when he is standing in their living room.

"I'm kind of mad that he took advantage of me," said Darrel Johnson, who knew Mr. Harlow from the country club and the Elks. "I'm mad at myself, too, for leaving the house open."

"Not any more," Johnson added; that's the power of a thief.

Mr. Harlow did not clean people out, the police say. He is accused of taking a few valuables for sale to dealers and rearranging the rest to hide the theft.

"It was a very slick operation, and so nobody suspected him for a long, long time," Chief Davis said. "If you knew the guy and talked to the guy, you wouldn't suspect it either. He's very pleasant, friendly."

After being arrested coming out of Mr. Johnson's house with a pocketful of coins in August, Mr. Harlow gave the police a 26-page statement detailing dozens of burglaries. Freed on bail, he began contacting victims to apologize and ask if they would pressure the authorities for leniency, the *Kewanee Star Courier* reported. Those repeated contacts with potential witnesses got him sent back to jail, where he awaits trial for early next year.

Mr. Harlow, who is married and has two children, has pleaded not guilty. His lawyer did not return repeated telephone calls.

One resident here . . . has known the Harlows for 15 years. The families attended high school football games together, spent Christmas Eves together, even planned to start a joint vacation. . . . "It still hurts a lot," [she] said. "It's like a death in the family."

I went to talk to my former undergraduate adviser, Perry Miller, about the situation. He said, "Look what you are going through; we all go through in this life. Let him do it. There will be a time when he'll pay." Well, he was offering judgment and retribution to me over *time,* and I guess that appeased me. I knew in my heart that what that guy was doing was something I was tempted to do. There is a difference between people who want to do things and don't do them and people who actually do the things that we all are tempted to do but don't. With the power of his story Cheever connects with us, reminds us of our lusts, and some of the desperation that prompts those lusts—lest we become all too self-righteous, full of ourselves, unwilling to take a peek at our never-ending temptations.

In "The Housebreaker of Shady Hill," Cheever switches into the French mode: "Shady Hill, as I say, a *banlieue* and open to criticism by city planners, adventurers, and lyric poets, but if you work in the city and have children to raise, I can't think of a better place." Some sociologists have been saying that for years. Cheever continues:

> My neighbors are rich, it is true, but riches in this case mean leisure, and they use their time wisely. They travel around the world, listen to good music, and given a choice of paper books at an airport, will pick Thucydides, and sometimes Aquinas. Urged to build bomb shelters, they plant trees and roses, and their gardens are splendid and bright. Had I looked, the next morning, from my bathroom window into the evil-smelling ruin of some great city, the shock of recalling what I had done might not have been so violent, but the moral bottom had dropped out of my world without changing a mote of sunlight.

And so it can go for us as we in our various ways sweat out this life, and in our various moments sometimes stumble, our "moral bottom" all too evidently upon us. Johnny Hake had become, as he said, "a common thief" and an "impostor." And then what happens? He listens in new ways to the language. Williams used to say, "The language, the language"—desperately trying to reconnect that language to our lives, the language that had become sterile with all the jargon from psychology and sociology and economics, distorted with all the passing voices and the clever distancing, so that we were lost from these moral and emotional challenges of our lives.

Hake's parachute, as it were, opened, and he was rescued. What would have happened if he hadn't gotten the deal? That is the reader's question. Here's how it happens:

> "Hakie, I've been looking for you everywhere! You sure folded up your tents and stole away."
>
> "Yes," I said.

"Stole away," Howe repeated. "Just stole away. But what I wanted to talk with you about is this deal I thought you might be interested in. It's a one-shot, but it won't take you more than three weeks. It's a steal. They're green, and they're dumb, and they're loaded, and it's just like stealing."

Anyway, Johnny Hake took a wallet, and having had the wallet in his pocket enables his ears to be finely tuned so that he can listen now to others and to himself in ways not before possible for him. The wallet, the stolen wallet, in this paradoxical way becomes an instrument of moral self-scrutiny and the fathoming of the self. There he is alone and at rock bottom, as you and I have known ourselves, in our own ways, to be. Listen to this moment:

I walked around the streets, wondering how I would shape up as a pickpocket and bag snatcher, and all the arches and spires of St. Patrick's only reminded me of poor boxes. I took the regular train home, looking out of the window at a peaceable landscape and a spring evening, and it seemed to me fishermen and lone bathers and grade-crossing watchmen and sand-lot ball players and lovers unashamed of their sport and owners of small sailing craft and old men playing pinochle in firehouses were the people who stitched up the big holes in the world that were made by men like me.

This neighbor's wallet is burning a hole in the consciousness of a man, bringing him up short not only with respect to that middle-of-the-night theft, but also about something much larger: How ought he to live, with what values decisively in mind? What about a life's meaning, its destiny? It's as if that wallet could bring that on so that he could see; he could see you and me and himself in those small moments of ordinary goodness and moral possibility—all helping someone move along, taking someone for a sail, making sure that if there is a fire there is a fire truck that will go, and that the grading will work and the signals will work, and that a person strug-gling just to swim can be our teacher as we struggle to stay afloat in many ways, to stay afloat with some self-respect, to stay afloat in such a way that we take a measure of the swim of this life.

In "The Sorrows of Gin," Cheever gives a fancy name to a rela-tively impoverished family. They may have a fancy name and they may have all the money in the world and they may live in the place that you and I want to live, would be glad to live, to enjoy; but there is that little girl Amy and the gin she empties down the drain—talk about a youngster's wordless defiance. Here Cheever is again, reveal-ing to us our conceits, our deceits, and those small moments that are revelatory. This is bleeding close to the bone, close to the bone of ei-ther what we are or what we want to be. Yet there are pitfalls—signs warning us of trouble, near at hand or around the bend. Cheever's stories italicize some of those dangers—how we occasionally may take so much for granted.

Take Cheever to heart. Let the poignancy, the poetry, and the power of his language and his visionary moments stay close to you through this time, and in future times.

PART V

Boundaries, Borders, and Breakthroughs

Finding simple clarity amidst moral, psychological, and social complexity.

Featured: Paul Gauguin, Charles Dickens, Thomas Hardy, and George Eliot

NINETEEN

Taking Aim

Paul Gauguin, French, 1848–1903, *Where Do We Come From? What Are We? Where Are We Going?*, 1897–98, oil on canvas, 139.1 x 374.6 cm. (54¾ x 147½ in.), Museum of Fine Arts, Boston, Tompkins Collection-Arthur Gordon Tompkins Fund, 36.270. Photograph © 2010 Museum of Fine Arts, Boston.

D'*où venons-nous? Que sommes-nous? Où allons-nous?* That is the French title of a painting by Paul Gauguin—a title I vividly recall my mother translating for us: *Where Do We Come From? What Are We? Where Are We Going?* I remember my mother telling me that when a painter has to use language, there's trouble. But there it is— not trouble but a big success. I'd like to share with you what Gauguin himself said about this painting.

The two upper corners are chrome yellow, with the inscription on the left and my signature on the right, like a fresco which is appliquéd upon a golden wall and damaged at the corners. To the right at the lower end, a sleeping child and three crouching women. Two figures dressed in purple confide their thoughts to one another. An enormous crouching figure, out of all proportion, and intentionally so, raises its arms and stares in wonderment upon these two, who dare to think of our destiny. A figure in the center is picking fruit. Two cats near a child. A white goat. An idol, with its arms mysteriously raised in a sort of rhythm, seems to indicate the Beyond. A crouching figure seems to listen to the idol. Then lastly, an old woman, nearing death, appears to accept everything, to resign herself to her thoughts. She completes the legend. At her feet a strange white bird, holding a lizard in its claws, represents the futility of vain words. All this is on the bank of a river in the woods. In the background is the ocean, then the mountains of a neighboring island. Despite the changes of tone, the coloring of landscape is constant, blue and Veronese green. The naked figures stand out in orange. . . . So I have finished a philosophical work on a theme comparable to that of the Gospel, and so I have tried to understand life.

What this painter tried to do is what some of the writers in this book have been trying to do: to understand the progression of life and its meaning. This goes into the best of psychoanalysis—what, for example, Erik Erikson did in his efforts on human development, given to us in *Childhood and Society* and in *Insight and Responsibility*, important contributions to psychoanalytic thinking.

What is it that makes for awareness? Some of us tend to think of awareness as connected to intellectuality. We become increasingly aware as we take more courses, as we make our way from one grade to the next in school, and become certified and go on and become certified yet again, collecting diplomas and promotions; on and on and on this progression of "awareness" goes. Walker Percy helps us to think of awareness in a different way, courtesy of Kierkegaard. He gives us awareness not about molecules or legal or financial news, but awareness of life's significance, or a lack of awareness that puts us into a kind of psychological or moral stupor. But there are other kinds of awareness—ones that have to do with class and race, with neighborhood, and/or with one's situation in society.

Let's now turn to *Great Expectations,* which tells the story of a boy named Pip. Charles Dickens was very good with children. Pip is living with relatives. He's one of Dickens's orphans. The relative to whom he is closest is a blacksmith. Ultimately, Pip will meet up with a girl of high background and fall in love with her, and in so doing he will become aware of himself in ways hitherto not possible.

Here is Pip talking: "And then I told Joe"—who's the blacksmith and the dearest person in the world to him—"that I felt very miserable and that I hadn't been able to explain myself to Mrs. Joe and Pumblechook who were so rude to me, and that there had been a beautiful young lady at Miss Havisham's who was dreadfully proud, and that she had said I was common and that I knew I was common, and that I wished I was not common, and that the lies had come of it somehow, though I don't know how."

Pip begins to tell stories to himself and to others in order to make himself more pleasing and acceptable. Later on he says, "It is a most miserable thing to feel ashamed of home. There may be black ingratitude in the thing, and the punishment may be retributive and well deserved; but, that it is a miserable thing, I can testify."

Fate would beckon him, however. In the early part of the novel, he showed a little concern for a criminal on the lam, running from the police. He got some food for the criminal, and this criminal went off to Australia—and eventually, from distant Australia, the criminal will adopt the lad who had befriended him. Soon a lawyer will come and take Pip on and he will go to London, be tutored and educated privately and become a member of the upper class, so that now he is eligible for Miss Havisham and her daughter. The novel wants us to think about what our values are and what it is that makes us aware of whom and in what way: who is eligible for our approval, for entrance to our family, and why.

Dickens spent his childhood in prison with his family; they were taken to jail because his father couldn't pay his debts. He never went to school, never took writing courses, English courses. He learned to read on his own and write on his own—he was what we call a "self-made man," and is now one whose words are taught by very well educated teachers to eager, interested students. Thomas Hardy, on the other hand, came from a poor rural family in the southwestern part of England. His father was a stonecutter by trade, but Hardy wanted to write, and did. He came from a menial family, a "rustic" family, as George Eliot calls such folks in *Middlemarch,* but was buried in Westminster Abbey in 1928—a big deal then and now. Hardy took hard aim at rarefied fancy institutions in England. *Jude the Obscure* was the last novel he was able to write—he was excoriated for it and somehow thus unable to publish ever again. The opening chapters will show you why the novel stirred up enormous resentment among fancy literary critics; the entire section called "At Christminster" is a direct send-up of Oxford.

Hardy gives us Jude, the country bumpkin, who yearns to read and write and think, who wants to go to school, dreams even of going to college. Jude tries to get a job at Christminster, visiting a stonemason's yard: "For a moment there fell on Jude a true illumination; that here in the stone yard was a centre of effort as worthy as that dignified by the name of scholarly study within the noblest of the colleges."

That perception leaves him because he wants more. So he goes to the streets and he applies: "Descending to the streets, he went listlessly along till he arrived at an inn, and entered it. Here he drank several glasses of beer in rapid succession, and when he came out it was night. By the light of the flickering lamps he rambled home to supper, and had not long been sitting at table when his landlady brought up a letter that had just arrived for him." He had applied, he had written, he had asked to join their community. "She laid it down as if impressed with a sense of its possible importance." It was a nice bit of stationery, and "on looking at it Jude perceived that it bore the embossed stamp of one of the colleges whose heads he had addressed. '*One*—at last!' cried Jude. The communication was brief, and not exactly what he had expected; though it really was from the master in person. It ran thus: 'Biblioll College.' "What Hardy means, with regard to actual life, is Oxford's Balliol College, for those of you who know the score over there. "Sir—I've read your letter with interest; and judging from your description of yourself as a workingman, I venture to think that you will have a much better chance of success in life by remaining in your own sphere and sticking to your trade than by adopting any other course. That, therefore, is what I advise you to do. Yours faithfully, T. Tetuphenay." Under the signature is this: "To Mr. J. Fawley, Stone-mason." So a snotty-named official spells it all out to a stonecutter.

Jude goes and drinks more beer after that. Why not, after you're rejected? Then he gets to thinking about things. "He began to see that the town life was a book of humanity infinitely more palpitating, varied, and compendious than the gown life." Town versus gown, a hundred years ago, being chronicled.

Hardy then refers to the university—noting the irony: Oxford was originally founded to spread the Christian Gospel. Jude thinks to himself of the Bible, which he had used in learning to read. The gates were shut and on an impulse he took from his pocket a lump of chalk, which as a workman he carried. He wrote on the walls: " '*I have understanding as well as you; I am not inferior to you; yea, who knoweth not such things as these?*'—Job xii.3."

What might we want to write on *our* walls? Would we dare think of writing what was said in Matthew, that "the last shall be first and the first last?" Where would that place us? What does one do with these truths handed down to us in religious institutions, even in great novels, such as *Jude the Obscure*? What does one do with what one reads from certain "texts" listed on reading lists? I suppose in some Utopian moment, those people who award Rhodes scholarships might give each person who wins one copy of *Jude the Obscure* to read as a proper kind of moral preparation for that trip across the Atlantic. The ironies of all of this are hard for us to deal with, but they are here for us in this tradition of the nineteenth century.

What we do with Jude and Pip, their embarrassment, their sense of being unfairly judged and condemned—do their stories have any bearing on our lives? And should that be the case, that we link them to our present-day America?

Now we move to *Middlemarch* and the age of reform; we will retrospectively look into the middle of the nineteenth century, back when England began to change politically, socially, and culturally. The hero of this novel is the village itself, a community called Middlemarch, and the people who populated it. There is a doctor in this novel, Dr. Lydgate, who starts out as a highly idealistic young man. By the time George Eliot is through with Lydgate we have a lot to consider, as we try to explain what happened to him. She weaves the story of his loss of idealism, his compromises into moral descent—a story that isn't so much judgmental as eye-opening, thought-stirring. Was this outcome necessary or inevitable, and how does one explain what happened?

Here is a novel that also offers us a couple of sisters, one intensely idealistic, the other very practical; and Eliot develops character in this novel with great psychological and moral savvy. She was aware of the unconscious and how it worked, well before Freud developed his thinking. This novel was published twenty-five years before *The Interpretation of Dreams*. A generation before Freud's writing, she uses the word "unconscious" and she offers all the "defense mechanisms" right there in this story. Here she writes of life. There is sophistication in this account of psychology and sociology:

Every limit is a beginning as well as an ending. Who can quit young lives after being long in company with them, and not desire to know what befell them in their after-years? For the fragment of a life, however typical, is not the sample of an even web: promises may not be kept, and an ardent outset may be followed by a declension; latent powers may find their long-awaited opportunity; a past error may urge a grand retrieval.

Eliot is bringing you closer to your own lives and the lives of people you know. She is exploring the mystery of time, of moving through it: what happens to people, to people you know, to people you love, to people you don't particularly like at all, to people you work with, to people you envy, to people you detest, to people you admire? You may already know this from your experiences in school and in work: the trajectory and how it takes place, and why it takes place, and who ends up doing what and why. These are huge mysteries, and she is not about to settle for reductionist explanations, whether they be psychological, sociological, economic, racial, whatever. She insists, in this novel, on allowing for complexity and ambiguity and irony and paradox in such a way that we ourselves, as we go through it, are surprised, as character develops and change catches us up in various ways. As she observes at one point: " 'But, my dear Mrs. Casaubon,' said Mr. Farebrother, smiling gently at her ardor, 'character is not cut in marble—it is not something solid and unalterable. It is something living and changing, and may become diseased as our bodies do.' " Dorothea then responds, " 'People glorify all sorts of bravery except the bravery they might show on behalf of their nearest neighbors.' "

"What do we live for, if it is not to make life less difficult to each other?" she has Dorothea ask later. Eliot is always asking those questions—a philosophical novelist of sorts, a woman in the nineteenth century daring to write, under an assumed name, a man's name, so that she would be taken seriously.

As we get further into *Middlemarch* we see how very tough Eliot can be on her explicit idealists, and much more generous to the ordinary people who don't have the kind of pretensions that some of us have, who want to change the world and tell the world that we know how it ought to be changed. Put differently: she is suspicious of ideologues, be their motives psychological, political, or social. I guess she is looking for some clay feet in the people who present themselves to the world as our teachers and our leaders. She is interested in turning cards over, in turning the tables on society and on us readers. I suppose, ultimately, in her own way, she is urging her own kind of populism, one that goes well with that of Dickens and of Hardy. The only central figures in this novel who get by without criticism are some of the poorest people, a man named Callid and others. These are the people she holds up high, just as Cheever does in that epiphany in "The Housebreaker of Shady Hill," when he talks about people who enable the railroad cars to go through railroad crossings without people being hurt—the ordinary people, the common folk, those whose labor and lack of pretentiousness mean so much to some of these writers, to us, the recipients of their presence, their work, their efforts. The question for us is how we can continue on our personal and educational trajectory; learning and achieving, and how we can become the people we want to become in various professions and in business, while holding on for dear life to some capacity for personal and moral reflection that keeps at a distance the temptation to become full of ourselves and thus lose those aspects of ourselves.

It can be painful and illuminating to go through these novels because these literary figures enter our pantheon, our company, our consciousness, initially, as outsiders who are often taking aim at us. But then they became an integral part of our own lives, as we absorb them, take in their summoning moral fire, aimed so adroitly: there for us to behold in our reading, and respect and reflect on and, most of all, respond to in our reading and in our lives.

TWENTY

Be Kind

When I was a college student, I took a writing course; it scared the daylights out of me. There were all these very able young writers. I don't know how I ever got into the course, much less the business! One of my fellow students had been in the navy during the Second World War, and he was older than all of us who had come to college straight out of high school.

This older student used to tell us about fighting and seeing his friends die. His name was Frank O'Hara, and he became a great "New York poet." He died of a terrible accident at the age of forty, but for a while he was a very promising and important younger American poet. He wrote a poem about Billie Holiday's death called "The Day Lady Died." She was known as Lady, not as just another singer.

> It is 12:20 in New York a Friday
> three days after Bastille day, yes
> it is 1959 and I go get a shoeshine
> because I will get off the 4:19 in Easthampton
> at 7:15 and then go straight to dinner
> and I don't know the people who will feed me

I walk up the muggy street beginning to sun
and have a hamburger and a malted and buy
an ugly NEW WORLD WRITING *to see what the poets*
in Ghana are doing these days
                                    I go on to the bank
and Miss Stillwagon (first name Linda I once heard)
doesn't even look up my balance for once in her life
and in the GOLDEN GRIFFIN *I get a little Verlaine*
for Patsy with drawings by Bonnard although I do
think of Hesiod, trans. Richmond Lattimore or
Brendan Behan's new play or Le Balcon or Les Nègres
of Genet, but I don't, I stick with Verlaine
after practically going to sleep with quandariness

and for Mike I just stroll into the PARK LANE
Liquor Store and ask for a bottle of Strega and
then I go back where I came from to 6th Avenue
and the tobacconist in the Ziegfeld Theatre and
casually ask for a carton of Gauloises and a carton
of Picayunes, and a NEW YORK POST *with her face on it*

and I am sweating a lot by now and thinking of
leaning on the john door in the 5 SPOT
while she whispered a song along the keyboard
to Mal Waldron and everyone and I stopped breathing

   I remember going to that bar and listening to the Lady, Billie Holiday, trying to interrupt the carbon molecules of organic chemistry facts and formulas that were in my head, that I was trying to hold there for the next exam. Part of me would have liked to just sit and listen to Billie Holiday during the entire lecture, and for many more hours to come. I remember dancing with my wife to her songs, which we both loved so much. I also remember the remarkable American artist who rendered it, the early Billie Holiday of the

1930s—her high-pitched, fragile, vulnerable voice trying to make a go of it, much as we do in our own lives, trying to find a direction for oneself and a career for oneself. Then there was the grown-up Billie Holiday, with her feet solidly on the ground, with a voice that could belt out those songs with that uncanny mix of tenderness and strength, no matter the pain in her own heart. And finally, there was the Billie Holiday of the 1950s, who was dying, and crying about a death that she knew was around any corner.

Years later I got to know a writer, Ed Sissman. We were both writing pieces for an editor named William Shawn at the *New Yorker,* and we'd send each other things before we'd send them off to this great god of sorts in New York. One day, Ed called me up and he said, "Bob, I just got some bad news." He was also a young man in his early forties, just like Frank O'Hara. Ed was by then a distinguished American poet, a writer for magazines, and a businessman who worked in an advertising agency in Boston, a vice president there. I said, "Oh. I'm sorry." He said, "I was just told by the doctor that I only have about a year or so to live." (Remember Raymond Carver's poem "What the Doctor Said.") I would get to talk with Ed. He would come over to my house and we would go to an ice cream place in Carlisle, Massachusetts, called Bates Farm, where, I can tell you, they have the most fantastic ice cream in the world. I eagerly swallow that ice cream and just laugh and laugh at the *New England Journal of Medicine*—at all their admonitory articles about cholesterol. Let them worry about cholesterol; I'll have my mocha chip!

Anyway, when Ed Sissman was a student at Harvard, he lived in Adams House in C-entry and wrote a poem called "Up All Night, Adams House C-55." It's in his collection called *Hello, Darkness*— what a title for a dying man to write. No one had to give him "grief therapy"; no one had to negotiate him through the "stages" of dying. He had read "The Death of Ivan Ilych" and he had read George Eliot and Dickens and *Let Us Now Praise Famous Men* and Orwell.

Dead on the dot of dawn, the Orient
Express steams in the window where we sit.
Its headlight hits Henry Kerr right in the eye.
Lightened by loosing the sandbags of sleep,
we blab about C Entry's ceilings like
so many free balloons, still full of gas.
From yesterday, while out in Plympton Street.
The air, recharged with light, proclaims
Today to its great public, and one rusty ray
Of sun, moon-bound, takes hold on Randolph Hall and caroms down,
    diluted, into all
Shades of Aurora on the brick sidewalk
Beside the charcoal street, all business—coal cards, milk wagons, and
    newspaper
trucks—at this ungodly and almighty hour. "Kant," Henry tries to say,
    producing just a
peanut-whistle husk, but we all know
which philosopher he means. "I don't buy Kant,"
says Parsons. "Now you take Descartes and see."
"You take Descartes," I interrupt, and down
the less of my rum Coke. "Let's all get down
And eat before it all gets too jammed, and take
a walk." "All right, let's go!" Each with his green
and inky copy of the Crimson *in*
His inky hand, a badge of editors, we march like marshals down the dusty
    flights
of stony steps to the subalterns' mess
In clouds of power and manly sleeplessness.

Later in his life, Ed would write a poem more pertinent to the books we are looking at. The poem, written after Orwell died, is titled "George Orwell, 1950–1965." Note how he refers to Orwell as an "unmet friend," just as the books we've read in this course are friends; the passage about Orwell's foe refers to *Homage to Catalonia* and the Spanish Civil War.

> *Dear George Orwell.*
> *I never said farewell.*
> *There was too much going on:*
> *Crabgrass in the lawn*
> *And guests to entertain,*
> *Light bantering with pain*
> *(But wait till later on),*
> *Love nightly come and gone,*
> *But always in the chinks*
> *Of my time (or the bank's),*
> *I read your books again.*
> *In Schrafft's or on the run*
> *To my demanding clients,*
> *I read you in the silence*
> *Of the spell you spun.*
> *My dearest Englishman,*
> *My stubborn unmet friend,*
> *Who waited for the end*
> *In perfect pain and love*
> *And walked to his own grave*
> *With a warm wink and wave,*
> *To all; who would not pull*
> *The trigger on the bull*
> *Elephant, and who,*
> *Seeing his foe undo*
> *His pants across the lines,*
> *Did not blow out his brains;*
> *Who served the Hôtel X*
> *As low man, slept in spikes*
> *With tramps, in Rowton Houses*

With pavement artists, boozers,
Boys, insomniacs;
Who spat on shams and hacks,
Lived in a raddled flat,
Passing trains hooted at,
And died for what we are,
Farewell, Eric Blair.

When I was a boy, I went with my mother and father and brother to Sioux City, Iowa, where my mother had lived her youth. Her younger brother had been in the American army in the Second World War and had been killed, and we went for the funeral. I remember the tears. I remember the eulogy. And I remember him. I remember my parents trying to makes sense of not only his death but the deaths of millions of people: young soldiers, and people who even then the world knew were being killed by those murderous dictators in Berlin and in Moscow.

How my mother loved this poem that Steven Spender wrote, saluting young idealists who had given their lives for democracy (with all its warts), and for decency, for this country, for other countries where (when one measures things) one is grateful for what they stand for.

I think continually of those who were truly great.
Who, from the womb, remembered the soul's history
Through corridors of light where the hours are suns,
Endless and singing. Whose lovely ambition
Was that their lips, still touched with fire,
Should tell of the Spirit clothed from head to foot in song.
And who hoarded from the Spring branches
The desires falling across their bodies like blossoms.

What is precious is never to forget.
The essential delight of the blood drawn from ageless springs
Breaking through rocks, in worlds before our earth.

Never to deny its pleasure in the morning simple light
Nor its grave evening demand for love.
Never to allow gradually the traffic to smother
With noise and fog the flowering of the spirit.

Near the snow, near the sun, in the highest fields
See how these names are fêted by the waving grass
And by the streamers of white cloud
And whispers of wind in the listening sky.
The name of those who in their lives fought for life
Who wore at their hearts the fire's center.
Born of the sun they traveled a short while towards the sun,
And left the vivid air signed with their honor.

This book started you, the reader, out in Alabama, went to York-shire and Lancashire, in England, came back to "the States," as my father used to call this country, all these fifty states, each a nation of sorts within a nation, with its own history and flag and flower and capital: half a hundred democracies within one democracy! How lucky we are. How lucky we are, as Carl Sandburg put it: "Americans All." We went on to Paterson, New Jersey, where the economy began with that first factory and met Dr. Williams, with his black bag and his typewriter. We met Raymond Carver, who admired Williams so much. I know that in some eternity those two surely have met and embraced. The love they both felt toward ordinary Americans, humble, hardworking, troubled, but sticking with it, their allotted life. We met Tillie Olsen and her feisty, insistent, lyrical, demanding, and reminding voice. We met Ralph Ellison, who gave us the limitations of sight—spoke of what we don't see and whom we don't see, thereby not seeing ourselves. We met cranky, inspired, inspiring, Christ-haunted Flannery O'Connor. We went through the religious side of the course with writers such as Dorothy Day and Bernanos and Simone Weil given hardly even a cursory glance compared to what they deserve. We met Hurston, who gave us Janie and her men in *Their Eyes Were Watching God*. We met Dr. Percy, and George Eliot in the infinity of her wisdom, and Dickens, whom we all know in various incarnations. We met Thomas Hardy. We met Tolstoy and Cheever. We met them all in a book—a book about life, about the course of life, this life we live, coming and going as it does.

There is the poem "Otherwise," written by Jane Kenyon just before she died of leukemia in New Hampshire, much too young to leave us. In this poem all of Walker Percy's riddles and ironies and troubles from *The Moviegoer* are worked out—she's got it all in just two stanzas; in fact, I dare say, the whole of Kierkegaard, to boot. He wouldn't resent that at all; maybe he'd be flattered, tied as a philosopher, a theologian, to a poet who sang so powerfully of herself, and to us.

> *I got out of bed*
> *on two strong legs.*
> *It might have been*
> *otherwise. I ate*
> *cereal, sweet*
> *milk, ripe, flawless*
> *peach. It might*
> *have been otherwise.*
> *I took the dog uphill*
> *to the birch wood.*
> *All morning I did*
> *the work I love.*
>
> *At noon I lay down*
> *with my mate. It might*
> *have been otherwise.*
> *We ate dinner together*
> *at a table with silver*
> *candlesticks. It might*
> *have been otherwise.*
> *I slept in a bed*

in a room with paintings
on the walls, and
planned another day
just like this day.
But one day, I know,
it will be otherwise.

How does one live with such knowledge? How to pick up each day with enthusiasm and insistence and pride and yet know, remember what that poem tells us—what Dr. Percy was trying to tell us, what Dr. Percy knew out of his own life: all that can threaten us, all the loss, the hurt, the pain, the vulnerability, and that eventuality for all of us (that "otherwise"). How, as Wordsworth put it, does one know those "intimations of mortality" and yet go on, leave the "magic mountains" and go into the valleys where people live in their homes and work and are part of that ongoing life?

This next poem is one my wife and I asked a friend of ours to read at our wedding. My wife's father was classmates with Robert Frost, who came to Harvard for a couple of years (another Harvard dropout). My wife used to teach Robert Frost to high school students, and she thought this might be a poem for all of us to hear that day. It's called "The Investment."

Over back where they speak of life as staying
("You couldn't call it living, for it ain't"),
There was an old, old house renewed with paint,
And in it a piano loudly playing.

Out in the ploughed ground in the cold a digger,
Among the unearthed potatoes standing still,
Was counting winter dinners, one a hill,
With half an ear to the piano's vigor.

All that piano and new paint back there,
Was it some money suddenly come into?

> Or some extravagance young love had been to?
> Or old love on an impulse not to care—
>
> Not to sink under being man and wife,
> But get some color and music out of life?

I have another Robert Frost poem to offer you; it's called "Reluctance."

> Out through the fields and the woods
>   And over the walls I have wended;
> I have climbed the hills of view
>   And looked at the world, and descended;
> I have come by the highway home,
>   And lo, it is ended.
>
> The leaves are all dead on the ground,
>   Save those that the oak is keeping
> To ravel them one by one
>   And let them go scraping and creeping
> Out over the crusted snow,
>   When others are sleeping.
>
> And the dead leaves lie huddled and still,
>   No longer blown hither and thither;
> The last lone aster is gone;
>   The flowers of the witch hazel wither;
> The heart is still aching to seek,
>   But the feet question "Whither?"
>
> Ah, when to the heart of man
>   Was it ever less than a treason
> To go with the drift of things,
>   To yield with a grace to reason,
> And bow and accept the end
>   Of a love or a season?

Let us please read that again.

> *Ah, when to the heart of man*
> *Was it ever less than a treason*
> *To go with the drift of things,*
> *To yield with a grace to reason,*
> *And bow and accept the end*
> *Of a love or a season?*

Finally, let me leave you with something that William James's son once learned. William James had five children, and one of them was named William. When William was in college he wondered (as his father's son, you would expect he would wonder) why and where and whither and for what reasons. He wondered as, I suppose, Gauguin did in Tahiti; as Cheever did while he wrote in the basement of an apartment house in Manhattan; as Agee did, bourbon by his side and his mind on fire; as Orwell did, coughing up blood but persisting with his pen; as Tillie Olsen did, when she had time after a working day; as Dr. Williams did, after his own kind of work; as Carver did, so grateful for sobriety and to be able to wing those stories out of his heart and mind and soul; and as you and I do—about those unforgettable stories that are so clear, lean, and clean, stirring and provocative, and those stories that break and heal your heart at the same time.

Anyway, like those people, like you and me, young William James, in his room at college, wrote to his uncle Henry—the famous novelist Henry James—to find out the answers to this life: how to live it. He got back from his uncle, the great portly, wise novelist, essayist, playwright, a few words of his most sage advice. The letter began:

My Dear One, I have your letter and here is my answer:
  Three things in human life are important. The first is to be kind. The second is to be kind. And the third is to be kind.

Let us all try in the important and the small ways in this life given us to be kind, even when it may be hard for us, even when we are challenged by the darkness that inhabits all of us and tears at us; even during those demanding, hurried times, let us try to be kind. Let us reach out to one another and think well of one another, knowing that the flaws in others we share in our own way. Let us, as W. H. Auden put it, "love one another or we die."

Hold on to these books; pick them up at times in your lives; remember them; keep in mind as good, strong, wise friends Agee and Orwell, and Dr. Bill Williams, and Flannery and Dorothy and Zora and Silone, and Walker, for they walked through shadows and sought, and sometimes found, the sun.

AFTERWORD

History of a Course

"Even college courses have their history," the child psychoanalyst Erik H. Erikson once remarked to me and some of us teaching assistants in his large undergraduate college course. Then came the elaboration: "The teacher has a personal history (and a thinking history) that gives shape to the course that the students take, though sometimes that 'variable,' as the social scientists say, is missing. I try to bring that up every year, in the first lecture—tell the students how I came to teach at Harvard, and with what hope and purpose in mind I teach the course that inspired this book; the point is to present them with some notion of what will be here for them to think about, if they decide to keep showing up in this place at this time, twice a week, to learn something about 'human development'—two words that can mean various things to various people (as I keep reminding myself and, naturally, them too)."

Soon enough, some of us teaching assistants wanted even more from Erikson: a conversation about qualifications for admission to a much-favored course, or about lecture schedules, the syllabus to be offered the students, and, inevitably, the "grading criteria" that ought to inform decisions as to who gets what letter (with sometimes a plus or minus) and why. Our professor was not eager to get into such detail—quite the contrary; he insisted that he had "no set lectures," that he responded to his own introspective life (what he learned, where, and how) and, yes, to the students he met walking to and from the lecture hall and (this was very important) during his office hours, which he held regularly, and for long enough to enable a solid meeting with one student after another.

Those office hours, we began to realize, enabled a clinician become teacher to straddle some fences built into his academic life (a highly unconventional one, which began in his fifties and came to him even though he'd never attended college or graduate school, as the students would learn during his lectures become personal storytelling). Though he called upon his psychoanalytic experience, he also reminded himself that he had been an artist before he encountered Dr. Sigmund Freud and his daughter Anna in Vienna during the 1920s. Indeed, he was at pains to draw on the blackboard during a lecture, to make a point by sketching a person or a place; even a thought became, in his artist's hand, a telling picture. He also had slides to share with his perceiving, as well as listening, audience—and not infrequently, he welcomed responses by his students, in a lecture hall, to what they saw or heard him say. "This course belongs to all of you, to each of you," he memorably said—and this engendered an immediate responsive interest in some, a sort of perplexity, even alarm, in others (and, as well, over time, the departure of a few youths who wanted a more conventional, predictable way of lecturing, of the lecturer's self-presentation, his manner of approaching his young, bright, privileged observers, heedful of what he had to say, mindful of their own opportunities, wishes, worries).

"I hope this course will be many things to many people," he once told us, as we talked about the young people in our respective sections—and then from our teacher came a not rare moment of candid self-appraisal: a rebellious insistence from our teacher of a kind of maverick will to improvise, to let things happen in response to a given day's unpredictable happenstances: a student's raised hand and public inquiry, the news of a particular day, and, not least, the lecturer's contemporary writing life (his work on a manuscript being prepared, realized for an editor's eyes). The point, he kept letting us know (kept keeping in his own mind, to inform his remarks), was to "convey factuality and feeling, with spontaneity permitted": √ a surprising, succinct comment spoken the day after one of his lectures, in his library office; his words stayed long and hard in our minds. Like the undergraduates, we tried to get into the mood of a course's rhythms, some obviously set by the professor but some prompted by the books we were all reading, discussing, pondering strenuously, as were the students, naturally, and the professor, who let us all know that "different parts of those books had a range of meanings" to him, depending on the yearly variations in the makeup of students and teaching assistants. "Like life, a course has its ups and downs, its changes of topicality, and presentation, and emphasis," he told his students and us (we who were anxious to pin him down, even as he wanted a certain elusive independence and unpredictability to inform a course). We began to understand that message through his demeanor and stated hopes, shifts of opinion and intention, all a declaration to us about a course's overall aim to stir, to prompt or provoke thoughts, yes, indeed, but also second thoughts, even some about the larger purpose of an expensive, much-touted experience called "higher education."

By the early 1970s Erik Erikson had left Harvard "to contemplate the world without the help of the students," he told us as he let us know that his "teaching days, in the classroom, are over." With those words he was his inimitable self—but still, we realized then and there, the teacher who wanted to say the obvious, yet while doing so, managed to tender no small amount of food for thought. (During his meetings with us teachers for his course, he invariably offered each of us some Swiss chocolate and even, now and then, a sip of brandy, which he kept in a hip flask and would pour into some nearby waiting paper cups—eyed by some of us fleetingly, even at times longingly.) The lecture was over, and we all were entitled to enjoy ourselves, relax, including the lecturer, who told us many times that "to speak in a course is to set a course, for the one talking and for those attending him or her" (vintage Erikson, the play on that word "course"). Indeed, playfulness, for him, was the pursuit of that theme.

I know some of us professors here stand and read over lectures, the same ones, year after year. I don't want to get self-righteous, but you do confine yourself (so I think) that way. I realize that the reader can be playful with his words while reading to the students; and a lecturer can avoid notes and say what comes to mind for an hour, and be full of himself, disorganized, self-indulgent: a performing fool! Each of us will get to our students in those lecture halls in our own way. For me, notes are a necessity. I write them down a day before the lecture, and then I try to talk them out to myself in silence (think them out, I guess you could say). I can hear myself talking, while I sit or walk around the house or outside, even though I'm not using my voice. When I'm walking to the lecture hall, I'm talking to the class in my mind, getting ready to speak to the students (not talking out loud to myself, I should add, just getting my thinking, re-membering head hitched to speaking, which is what a professor does, obviously, in a lecture hall, unless he comes in, opens up a notebook, and starts reading from it). When I do read in a lecture, from a book or notes, I always seem to break away at times—not by premeditation, by planning, but because I let my mind do a bit of wondering, wandering, as we do in psychoanalysis: the analyst and the analyzed.

But you have to be who you are, and that goes for teachers, too! When I'm walking to a lecture hall, I ask myself what I would like the students to be considering as they are walking away after the lec-ture. "Sure thing," as they say, there are other thoughts for them to be having, but sure thing I'm hoping they're turning some of what they just heard over in their minds—when they aren't getting rid of me or my words, so they can go about their lives, eyeing one an-other, overhearing one another. That's what a teacher does, through a course: tries to connect his head with the heads of the future, tries to make some headway with his students (who, in turn, help him or her to do that).

While teaching in Erikson's course, I also got to know the teaching that the sociologist David Riesman did at Harvard; I audited his lectures, met him and many of the young men and women who taught sections in his course. Over the years, I encountered students who had been lucky beneficiaries of that unique and productive pairing, Erikson and Riesman—two mavericks, one a psychoanalyst, one a lawyer, neither with a history of conventional academic training, both brought in by a dean, Mr. George Bundy, who did an end run around the usual fiefdoms that make up a professoriat, so as to offer "new voices, stir the waters for the students," as Dean Bundy later put it, during a discussion of academic politics at the Ford Foundation.

What a dean described as an aim, two professors vigorously pursued in their lecturing lives. David Riesman was willing to be articulate about the matter, as if he were in a courtroom, making a point or two with great conviction: "It didn't take long for Erik and me to realize that we had a mission, as well as a job—to give 'sanction' " (he liked that word!) "to the undergraduates, allow them to wander across certain borders, make their own mark on things, take the books to heart, live with them as well as try to use them in the eternal struggle for grades, for a 'record' that would enable future admission to graduate schools, and on and on! We encouraged the students to roam widely," he said,

> to offer their own renderings of the books, as well as to take in ours, to use their imaginations as well as their analytic skills, their ability to memorize and figure out what the teacher wants, then give it back to him, to her, in a blue book or a paper. So doing, we ourselves learned a lot about the world we'd just met, joined—the rules, the prerequisites, the possible administrative penalties, all so that these young Americans, so often called "the best and the brightest," would prosper here in their courses, to

be sure, but also take things into their own independent hands, as some did—"stand up to us in power," as Erik would say, an appreciative smile on his face. "You and I got here," he once told me, "by being balanced rebels—able to break ranks, be ourselves, yet be allowed to join a very traditional place, full of power, and sometimes full of itself!" We'd both contemplate that outcome of ours a lot—the struggle we each, in a different way, waged, with ourselves and in our teaching: the books we chose, and how we spoke of them, presented them to the students, with what other books for company. Erik was better at saying it: the balance between compliance and conformity, as against personal authority, independent thinking—a hard mix to make work for the best interests of these young men and women.

In 1975, I was asked to start teaching a course for Harvard undergraduates, a continuation of the teaching Erik Erikson, my own teacher, had done. The initial proposal had me using the same syllabus—with, of course, additions or subtractions based on my personal whims, interests. "As a child psychoanalyst who has studied Erikson's work, and written about it, you are the ideal successor," I was told. Tempted, I was ready to oblige—yet I had other, very strong interests, commitments. For years I had been doing documentary work, trying to understand how life goes for various kinds of Americans: children, their parents and teachers. My wife, Jane, a teacher of literature and history, and I spent our days at homes and in schools; on weekends, we tried to make sense of what we'd noticed, heard spoken; and, too, there were the drawings and paintings done for us at our behest (boys and girls telling us a lot by showing us persons and places and events, courtesy of crayons and paints applied to the paper we were glad to bring along).

During those years of "fieldwork," as it is described in the social sciences, we were always on the lookout for help from others, those who had tried to regard closely their fellow human beings, and because of Jane's long experience, we began to read books that might help us connect those families we were getting to know with others whose lives were portrayed by writers who had witnessed them firsthand or had approached them through the imaginative storytelling that enables short stories, novels, or the lyrics of music, poetry. Moreover, artists using canvases and paintbrushes, or photographers carrying cameras all over, with a thoughtful, sensitive willingness to use them in a place, at a moment, had also established a record of what was there (and now for the viewer, holding a book, becomes very much here, a sight available for an interested person's pensive scrutiny).

No wonder, then, when I began to think of teaching a college class, those photographs came to mind and, with them, the remarks of the men, women, and children whose appearances in far-off homes, fields, and streets became quite summoning presences in the classroom (where slides could be used) or in dormitories, where books opened sent forth so much for students to attend to. As a consequence, Jane and I, meeting with Joan and Erik Erikson and David Riesman, came up with a course titled A Literature of Social Reflection—with its syllabus as a rationale for its character, a statement of its purpose. So thinking, planning, I kept going back to a brief freshman seminar I'd taught, titled Moral and Social Inquiry—again, calling upon essayists, novelists, playwrights, poets as helpfully instructive witnesses to human scenes afar become available close-up through a book's words and pictures, or a film's. (No wonder, when some of us who taught in A Literature of Social Reflection wanted to extend our message beyond the college's walls, we came up with the term "double take" to convey the mind, heart, soul of our proposed initiative—a course's themes and dreams providing the energy for a magazine's daily life; and, indeed, many of the editors of *Double Take* once taught in the course whose lectures now appear in this book.)

This book holds those lectures, once taped, now transcribed and edited. I hope it conveys, as well, the visual moments from those lectures, as they got us all going, sitting in an auditorium's seats. There was music, too—Billie Holiday singing her heart out, catching us in our throats as her voice pierced the air, stopping us mentally in our tracks. There were chalked words on a blackboard, looming over the teacher's body: names, dates, words spoken—of alarm or annoyance or amazement or wonder. Again, the repetition: the doubling of the words to be read on the blackboard, and heard as the teacher's voice rendered them. Most of all, there were stories, incidents, events, connected to reading assigned—the lecturer letting others know what he'd experienced (when, where, and how) and what that moment in a life being lived had to do with something one of our assigned writers or photographers or artists had to offer us. All that is, needless to say, for this book's readers—the verbal and visual become a book's contents. Yet, one hopes and prays, a course's life is not the property of its teachers, the lecturer, or even of those wonderfully able and varied men and women, from all walks of life, who volunteered to help the weekly section meetings work amicably, productively, but belongs, finally, to the students themselves: how they carried forth, years afterward, their particular responses to moments and messages in a course's life, a student's participating membership in A Literature of Social Reflection transmuted into memories held and, at times, an enlivening heritage.

As I wrote these words, I recalled a recent exhibit at the Boston Museum of Fine Arts featuring Gauguin's Tahiti paintings: lo and behold, some visitors to that collection of Gauguin's work were huddled near one of his paintings, *Where Do We Come From? What Are We? Where Are We Going?* Standing there, looking, they were in fact held fast, conversing, remembering "like a class," a museum attendant commented, and then came this: "Those same young people also gathered," he remarked, "near two of Edward Hopper's pictures," also in that museum. Thus had a course been carried across time and space to another scene, prompted by pictures hung and waiting for visitors still in their minds taking in a course, their memories now bearing down hard on their everyday lives: art, respectfully addressed, celebrated, in a class, was extending a hand to life, becoming very importantly a part of it.

A Reading List for Life

The Syllabus from A Literature of Social Reflection

Many of the writers and photographers whose books and photographic collections are assigned, shown, or suggested in this course have struggled hard to reconcile scholarly, literary, or artistic interests and pursuits with moral concerns: the person of relative privilege or good education who wants to document the condition of those less fortunate or evoke their situation in short stories, poems, novels, or visually but who him- or herself lives "another life," so to speak. Still others whose work will be read or viewed have tried to understand not only how various people live but to what ultimate (explicitly avowed, implicitly held) moral or religious or philosophical purpose, if any, they adhere. In this course, we will try to compare various modes of social observation and at the same time explore the ethical issues that confront those men and women who want to change the world in one way or another, those ordinary people caught in a particular social crisis, and, not least, those who try to make sense of what others initiate politically, struggle with psychologically, endure socially.

RECOMMENDED READING

Agee, James, and Walker Evans, *Let Us Now Praise Famous Men:* Book
  Two up to "Shelter," plus the sections entitled "Education" and
  "Work"
Baxter, Charles, "Gryphon"
Bernanos, Georges, *The Diary of a Country Priest*
Boyle, T. Coraghessan, "Greasy Lake"
Carver, Raymond, *Fires*

Carver, Raymond, "Your Dog Dies" and "My Crow"

Carver, Raymond, *A New Path to the Waterfall*

Carver, Raymond, *Where I'm Calling From*

Cheever, John, *The Collected Short Stories*

Coles, Jane, and Robert Coles, *Women of Crisis*

Coles, Robert, *Children of Crisis,* volume II, *Migrants, Sharecroppers, Mountaineers*

Coles, Robert, *Children of Crisis,* volume V, *Privileged Ones*

Coles, Robert, *Dorothy Day: A Radical Devotion*

Coles, Robert, *The Moral Life of Children*

Coles, Robert, "Next Door but Across an Ocean" (reprinted from *Harvard Magazine*).

Coles, Robert, and Ross Spears, *Agee*

Coles, Robert, with photographs by Alex Harris, *The Old Ones of New Mexico*

Day, Dorothy, *The Long Loneliness*

Dickens, Charles, *Great Expectations*

Eliot, George, *Middlemarch*

Ellison, Ralph, *Invisible Man*

Gallagher, Tess, "My Father's Love Letters"

Hardy, Thomas, *Jude the Obscure*

Hurston, Zora Neale, *Their Eyes Were Watching God*

McPherson, James Alan, "Going Up to Atlanta"

Nemerov, Howard, "September, the First Day of School"

O'Connor, Flannery, "The Displaced Person," "The Artificial Nigger," "Good Country People," "Everything That Rises Must Converge," "The Enduring Chill," "The Lame Shall Enter First," "Revelation," and "Parker's Back"—all contained in *The Complete Stories*

Olsen, Tillie: the short stories that make up *Tell Me a Riddle*

Orwell, George, *The Road to Wigan Pier*

Percy, Walker, *The Moviegoer*

Silone, Ignazio, *Bread and Wine*

Tolstoy, Leo, *Confession*

Tolstoy, Leo, *The Death of Ivan Ilych and Other Stories:* title story and "Master and Man"

Weil, Simone, *Waiting for God*

Wiesel, Elie, *Night*

Wiesel, Elie, "Why Christians Can't Forget the Holocaust"

Williams, William Carlos, *The Doctor Stories,* compiled by Robert Coles

Williams, William Carlos, the long poem *Paterson,* Books One and Two
Williams, William Carlos, *White Mule,* the first novel in a series known as
    the Stecher Trilogy
Wolff, Tobias, *Back in the World*
Wolff, Tobias, "In the Garden of the North American Martyrs"
Yates, Richard, "Doctor Jack-o'-Lantern"

ADDITIONAL READING

Agee, James, and Helen Levitt, *A Way of Seeing*
America and Lewis Hine
Armstrong, Isabel, "Middlemarch: A Note on George Eliot's Wisdom," in
    Critical Essays on George Eliot, edited by Barbara Hardy
Berle, L. W., *George Eliot and Thomas Hardy*
Coles, Robert, *Doing Documentary Work*
Coles, Robert, *Dorothea Lange: Photographs of a Lifetime*
Coles, Robert, *Flannery O'Connor's South*
Coles, Robert, *Irony in the Mind's Life*
Coles, Robert, *Walker Percy: An American Search*
Coles, Robert, *William Carlos Williams: The Knack of Survival in America*
Coles, Robert, and Daniel Berrigan, *The Geography of Faith: Underground
    Conversations on Religious, Political, and Social Change*
Day, Dorothy, *By Little and by Little: The Selected Writings of Dorothy Day,*
    edited by Robert Ellsberg
Day, Dorothy, *Loaves and Fishes*
Double Take, issue 9, summer 1997
Ellison, Ralph, *Shadow and Act*
Evans, Walker, interview in the *New Republic,* November 13, 1976
Frank, Robert, *The Americans*
Hardy, Barbara, ed., *Middlemarch: Critical Approaches to the Novel*
Hurley, James, *Portrait of a Decade*
Lange, Dorothea, and Paul Taylor, *An American Exodus*
Liebow, Elliot, *Tally's Corner*
O'Brien, Tim, "Speaking of Courage"
Percy, Walker, *Lancelot*
Percy, Walker, *The Last Gentleman*
Percy, Walker, *Love in the Ruins*
Percy, Walker, *The Message in the Bottle*
Percy, Walker, *The Second Coming*

Percy, William Alexander, *Lanterns on the Levee,* with an introduction by
   Walker Percy
Petrement, Simone, *Simone Weil*
Pratt, Davis, ed., *The Photographic Eye of Ben Shahn*
Sigal, Clancy, *Weekend in Dinlock*
Speaight, Robert, *Georges Bernanos*
Stott, William, *Documentary Expression and Thirties America*
Walker, Alice, *In Search of Our Mother's Gardens;* specifically, "Beyond the
   Peacock: The Reconstruction of Flannery O'Connor," "Zora Neale
   Hurston: A Cautionary Tale and a Partisan View," and "Looking for
   Zora"
Warren, Robert Penn, *Who Speaks for the Negro?*
Wigginton, Eliot, ed., *The Foxfire Book*
Zola, Émile, *Germinal*

Permissions Acknowledgments

HARPERCOLLINS PUBLISHERS: Excerpts from *Their Eyes Were Watching God* by Zora Neale Hurston, copyright © 1937 by Harper & Row Publishers, Inc., and copyright renewed © 1965 by John C. Hurston and Joel Hurston. Reprinted by permission of HarperCollins Publishers.

HILL AND WANG, A DIVISION OF FARRAR, STRAUS & GIROUX, LLC, AND GEORGES BORCHARDT, INC.: Excerpt from *Night* by Elie Wiesel, translated by Marion Wiesel, copyright © 1972, 1985 by Elie Wiesel, translation copyright © 2006 by Marion Wiesel. Originally published as *La Nuit* by Les Editions de Minuit, copyright © 1958 by Les Editions de Minuit. Reprinted by permission of Hill and Wang, a division of Farrar, Straus & Giroux, LLC, and Georges Borchardt, Inc., for Les Editions de Minuit.

HENRY HOLT AND COMPANY, LLC: "The Investment" from *The Poetry of Robert Frost* by Robert Frost, edited by Edward Connery Latham, copyright © 1928, 1969 by Henry Holt and Company, copyright © 1956 by Robert Frost. Reprinted by permission of Henry Holt and Company, LLC.

HOUGHTON MIFFLIN HARCOURT PUBLISHING COMPANY: "Dear George Orwell 1950–1965" and scattered excerpts from *Night Music* by L. E. Sissman, copyright © 1999 by The President and Fellows of Harvard College; excerpts from *Let Us Now Praise Famous Men* by James Agee and Walker Evans, copyright © 1939, 1940 by James Agee, copyright © 1941 by James Agee and Walker Evans, copyright renewed © 1969 by Mia Fritsch Agee and Walker Evans. Reprinted by permission of Houghton Mifflin Harcourt Publishing Company.

HOUGHTON MIFFLIN HARCOURT PUBLISHING COMPANY AND A. M. HEATH & CO. LTD.: Excerpts from *Down and Out in Paris and London* by George Orwell, copyright © 1933 by George Orwell and copyright renewed © 1961 by Sonia Pitt-Rivers. Reprinted by permission of Houghton Mifflin Harcourt Publishing Company and Bill Hamilton as the Literary Executor of the Estate of the Late Sonia Brownell Orwell and Secker & Warburg Ltd. c/o A. M. Heath & Co. Ltd.

HOUGHTON MIFFLIN HARCOURT PUBLISHING COMPANY AND HAROLD MATSON CO., INC.: "The Artificial Nigger" from *A Good Man Is Hard to Find and Other Stories* by Flannery O'Conner, copyright © 1948, 1953, 1954, 1955 by Flannery O'Connor, copyright renewed © 1976 by Mrs. Edward F. O'Connor, copyright renewed © 1981, 1983 by Regina Cline O'Connor. Reprinted by permission of Houghton Mifflin Harcourt Publishing Company and the Mary Flannery O'Connor Charitable Trust via Harold Matson Co., Inc.

ALFRED A. KNOPF, A DIVISION OF RANDOM HOUSE, INC.: Excerpts from "The Housebreaker of Shady Hill" from *The Stories of John Cheever*, copyright © 1978 by John Cheever; "Poem for Hemingway & W. C. Williams," "What the Doctor Said," and "Gravy" from *All of Us: The Collected Poems* by Raymond Carver, copyright © 1996 by Tess Gallagher, introduction copyright © 1996 by Tess Gallagher, commentary and notes copyright © 1996 by William L. Stull. Reprinted by permission of Alfred A. Knopf, a division of Random House, Inc.

NEW DIRECTIONS PUBLISHING CORPORATION: Excerpt from *Paterson* by William Carlos Williams, copyright © 1946 by William Carlos Williams; "The Poor" and "The Young Housewife" from *The Collected Poems: Volume 1, 1909–1939* by William Carlos Williams,

Index

NOTE: Bold page numbers refer to picture captions.

ABOUT THE AUTHOR

ROBERT COLES is the author of many books, including *The Moral Intelligence of Children* and *The Spiritual Life of Children*. He won the Pulitzer Prize for his five-volume work *Children of Crisis*. He was awarded the Presidential Medal of Freedom in 1998, and the National Humanities Medal in 2001. He is the Emeritus James Agee Professor of Social Ethics at Harvard University, and Emeritus Professor of Psychiatry and Medical Humanities at the Harvard Medical School.

ABOUT THE TYPE

This book was set in Bembo, a typeface based on an old-style Roman face that was used for Cardinal Bembo's tract *De Aetna* in 1495. Bembo was cut by Francisco Griffo in the early sixteenth century. The Lanston Monotype Machine Company of Philadelphia brought the well-proportioned letter forms of Bembo to the United States in the 1930s.